"Thank you for taking the time to embark upon this peaceful coloring journey we have prepared for you. We hope it brings you calm and wonder."

-Mr. Michael and the art students of
Four Corners Montessori Academy 2017/2018

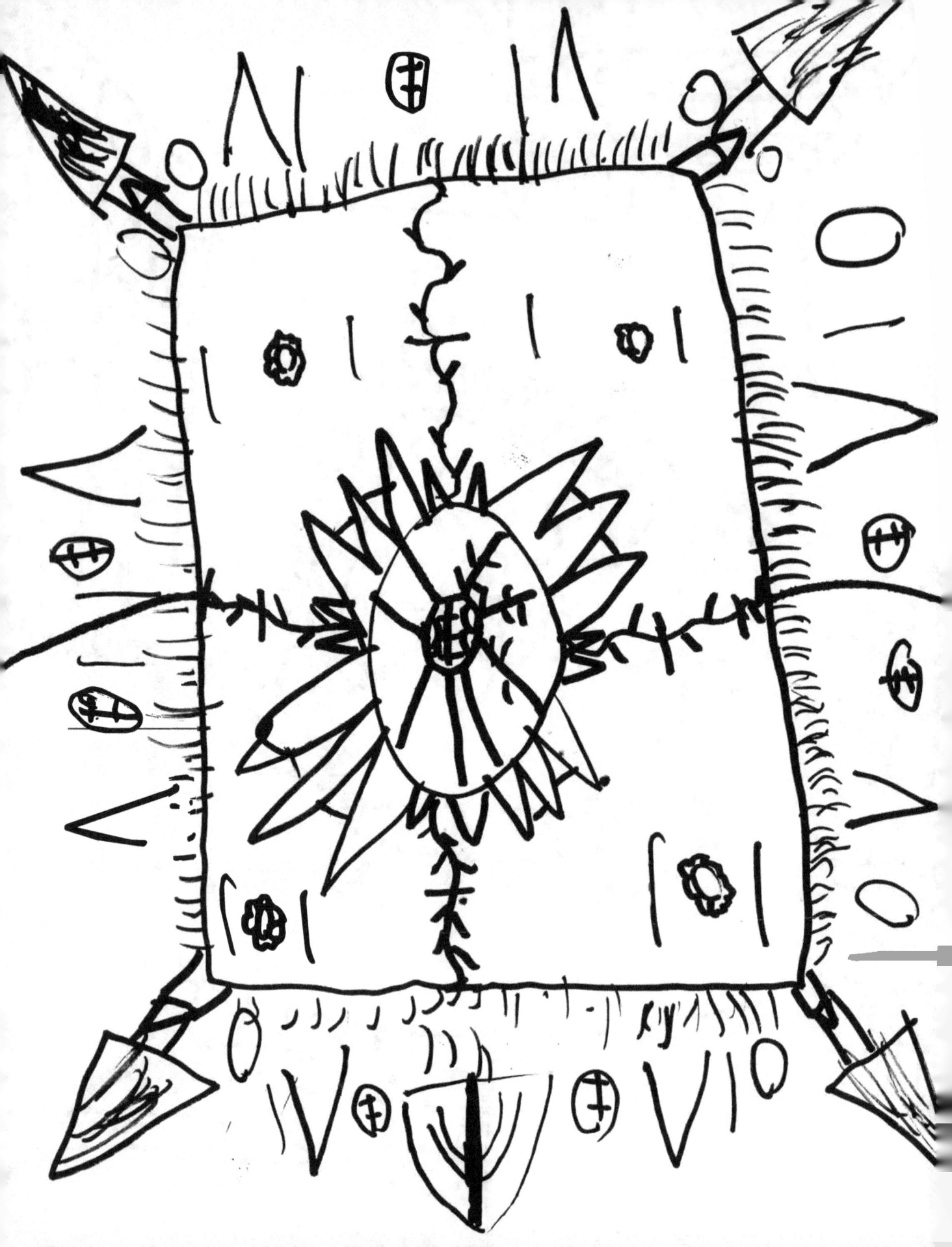

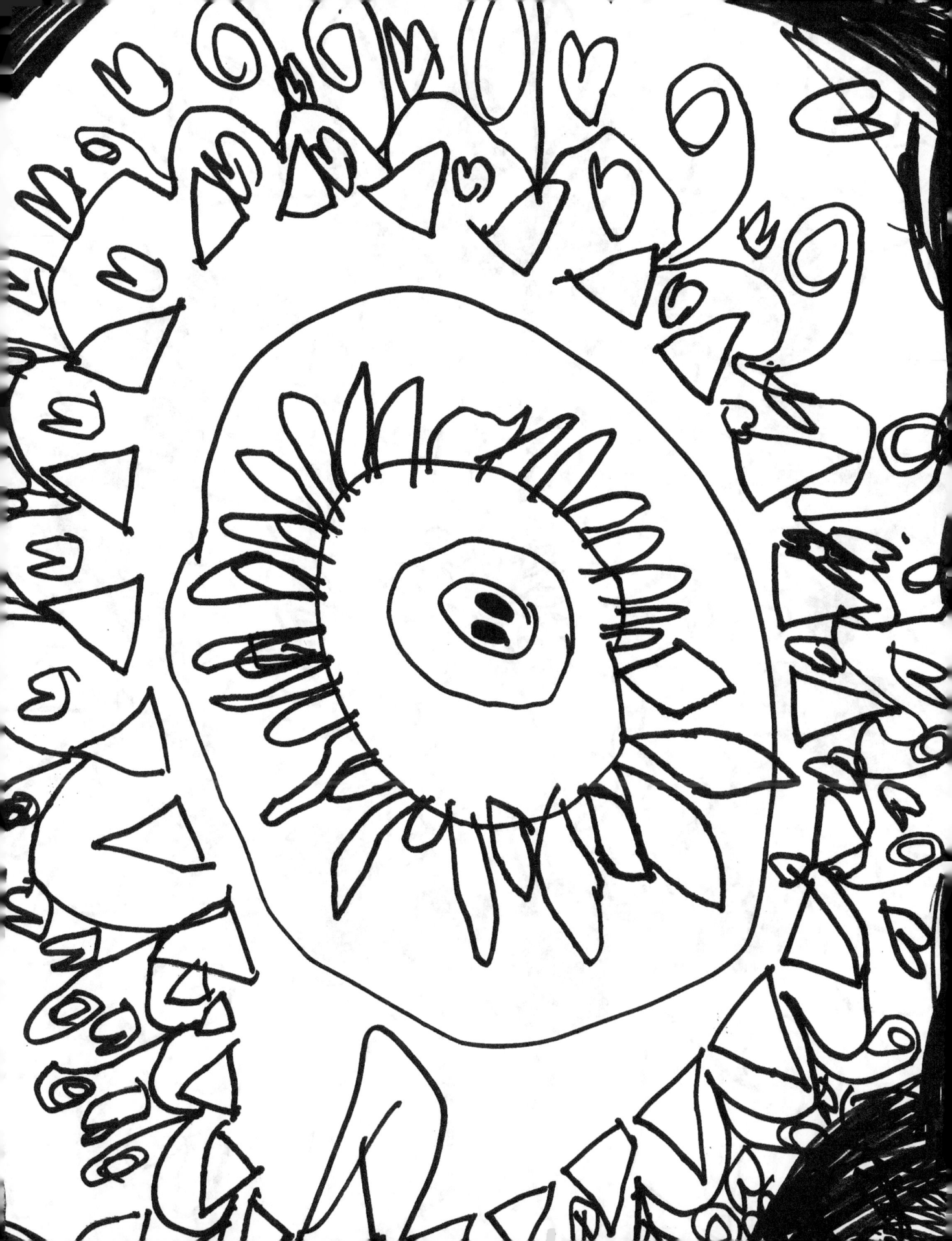

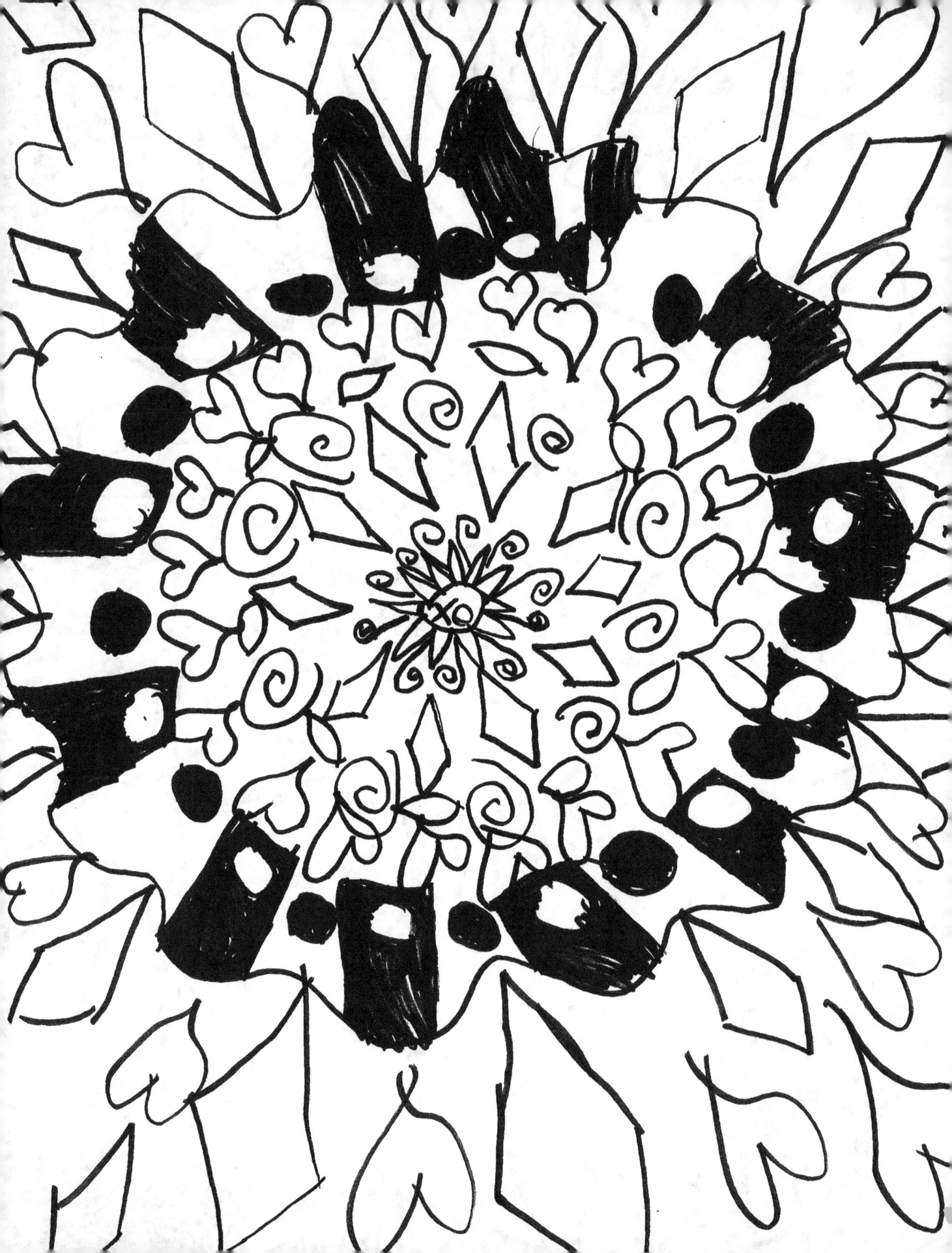

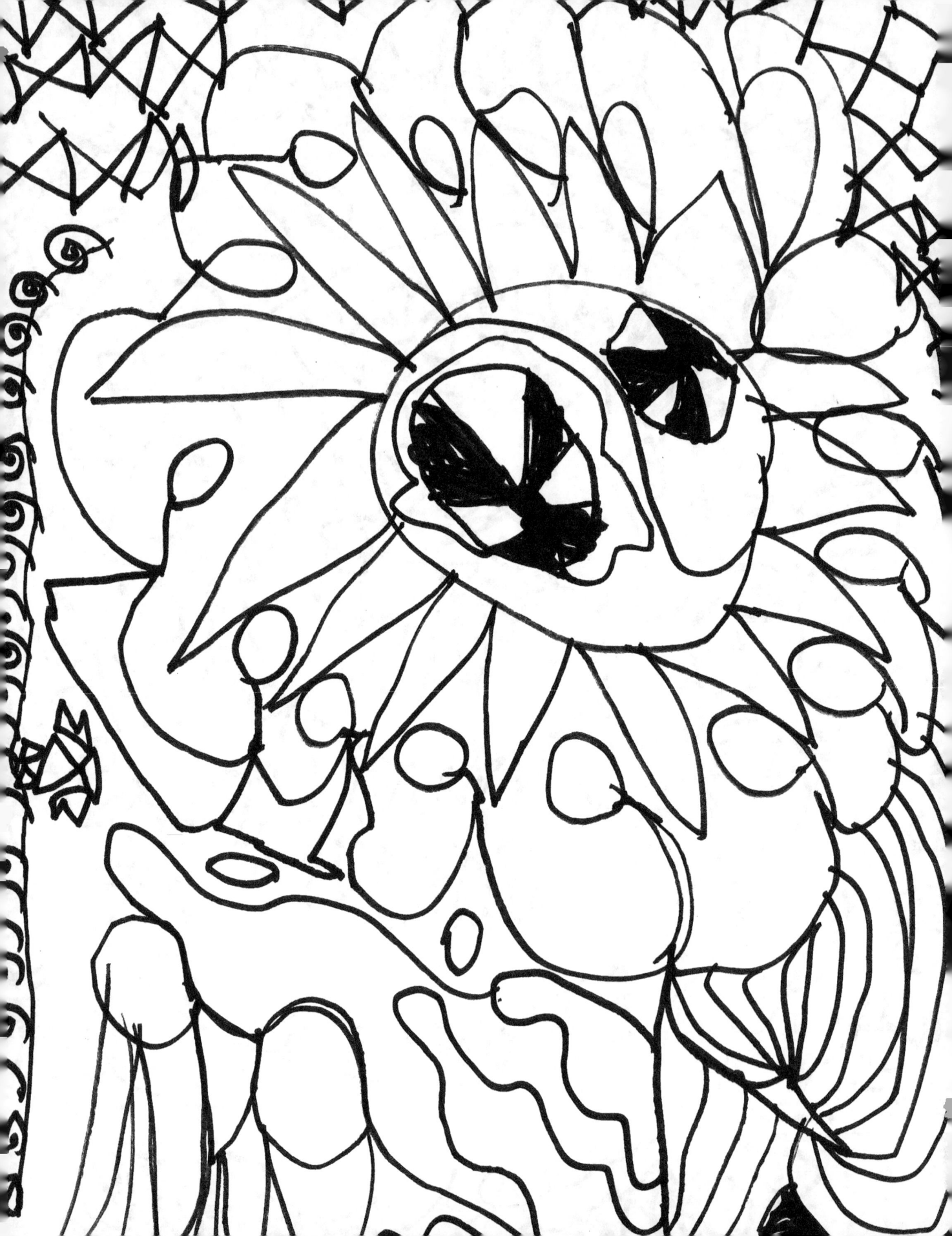

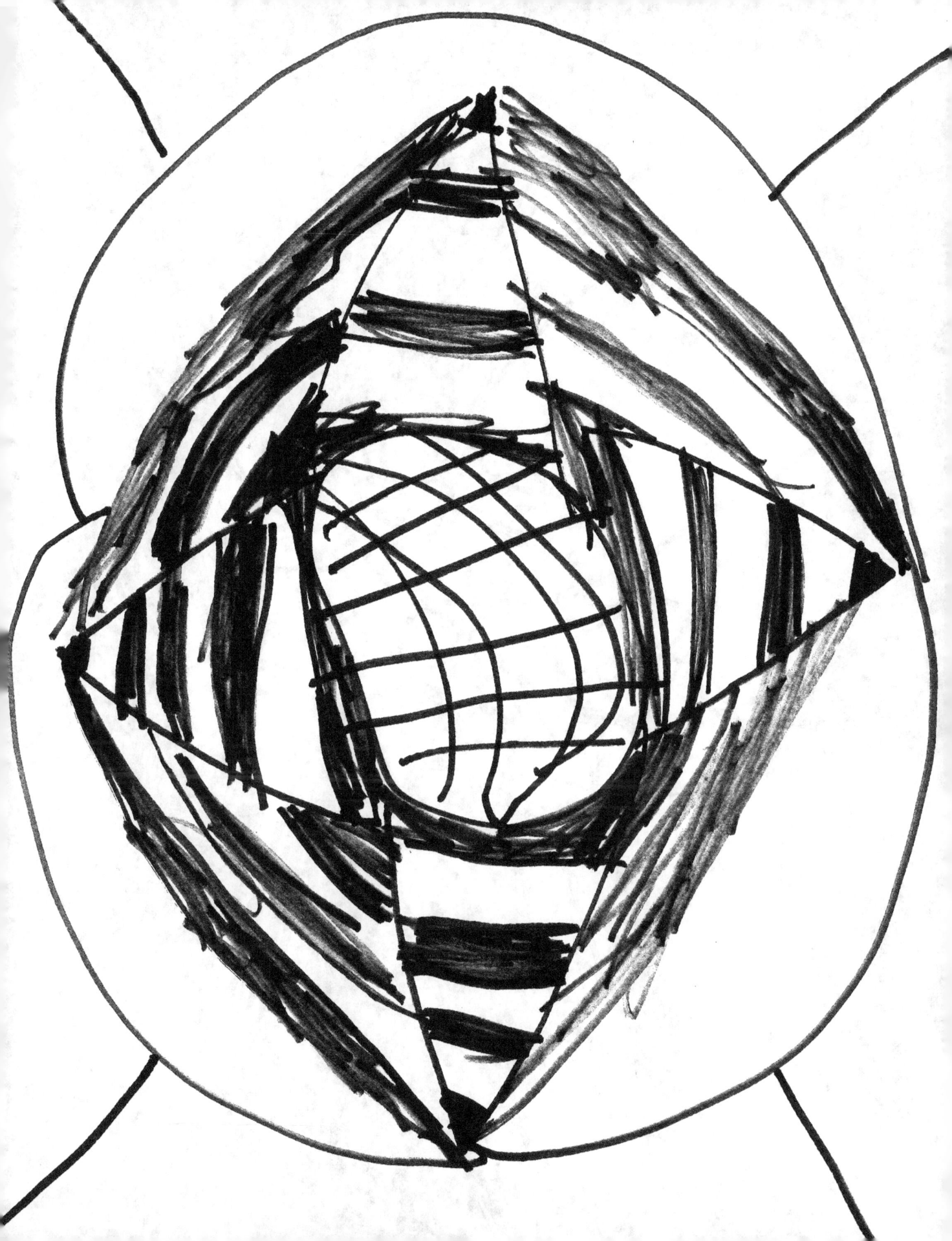

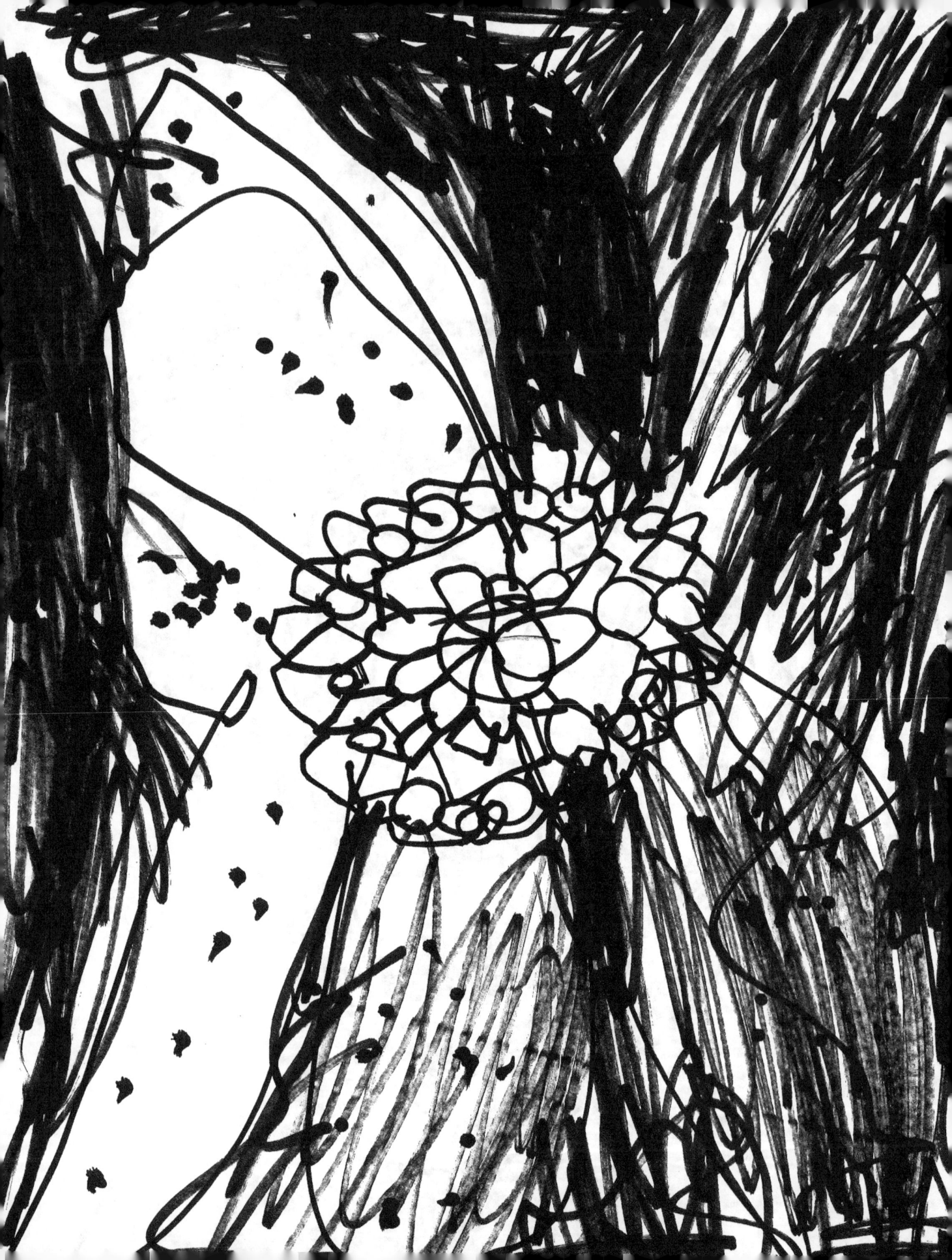

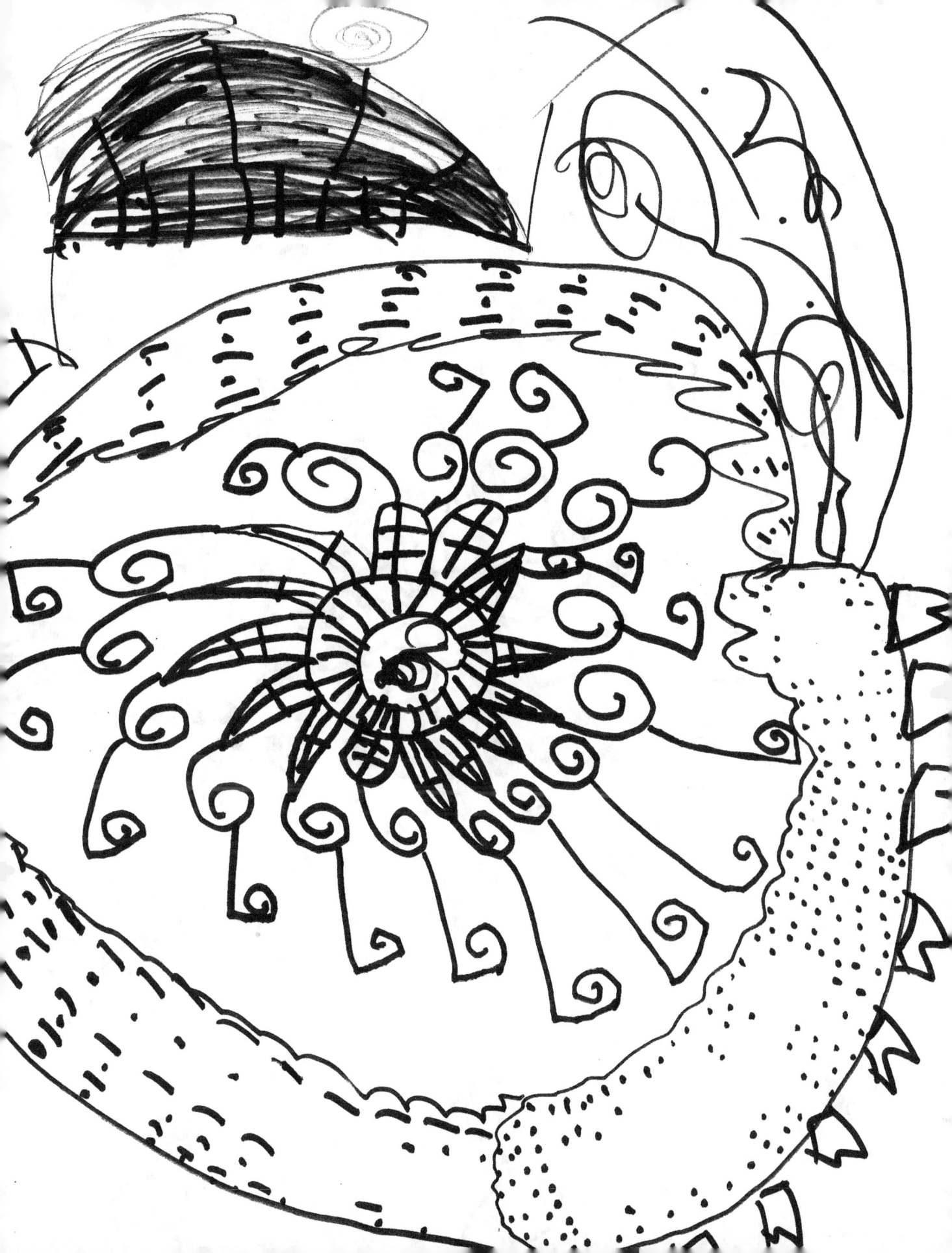

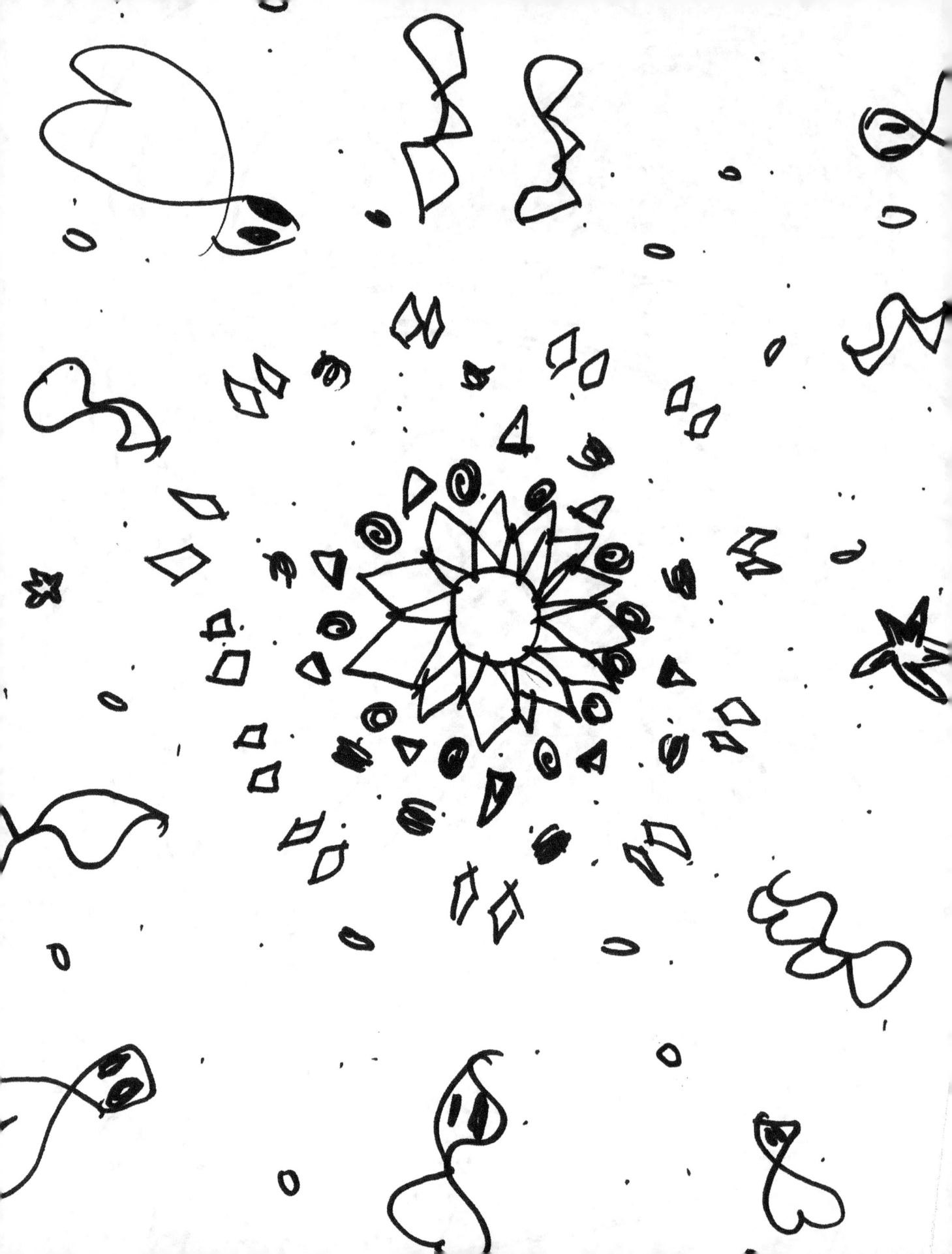

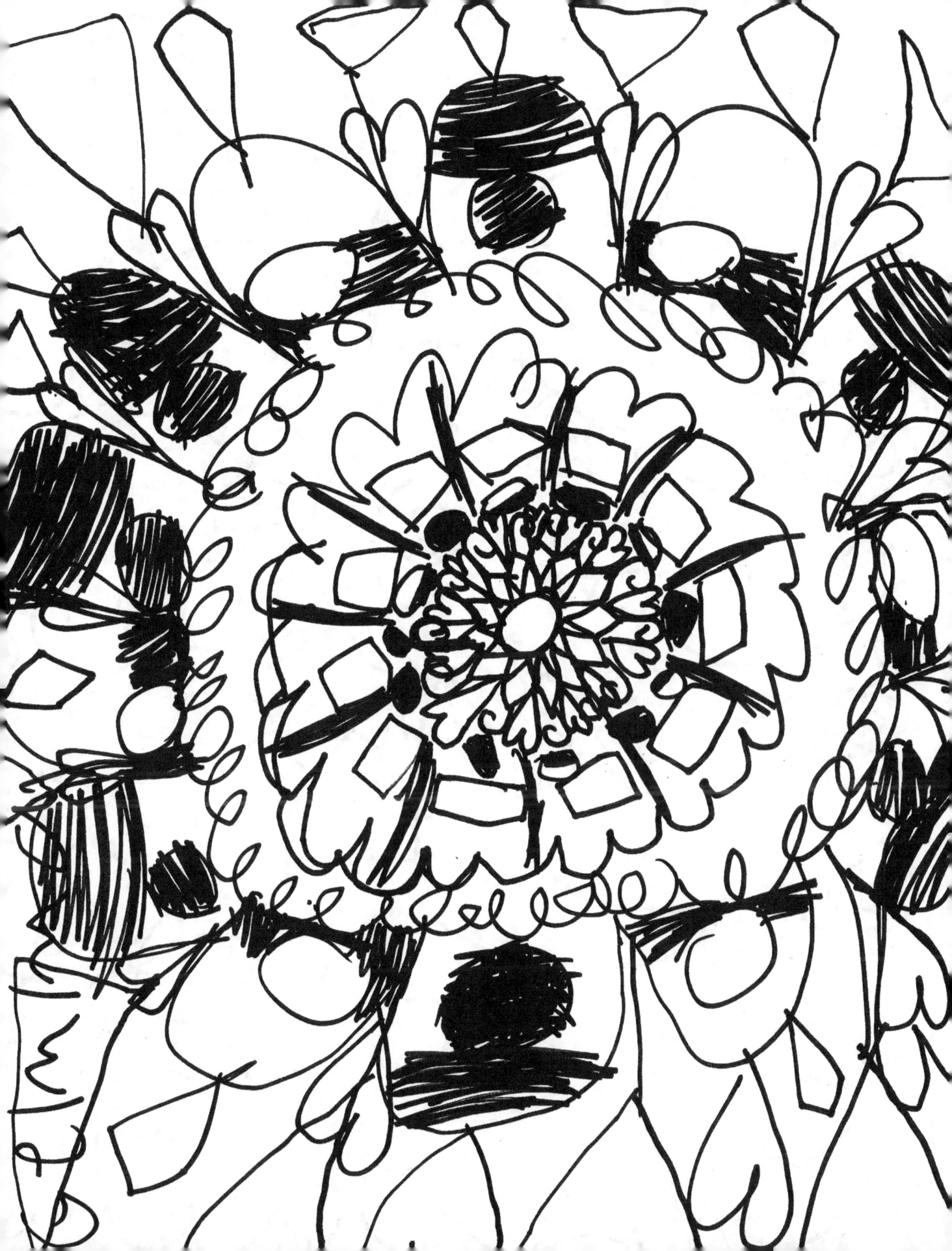

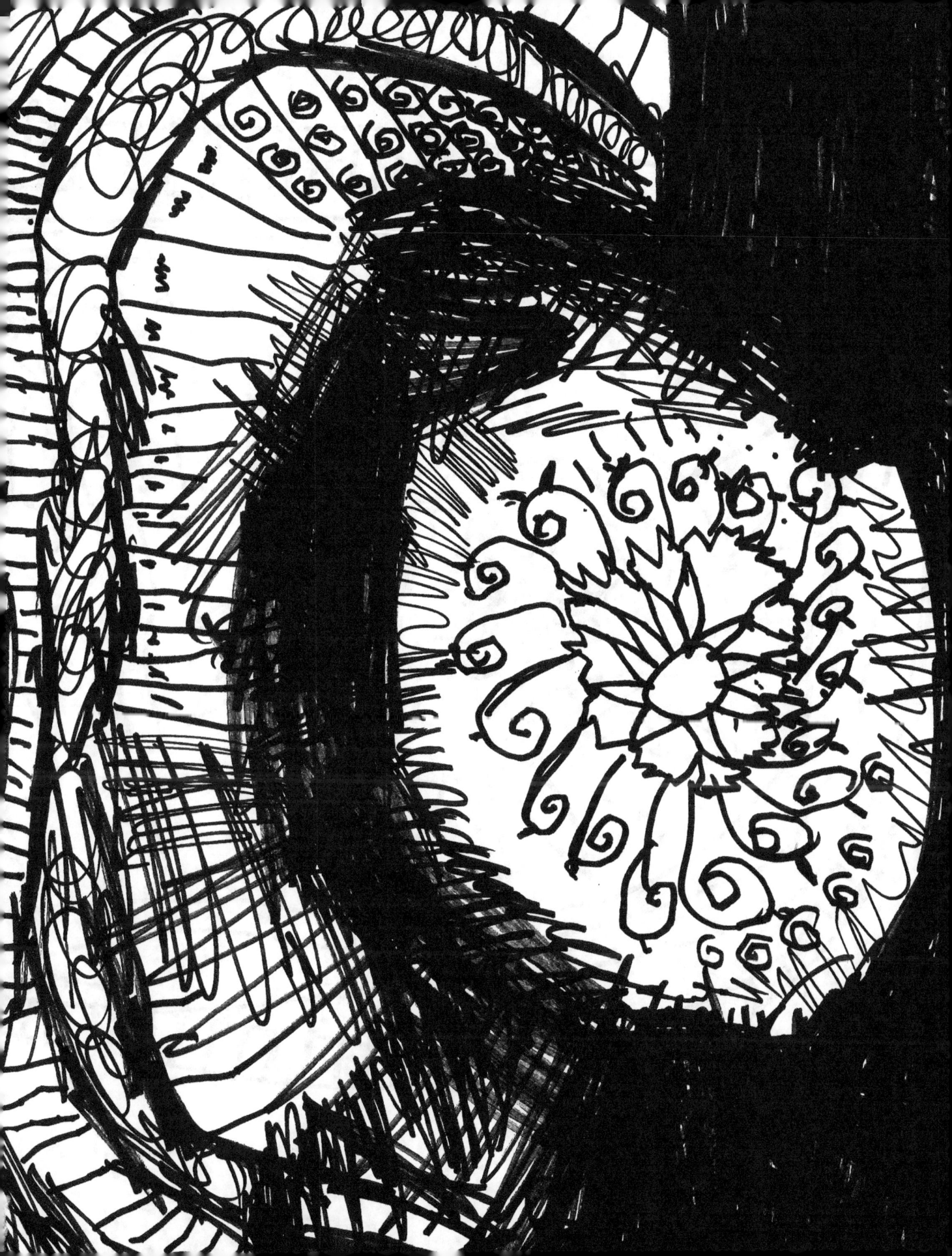

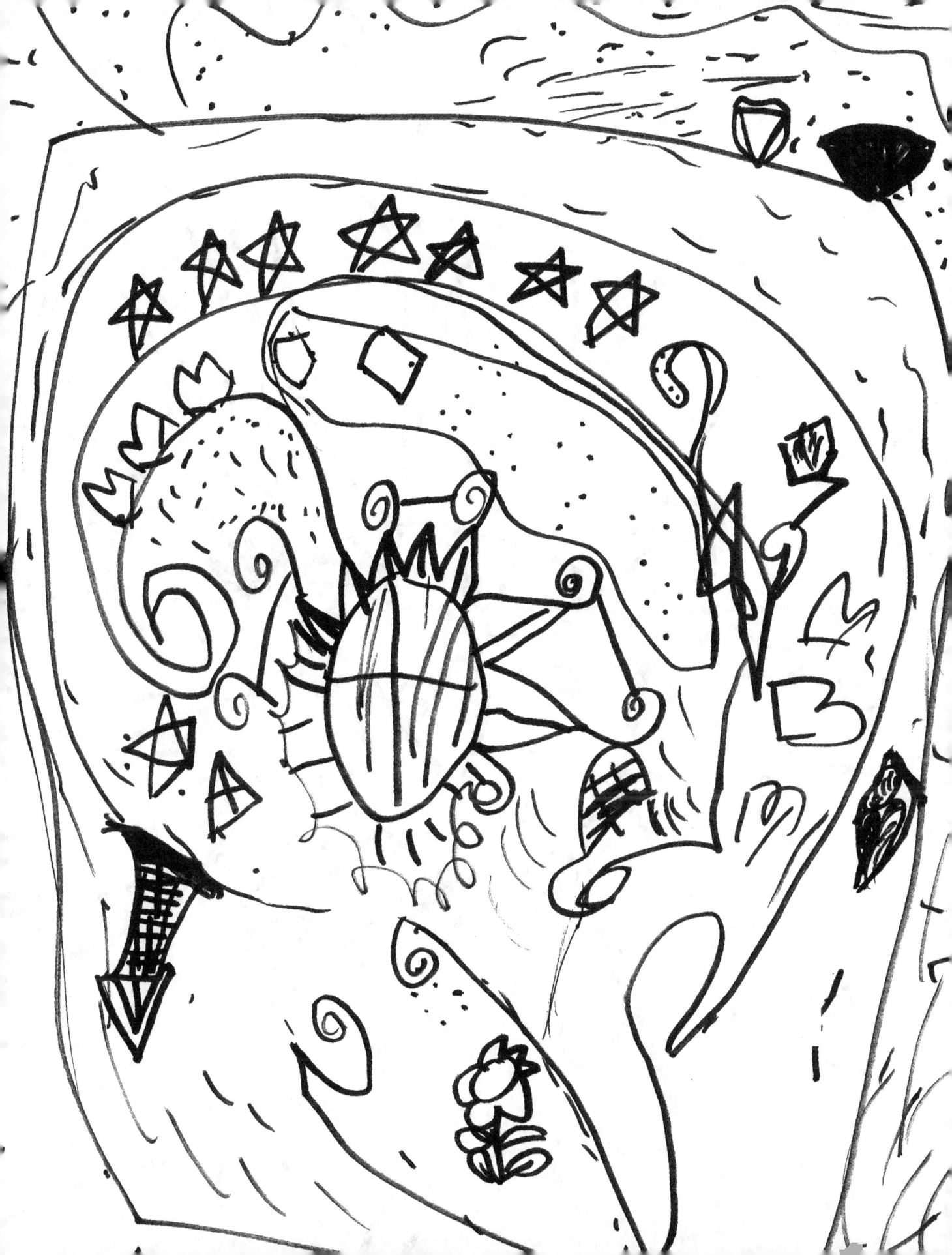

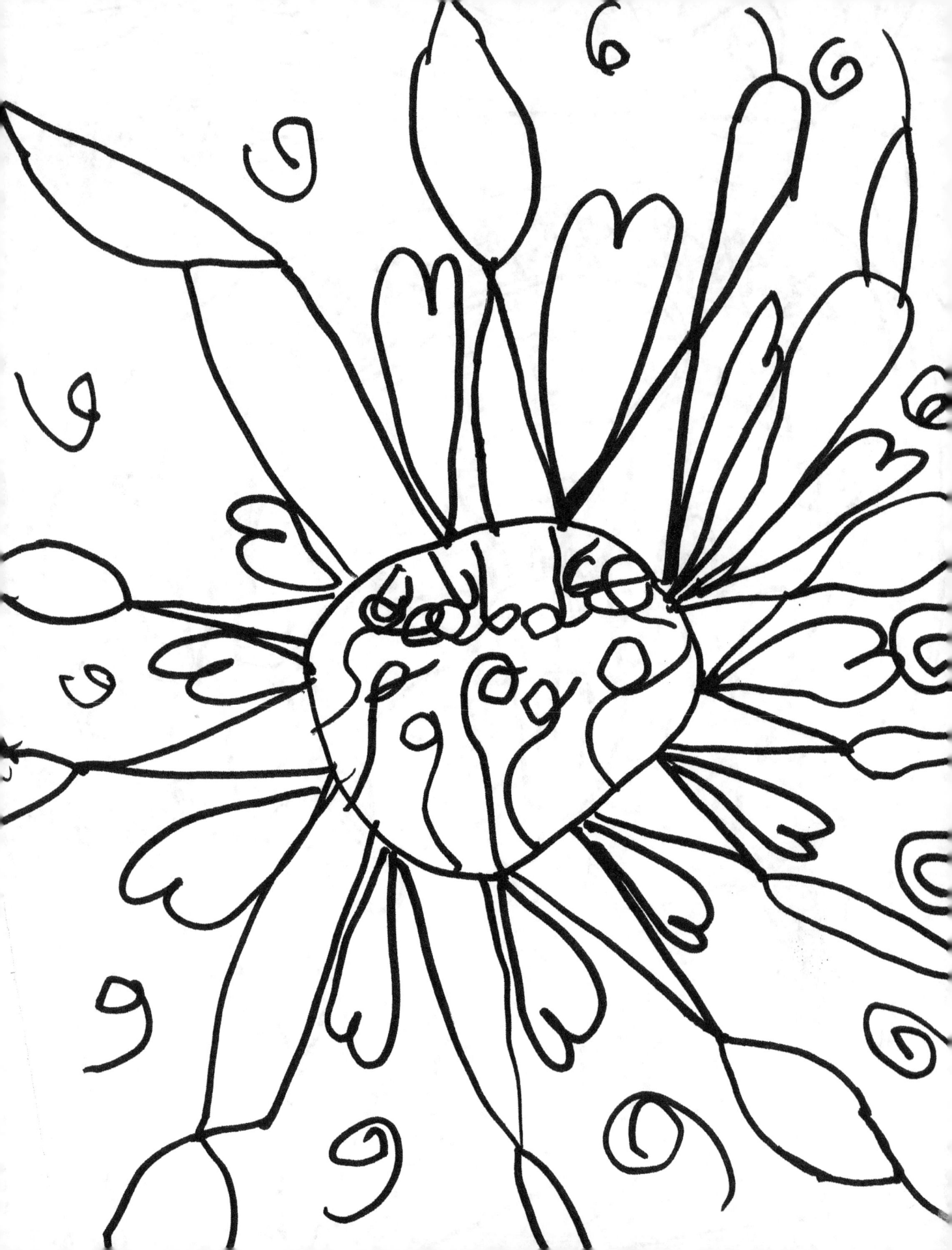

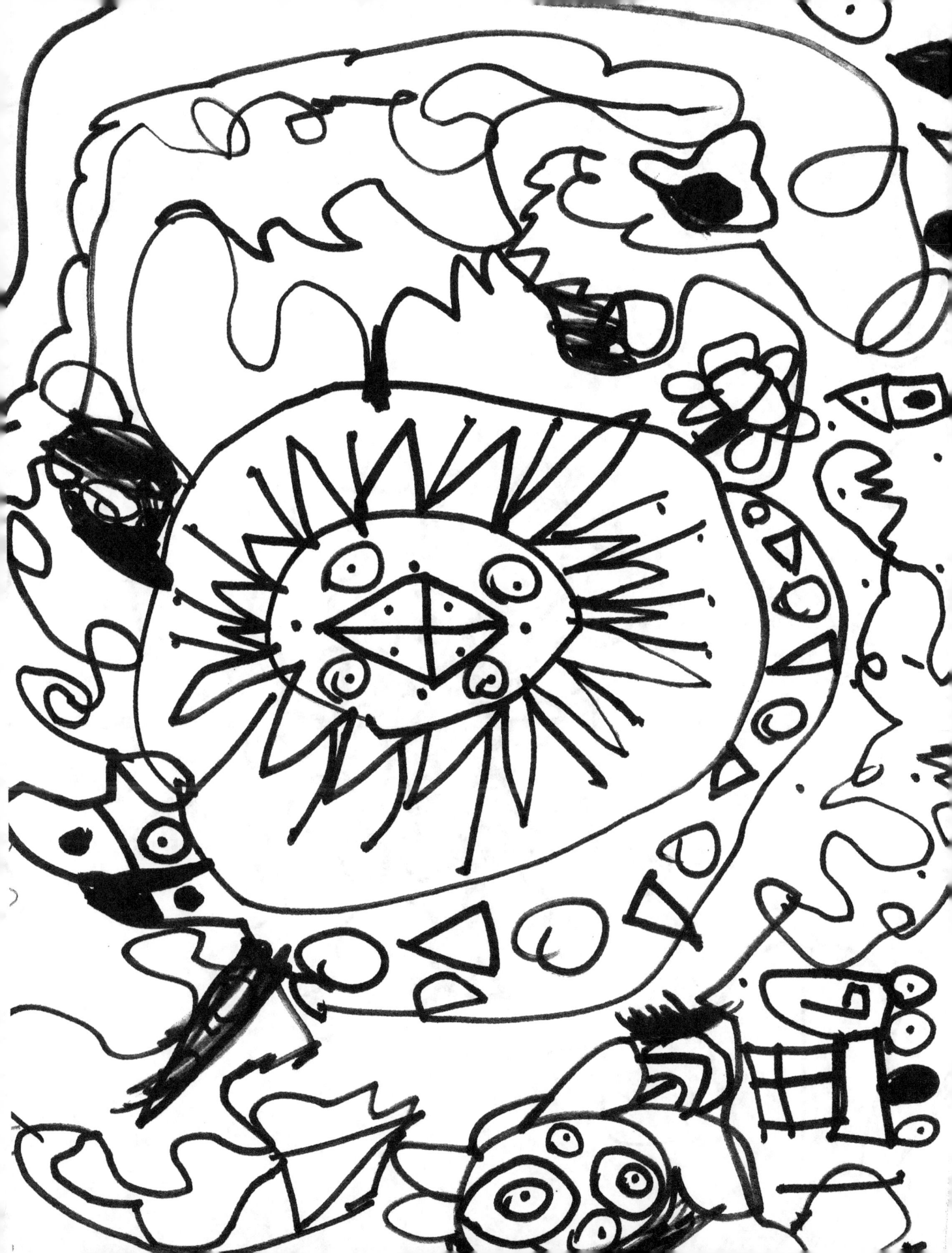

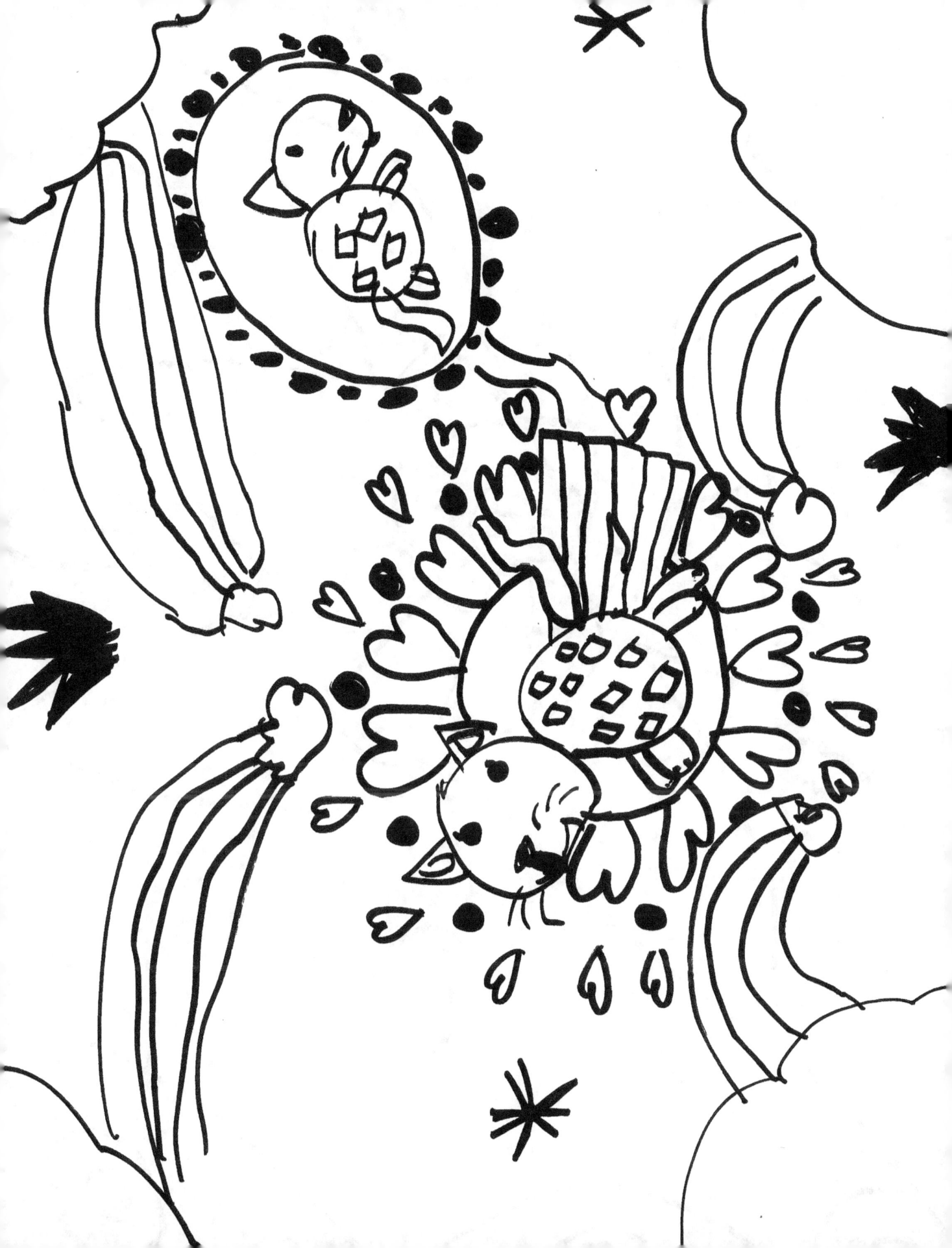

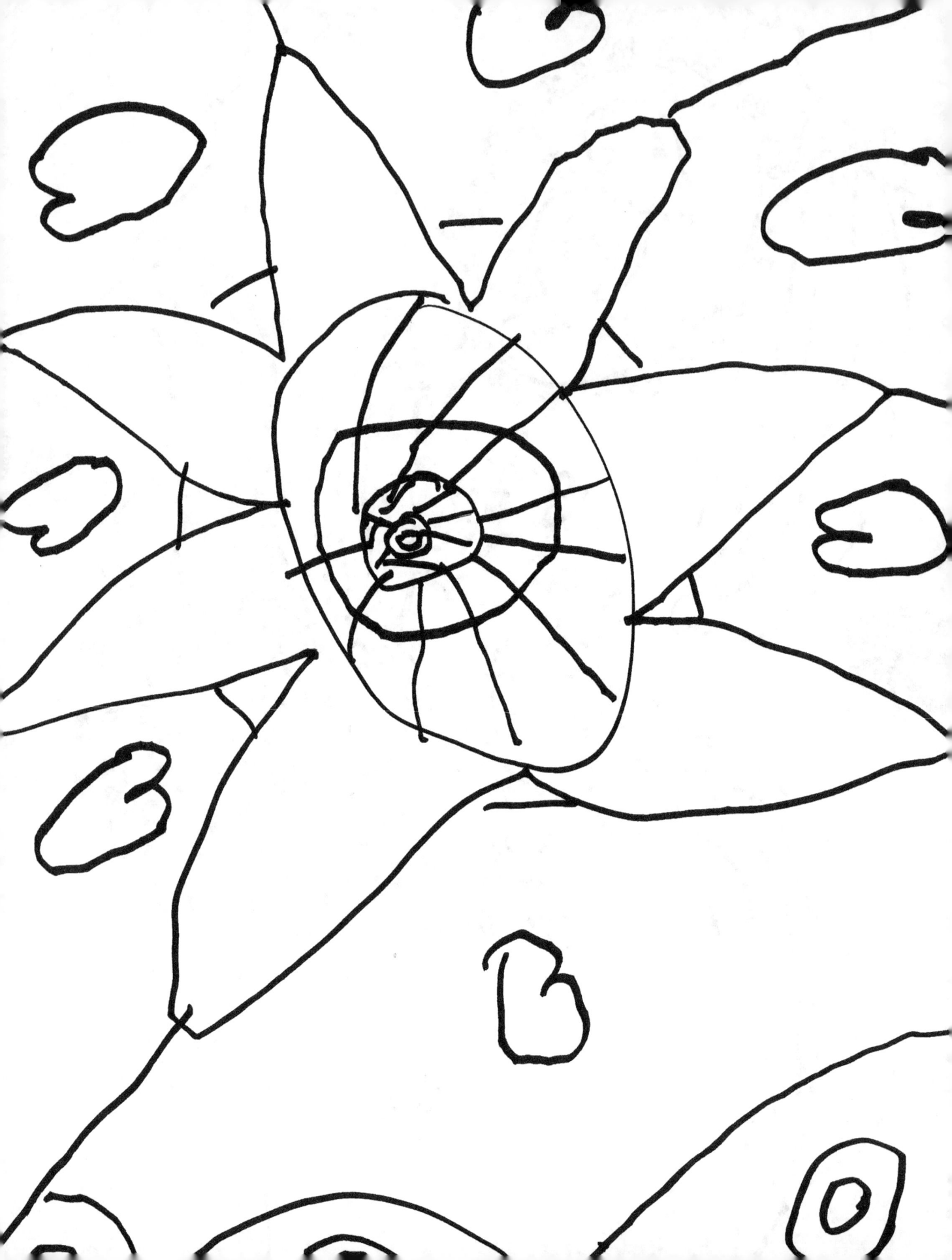

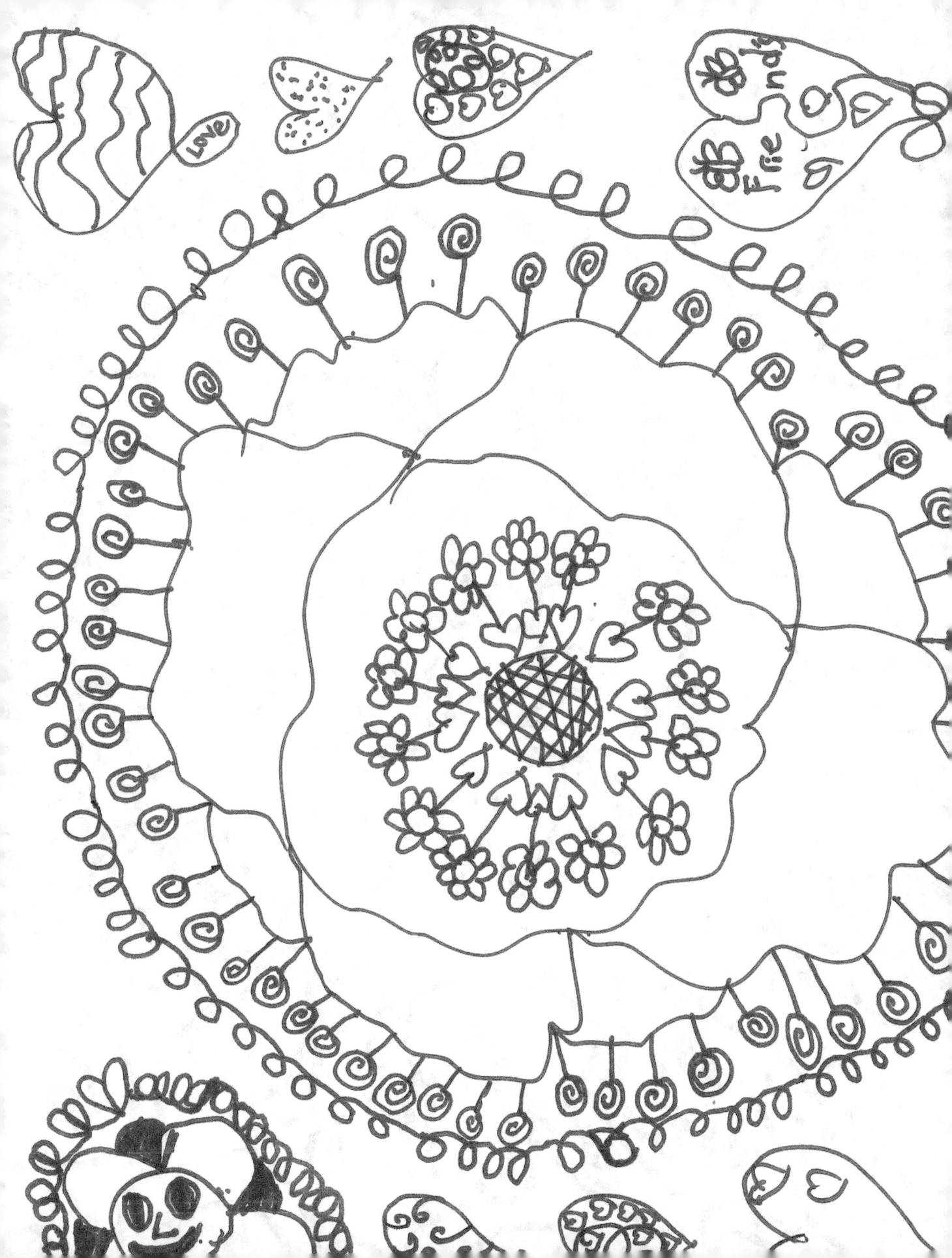

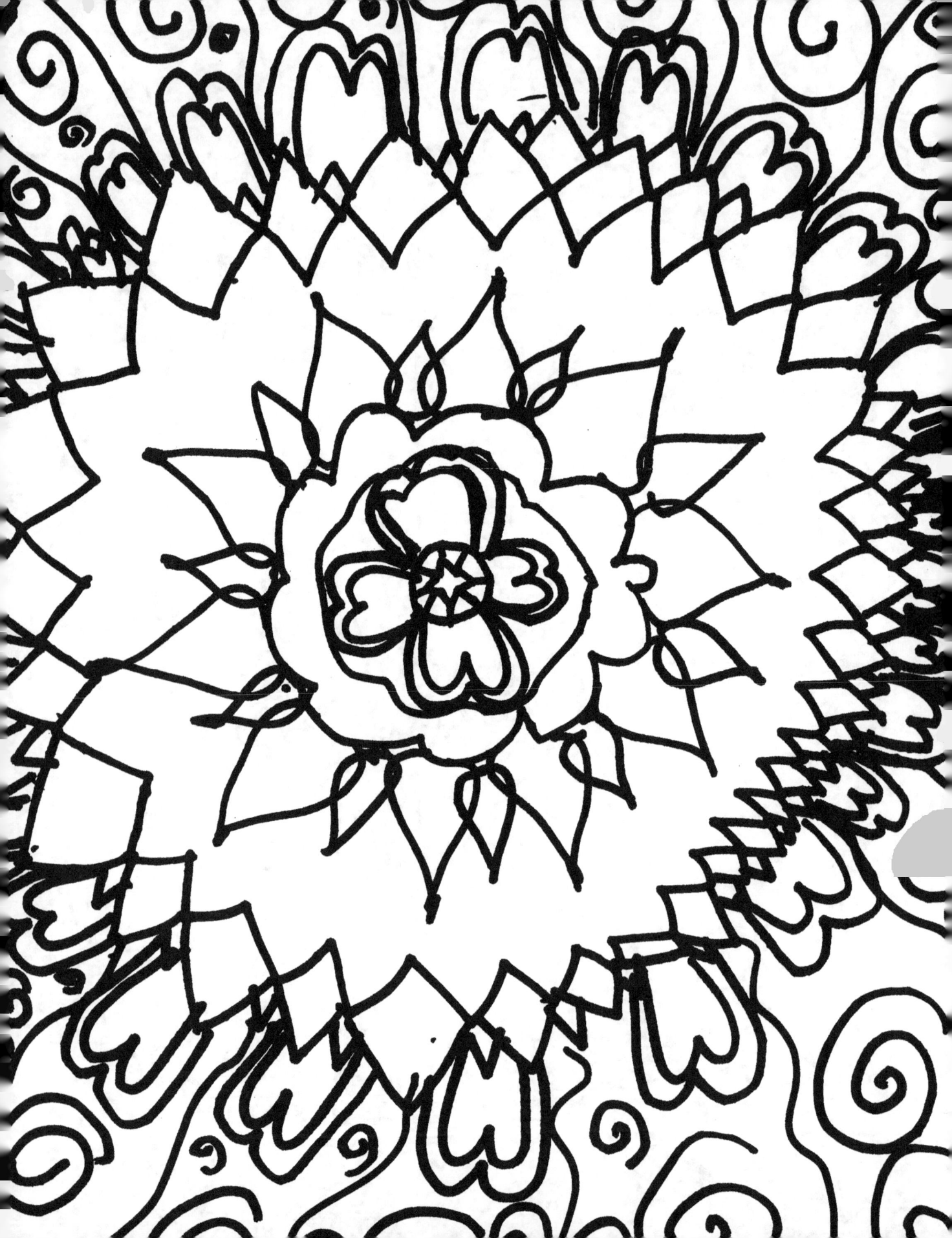

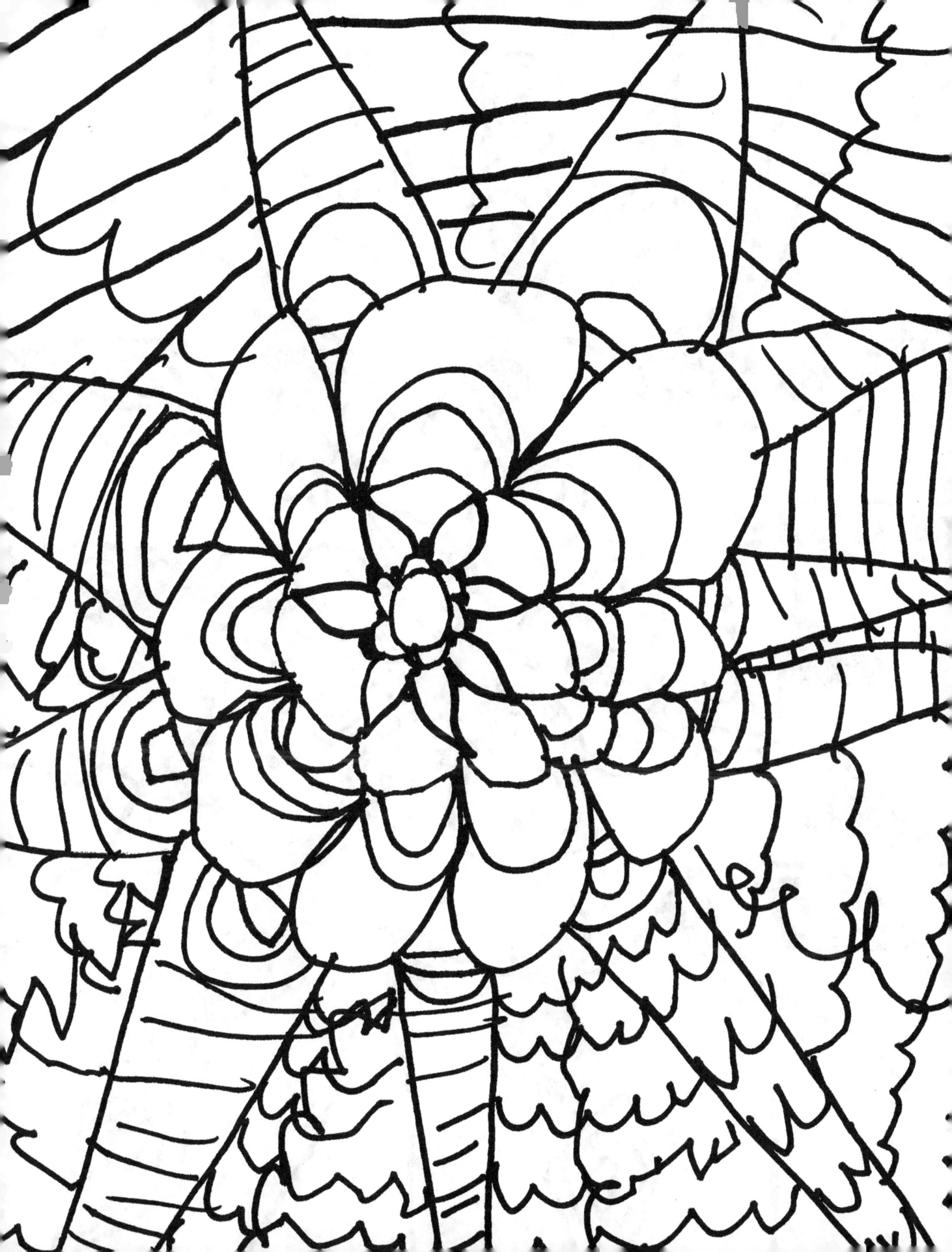

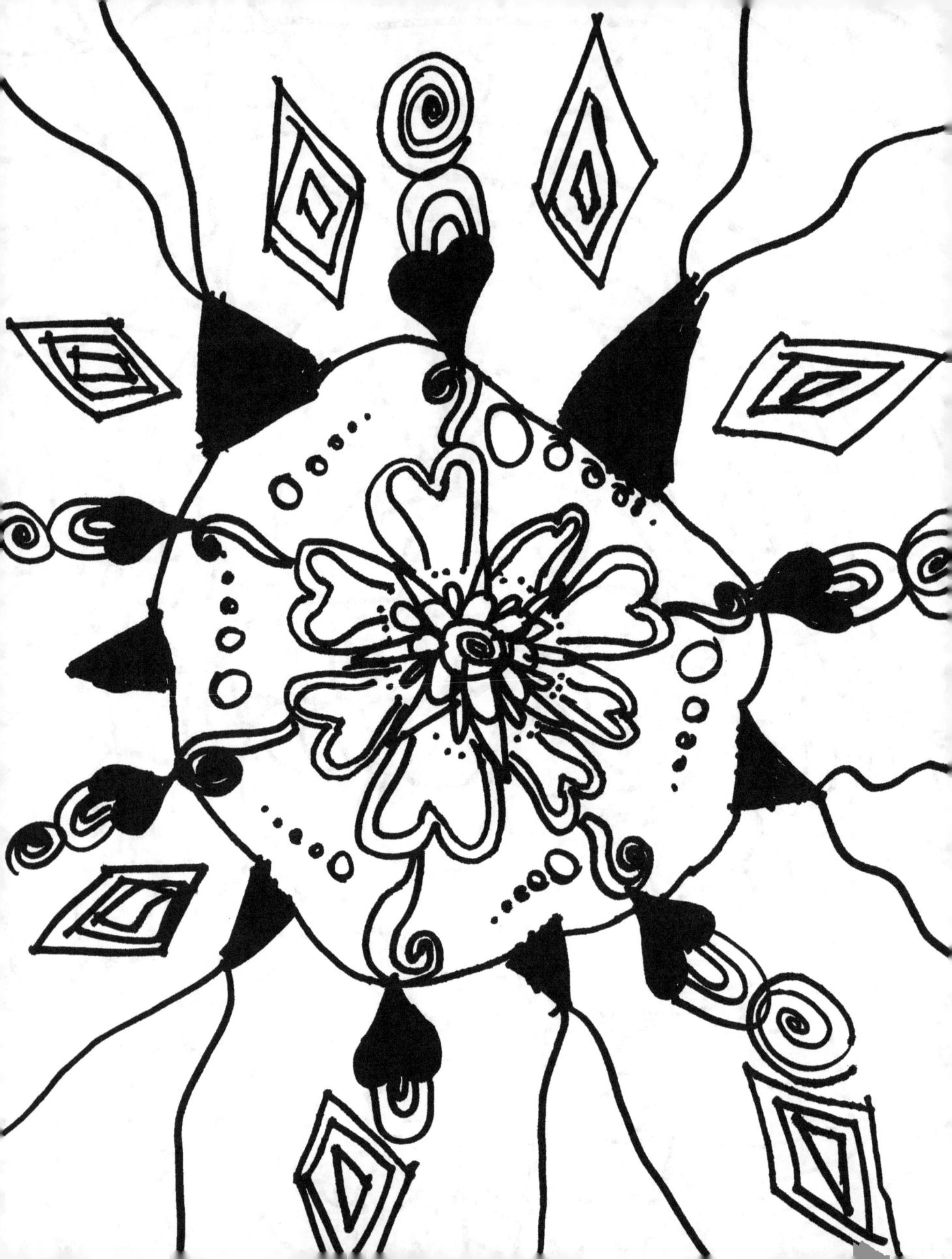

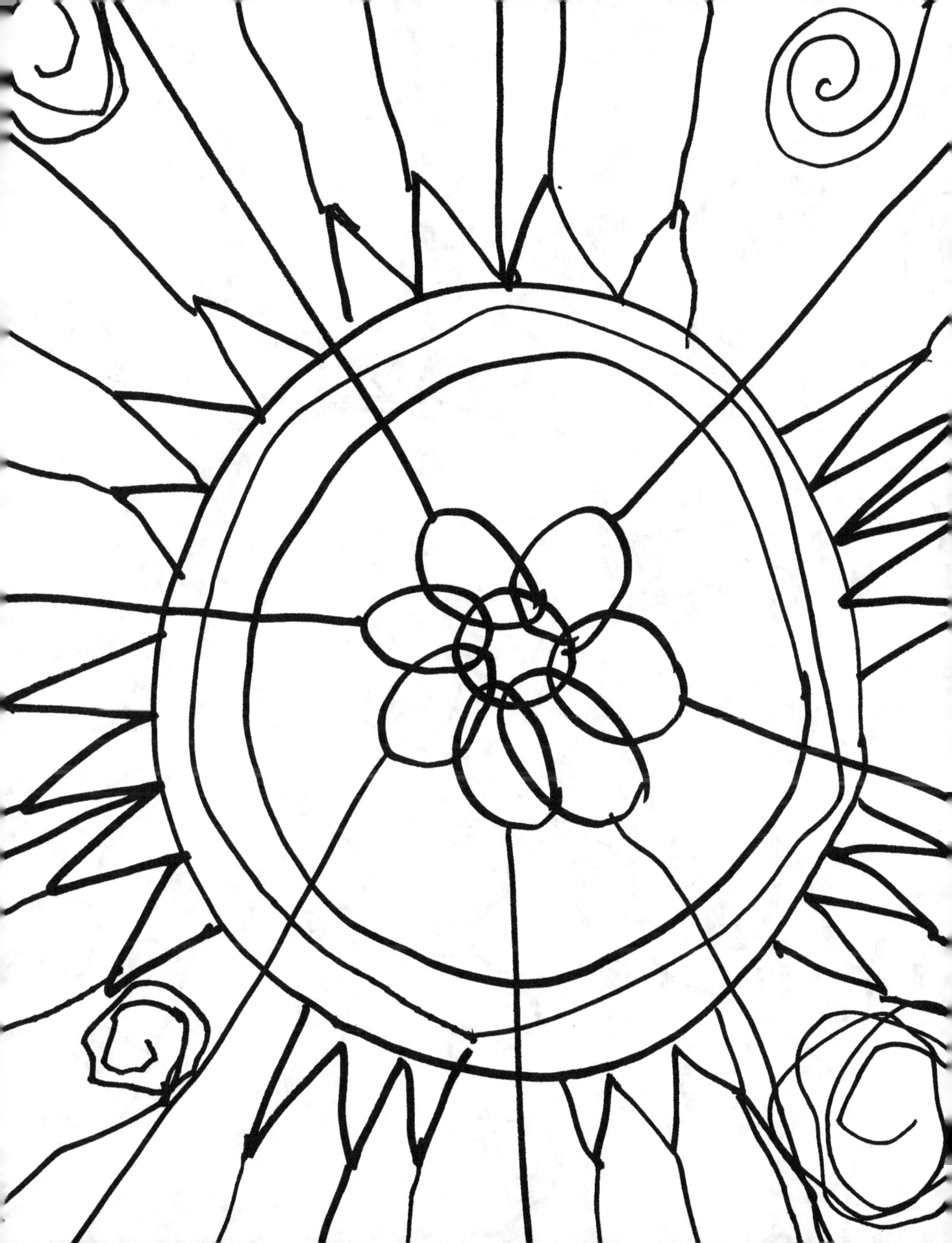

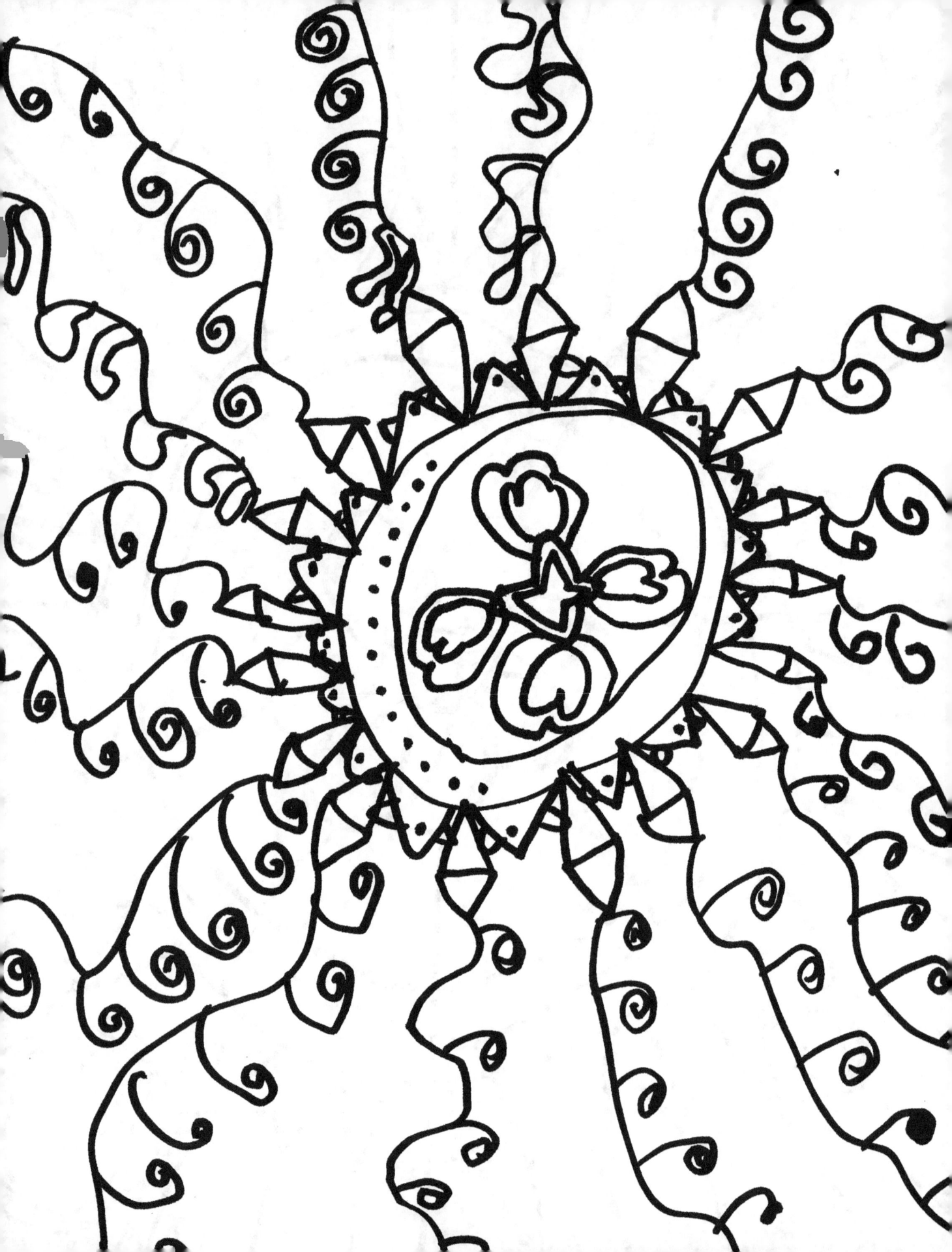

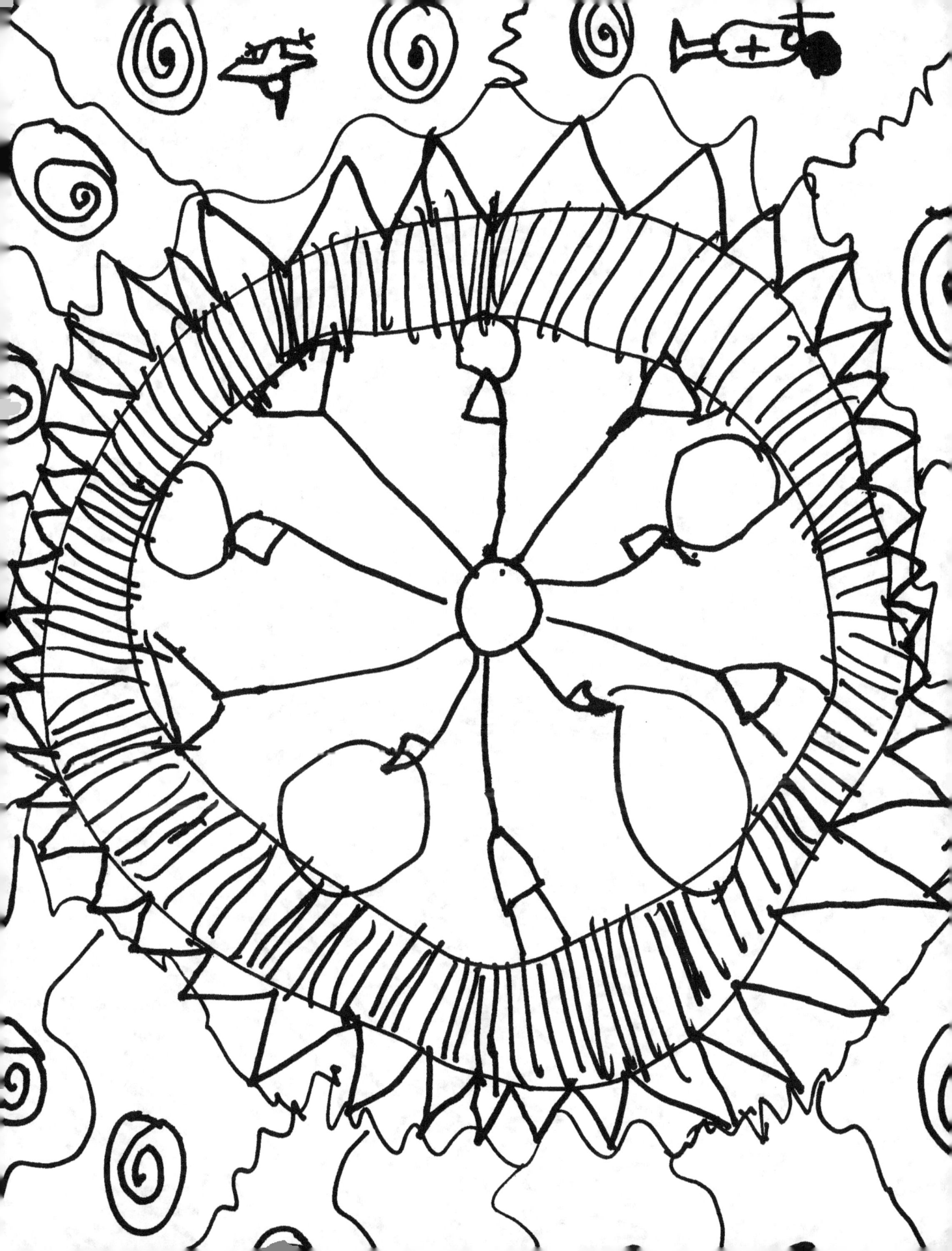

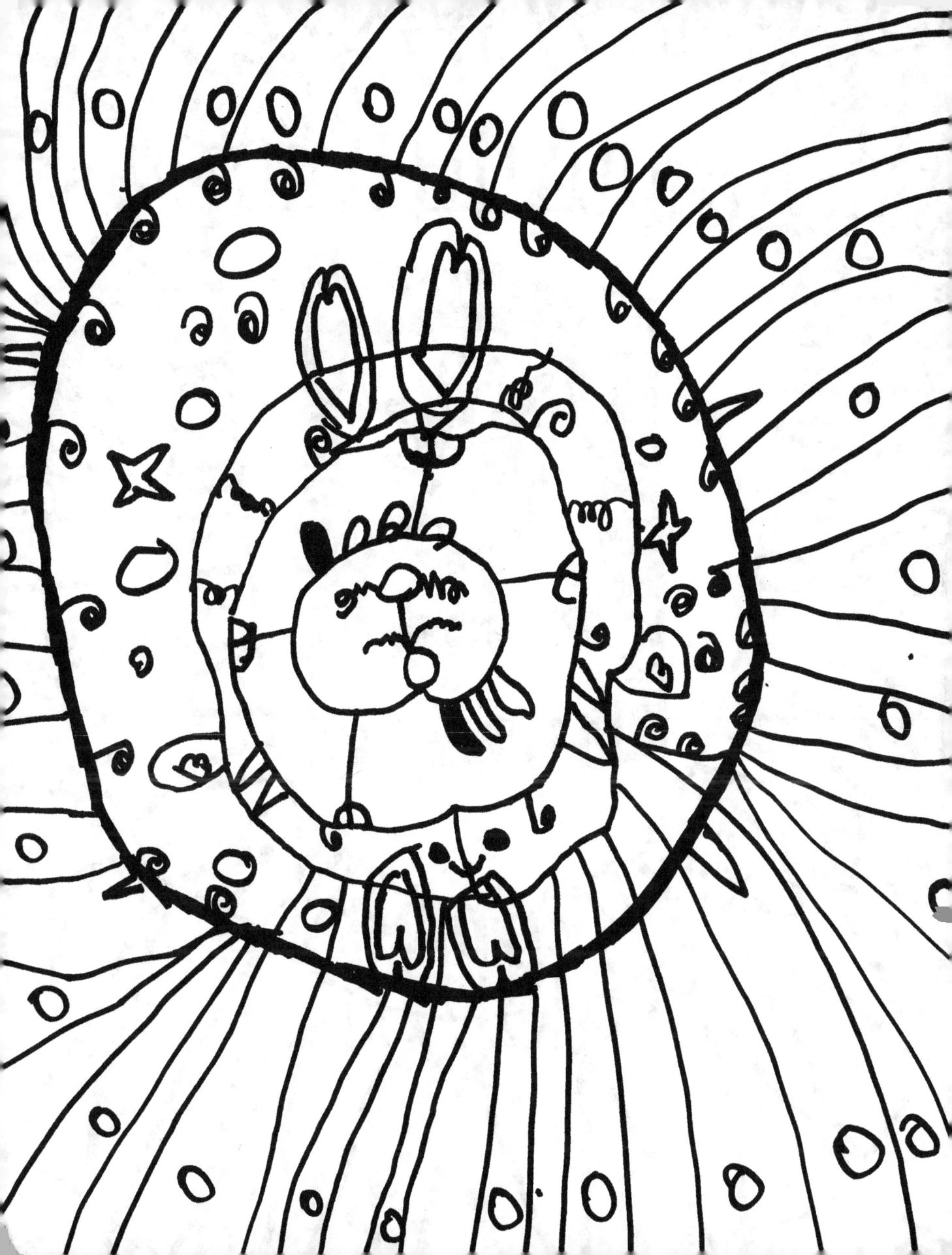

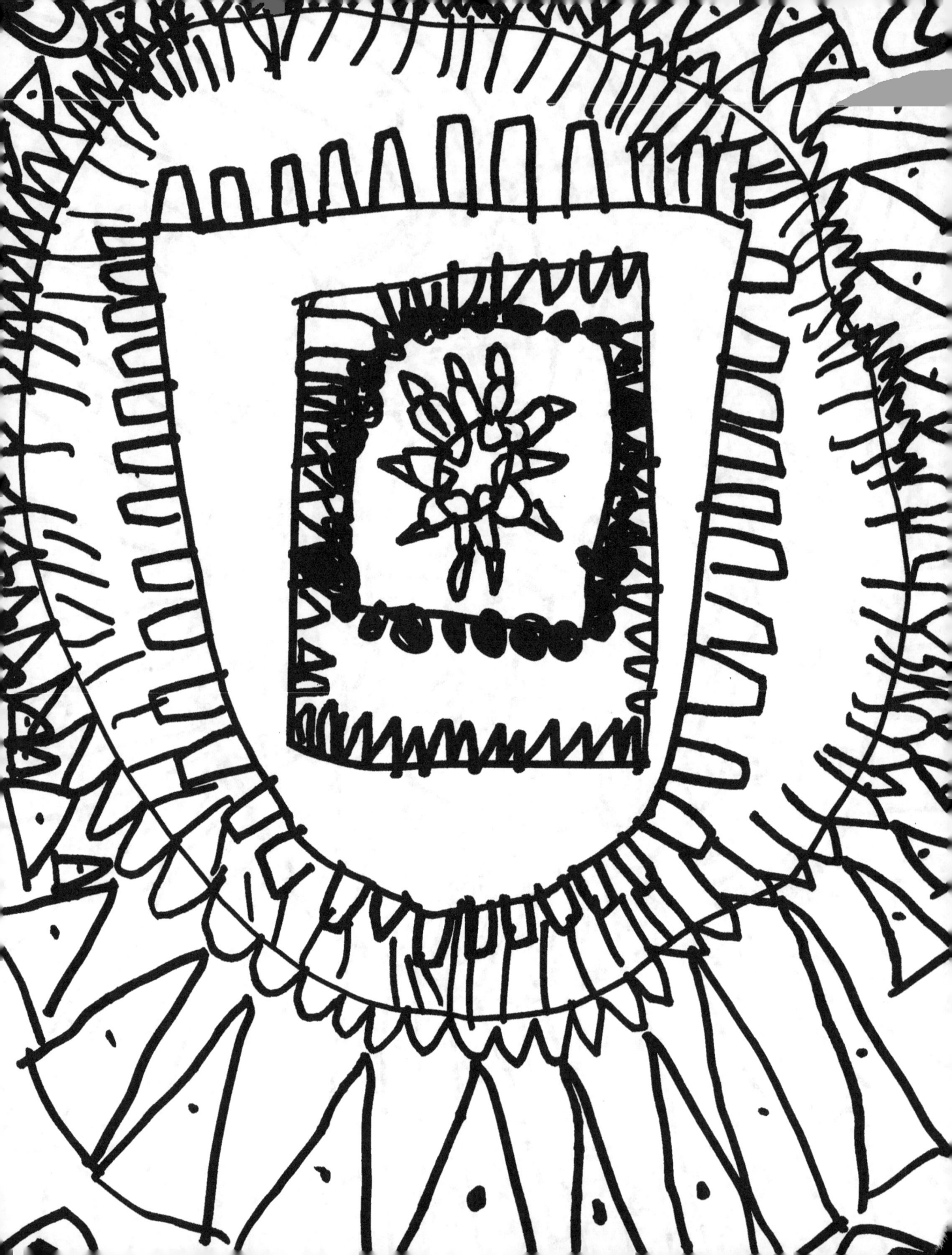

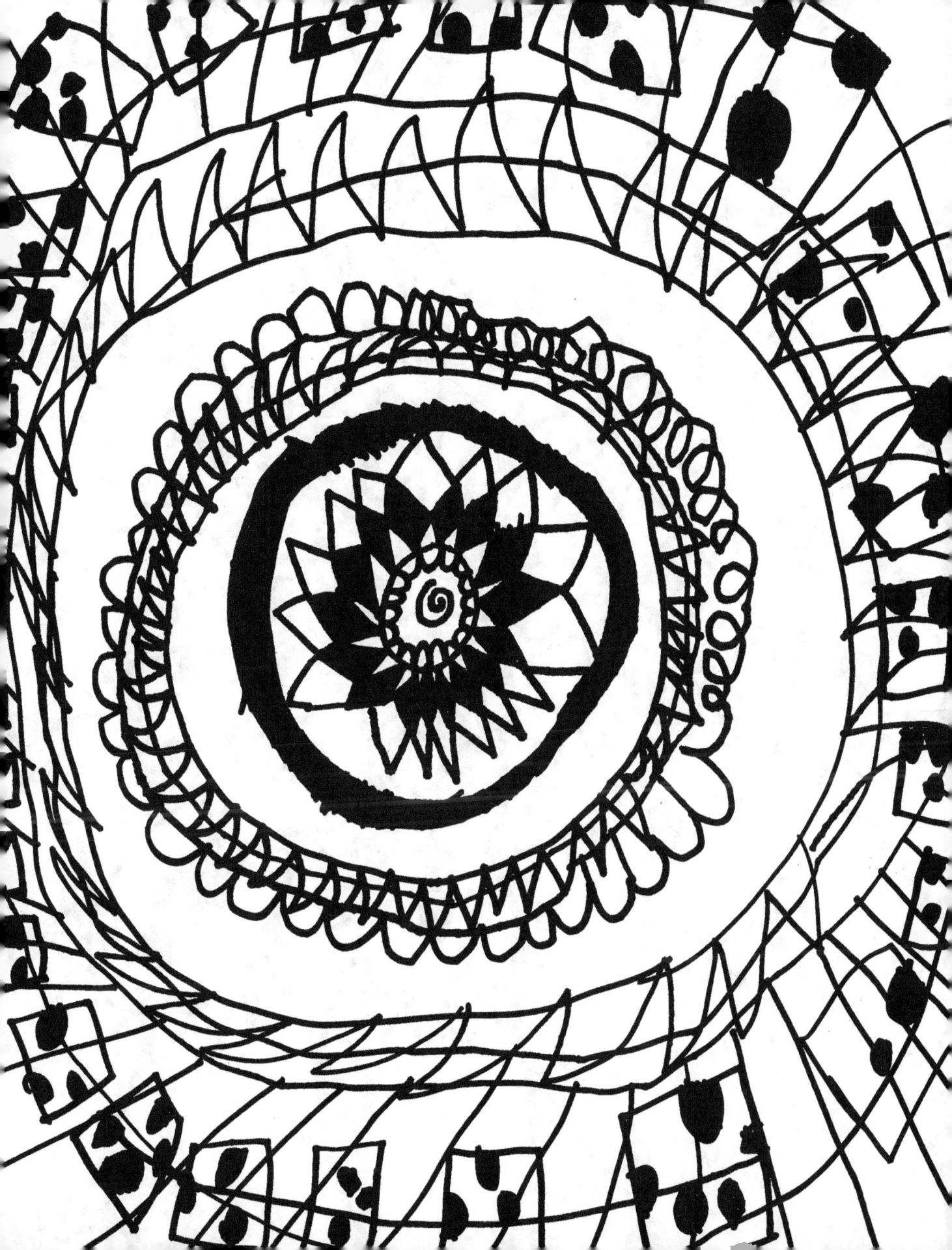

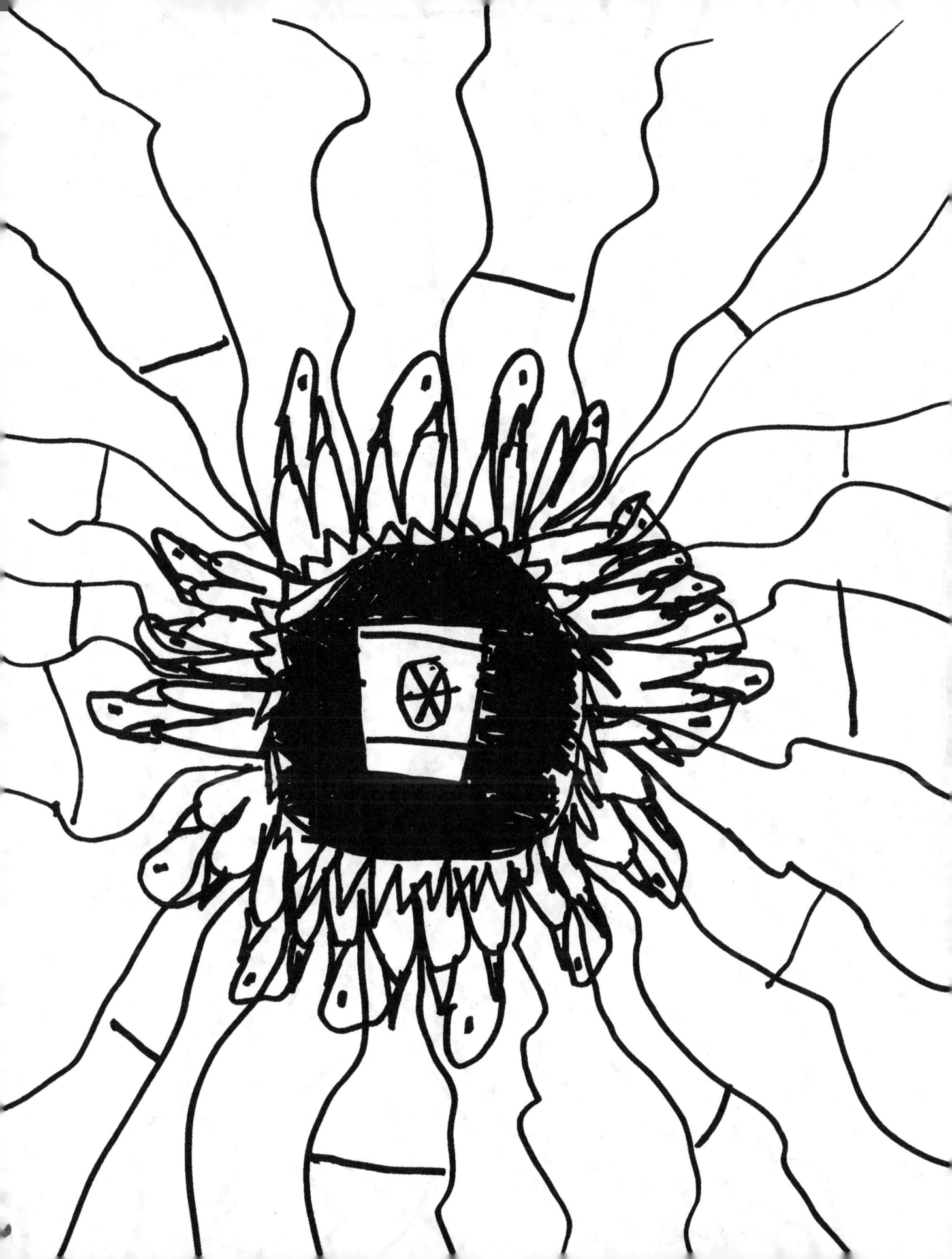

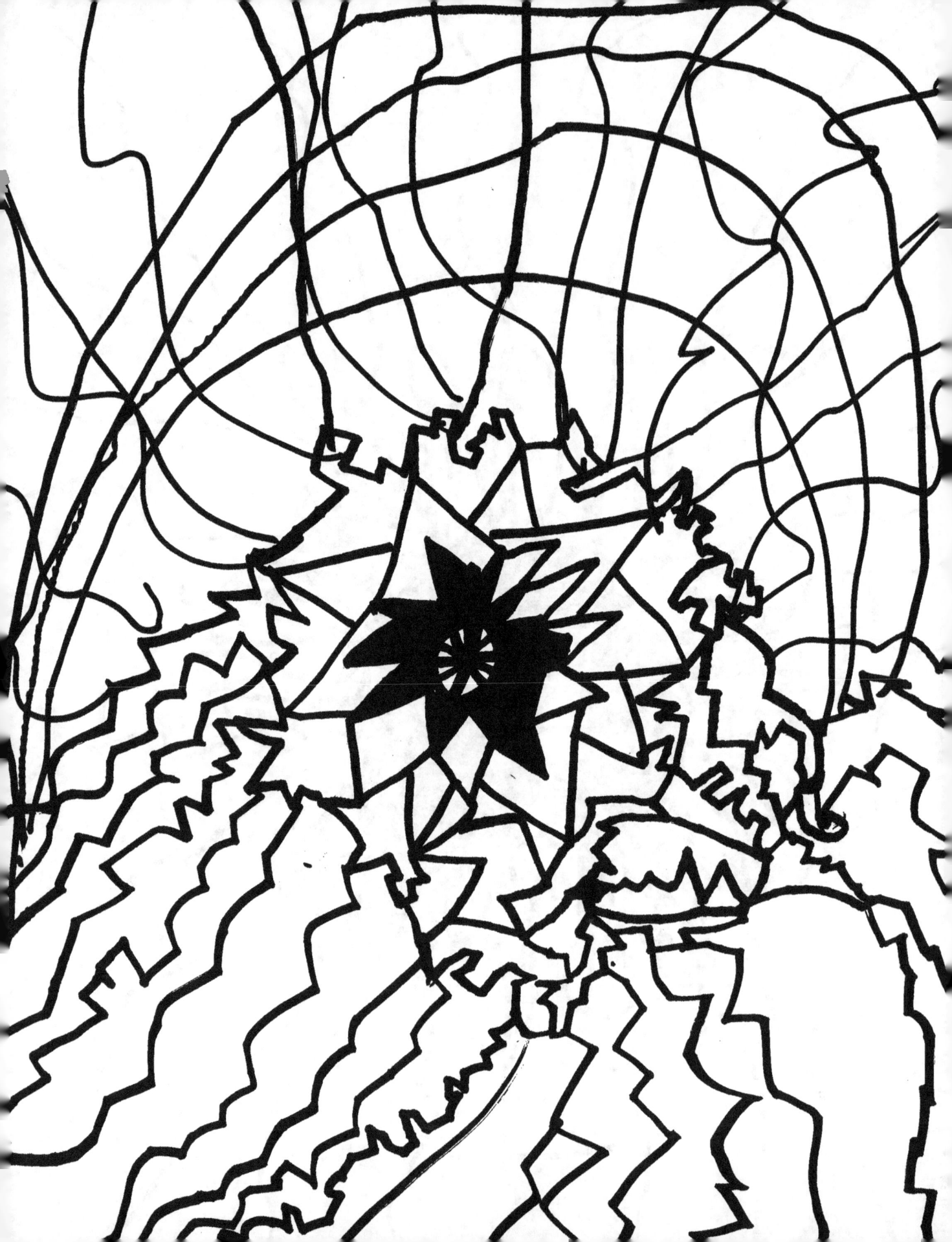

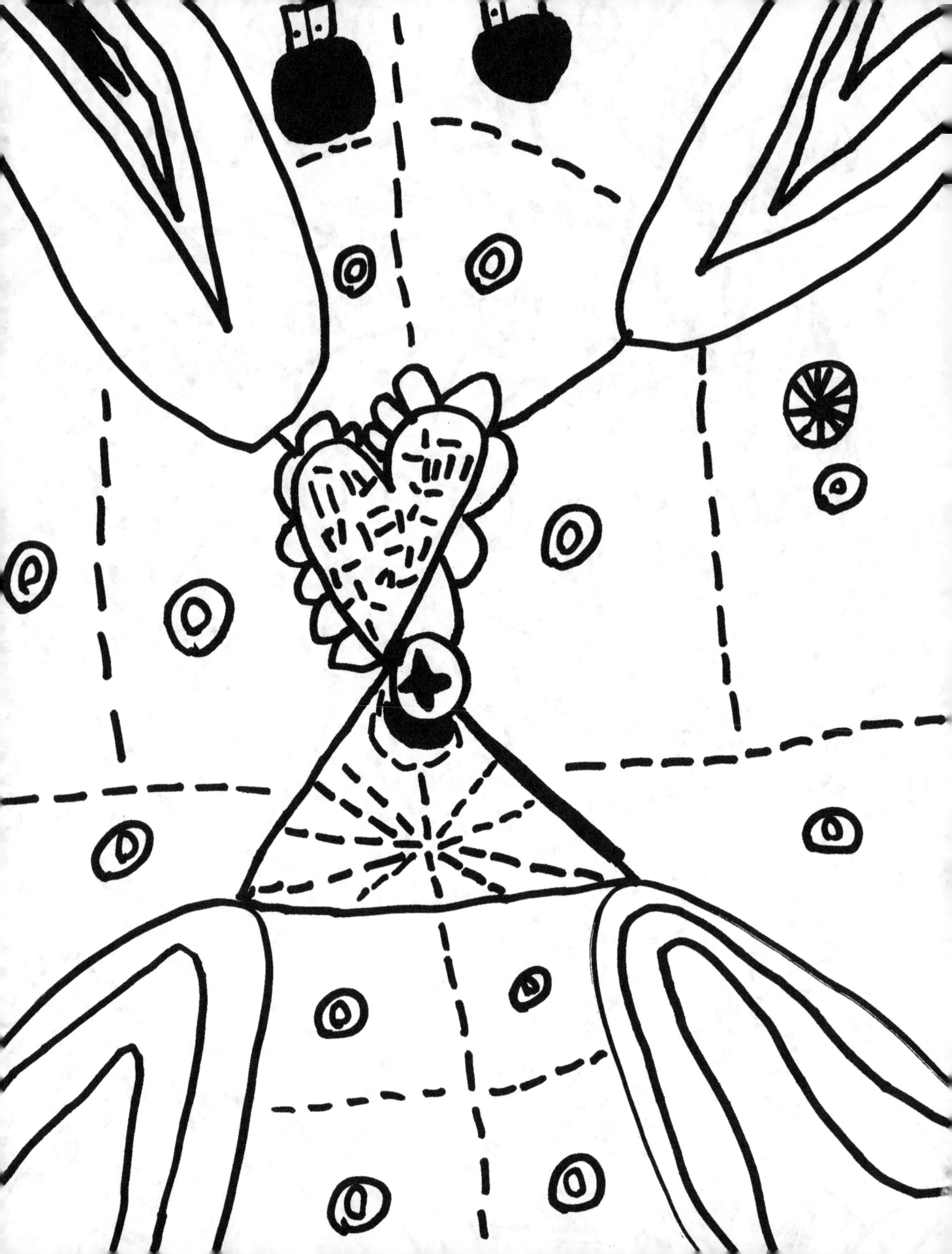

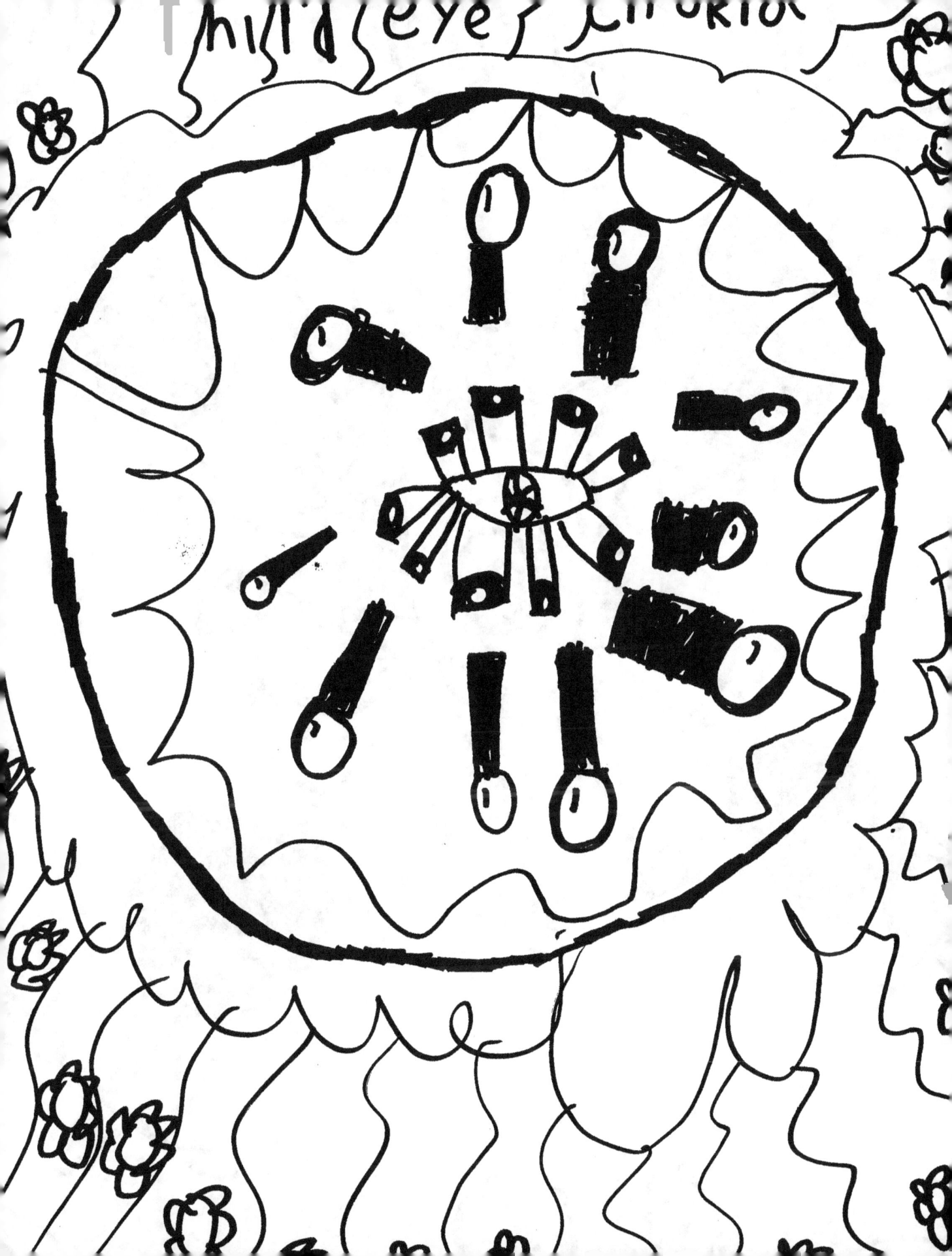

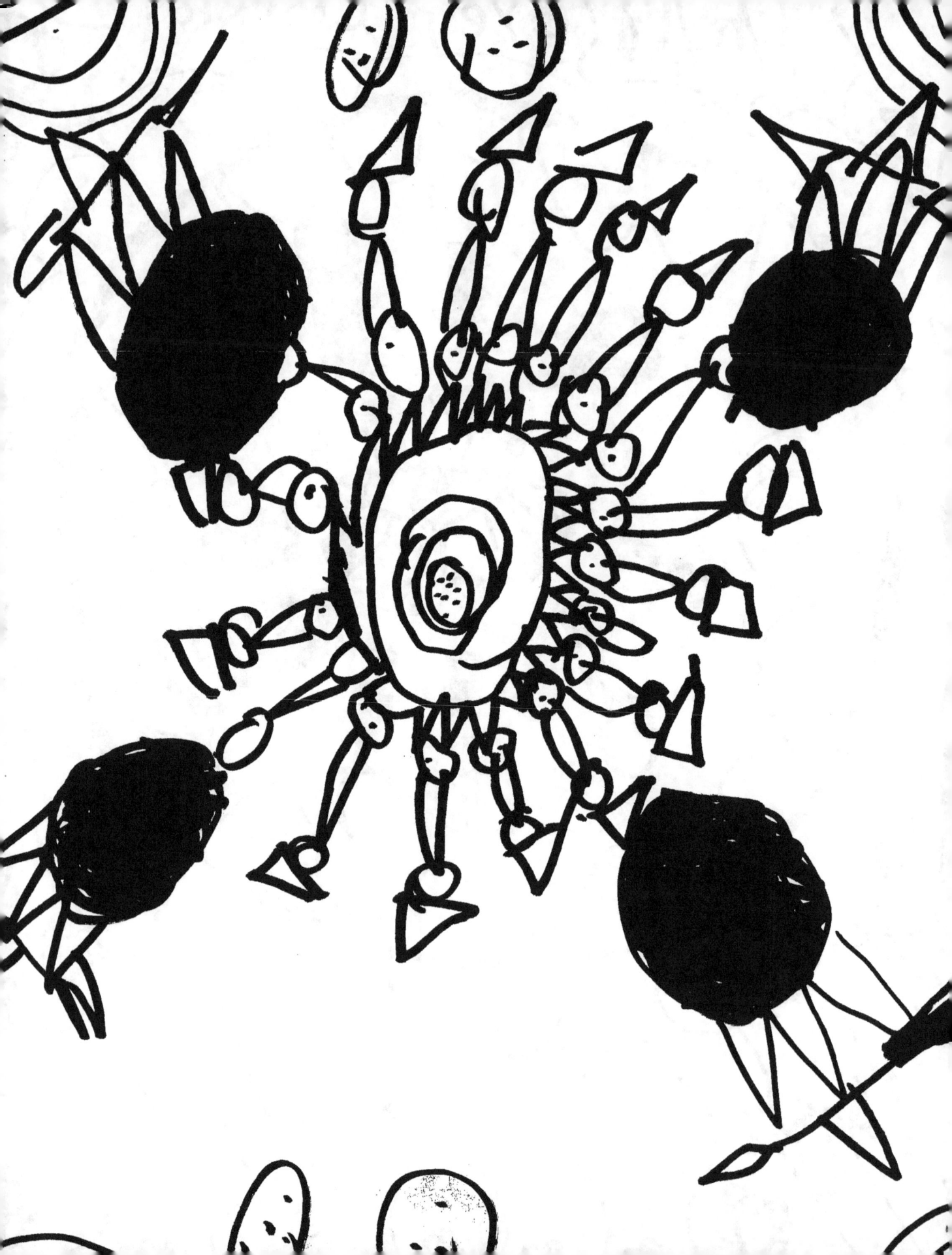

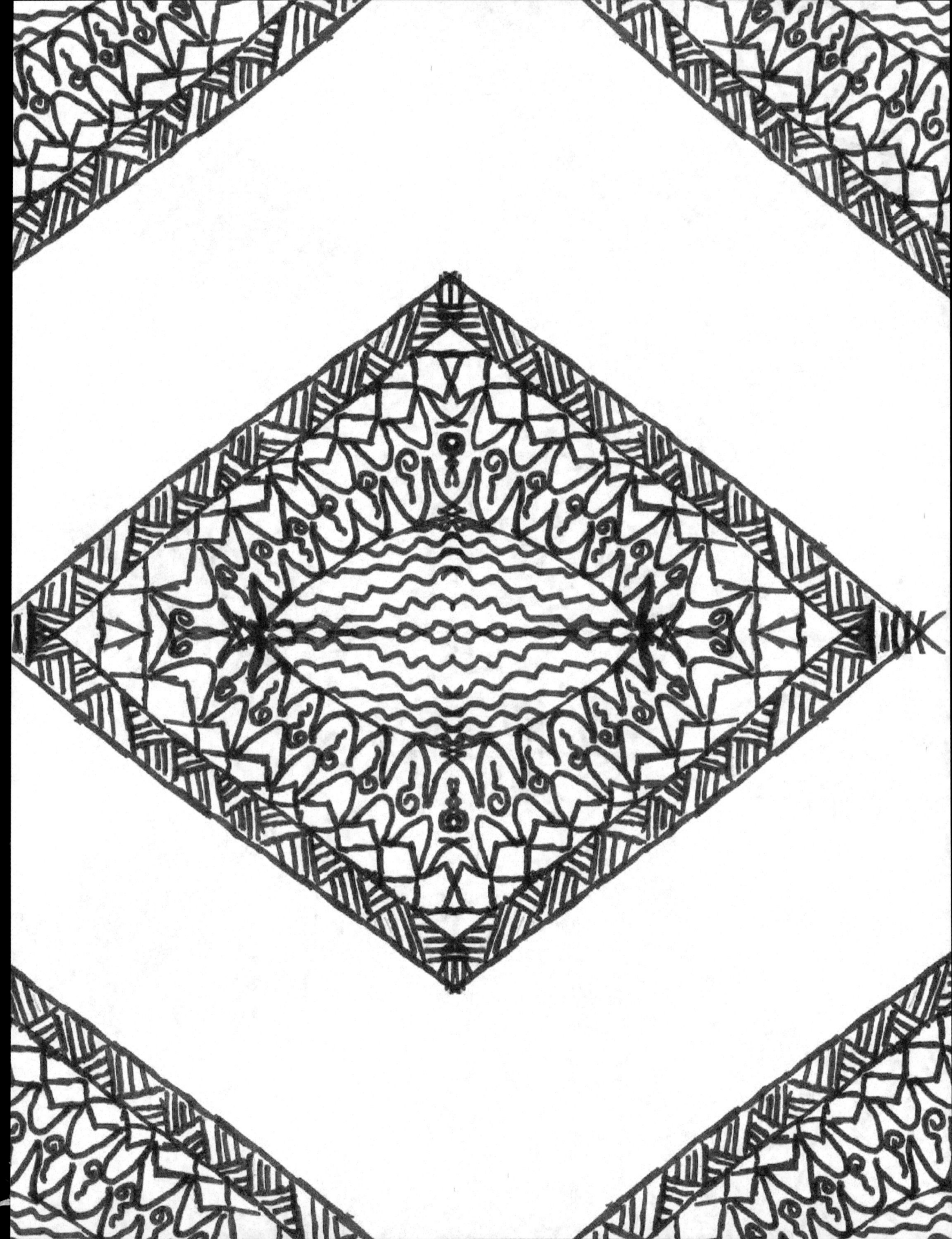

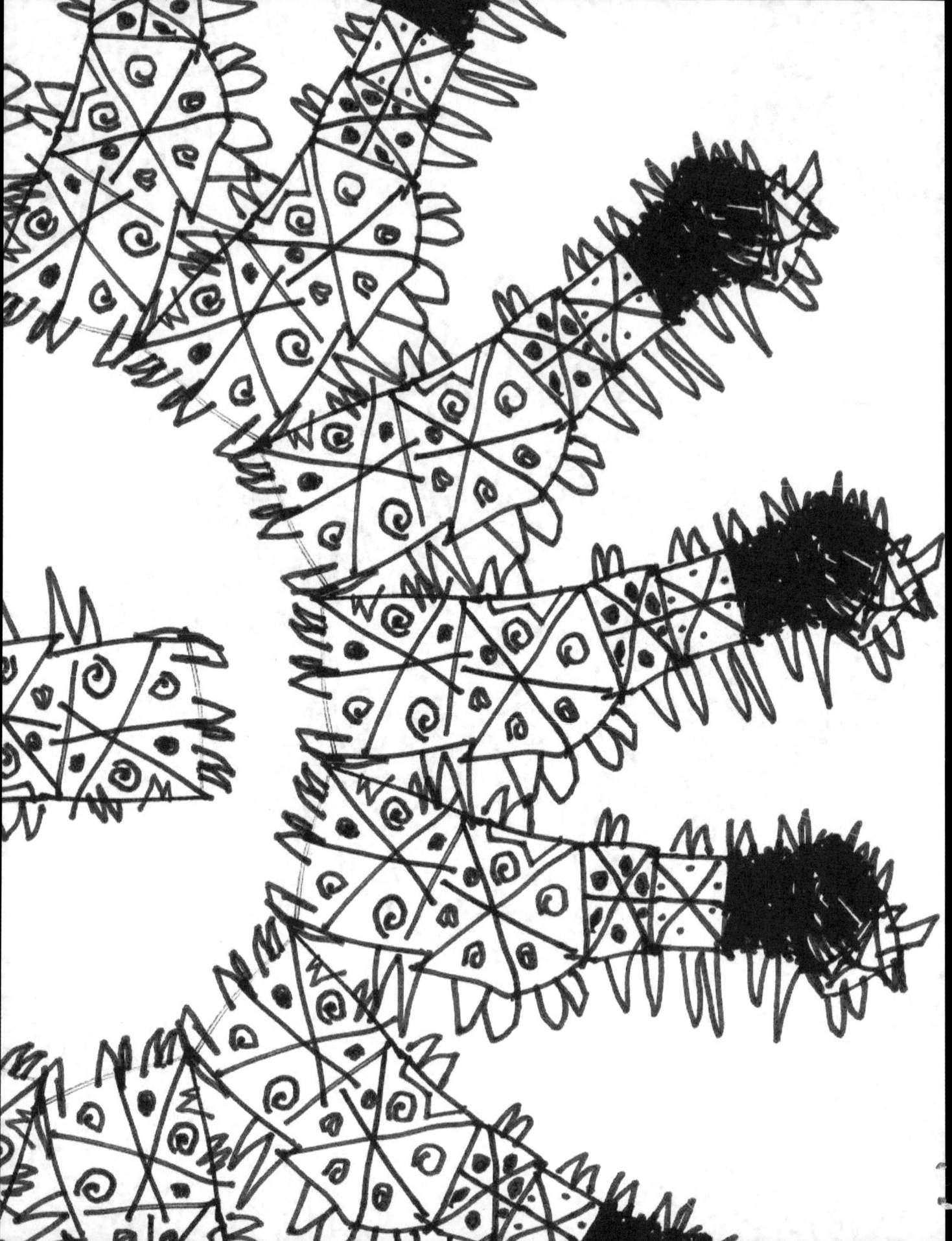

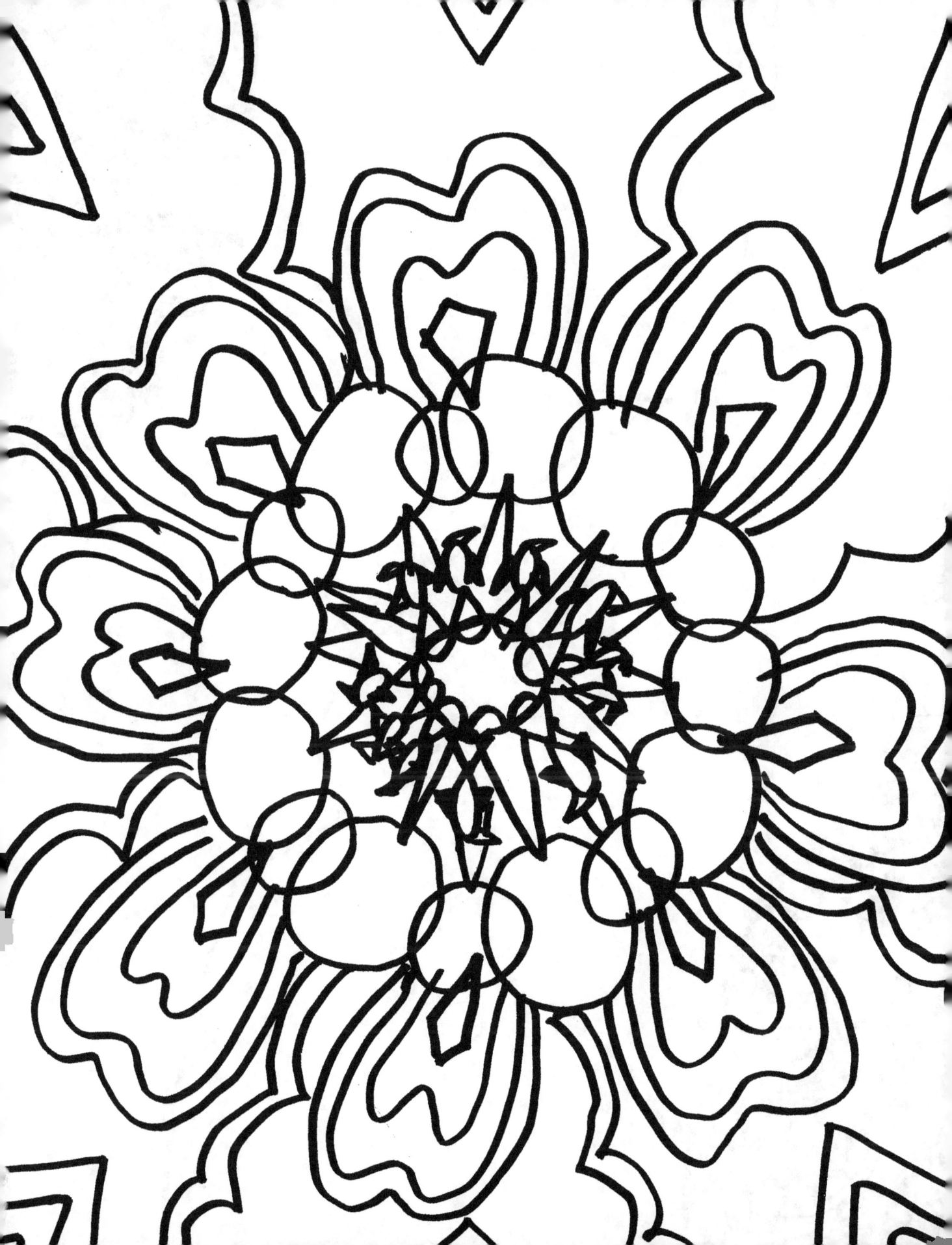

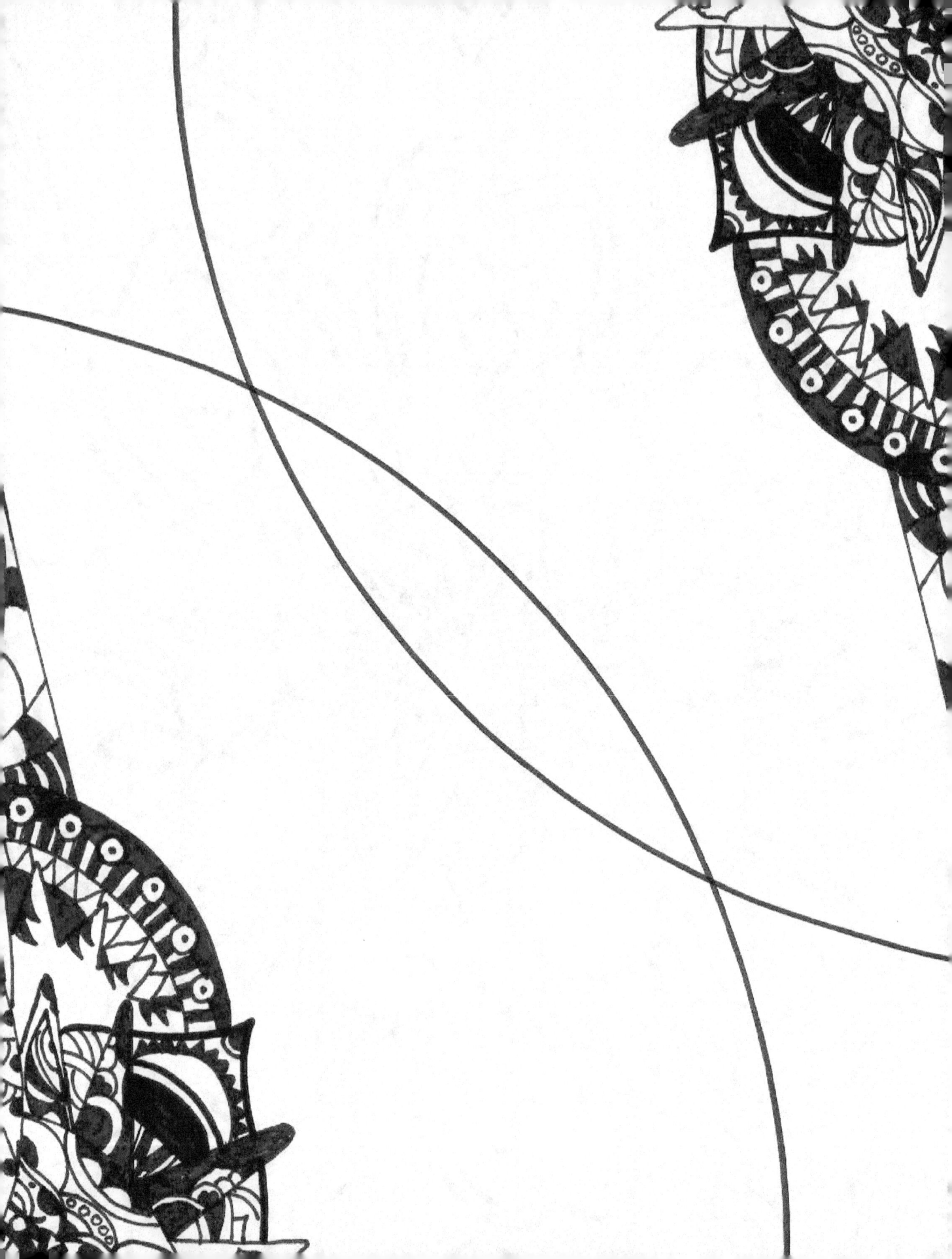

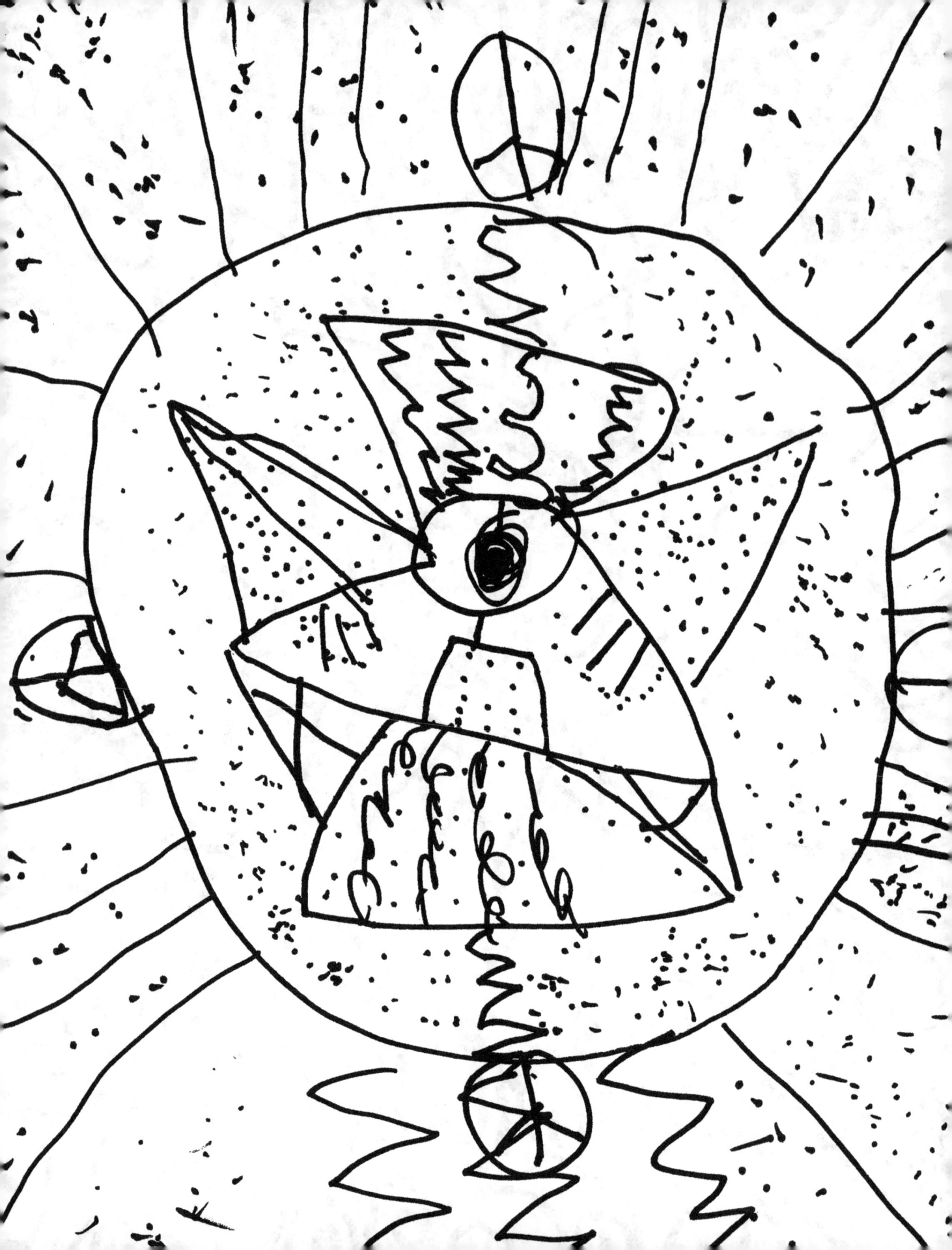

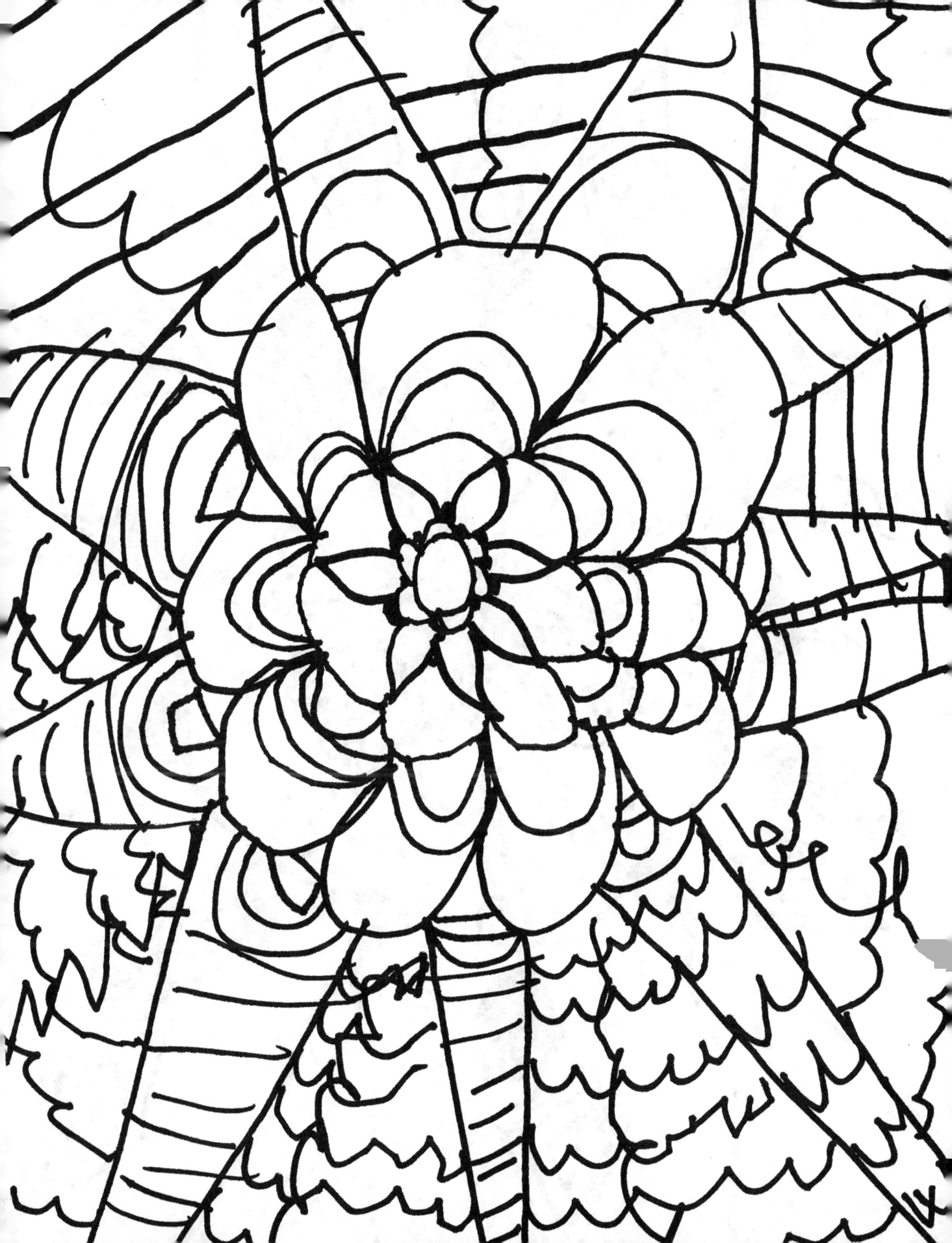

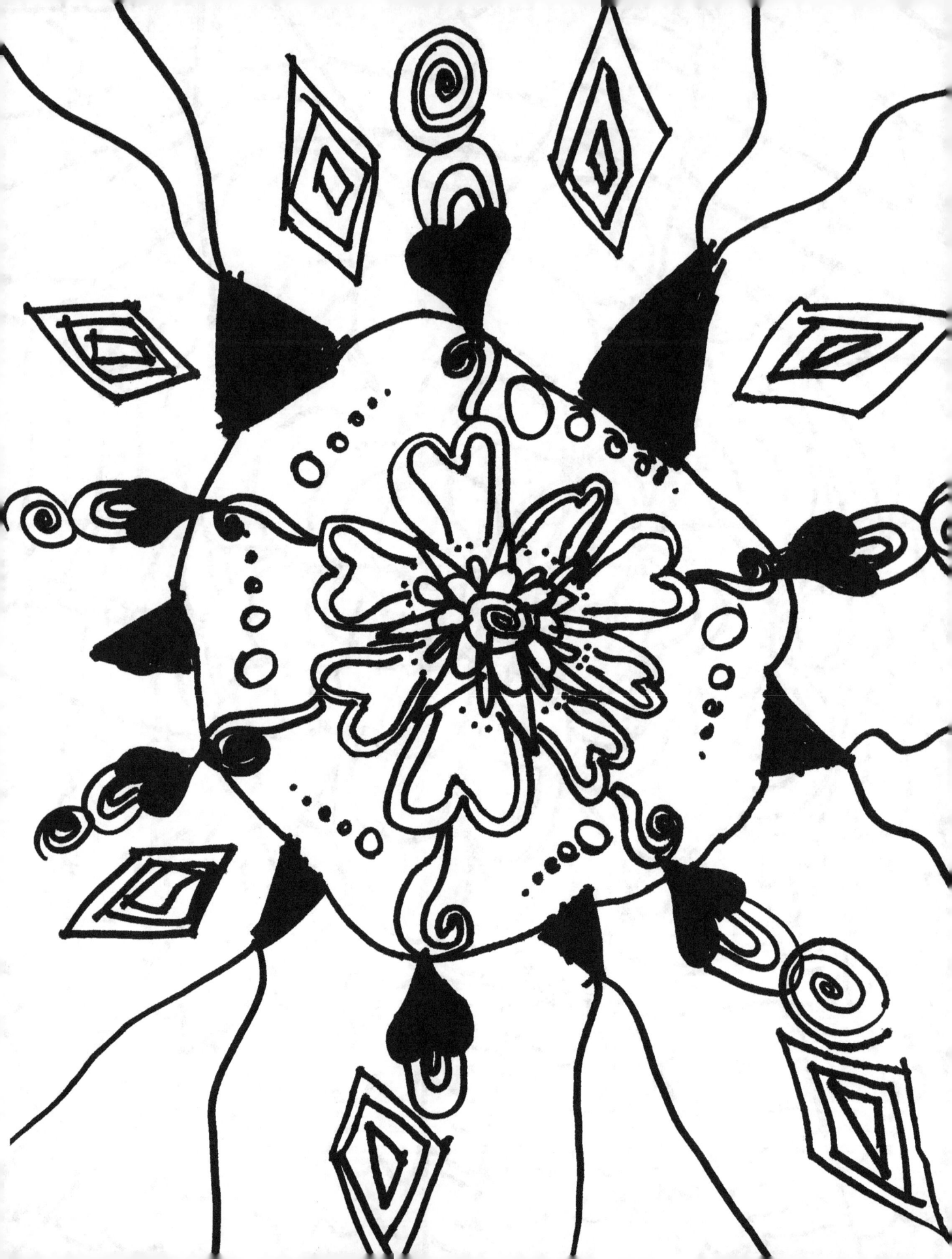

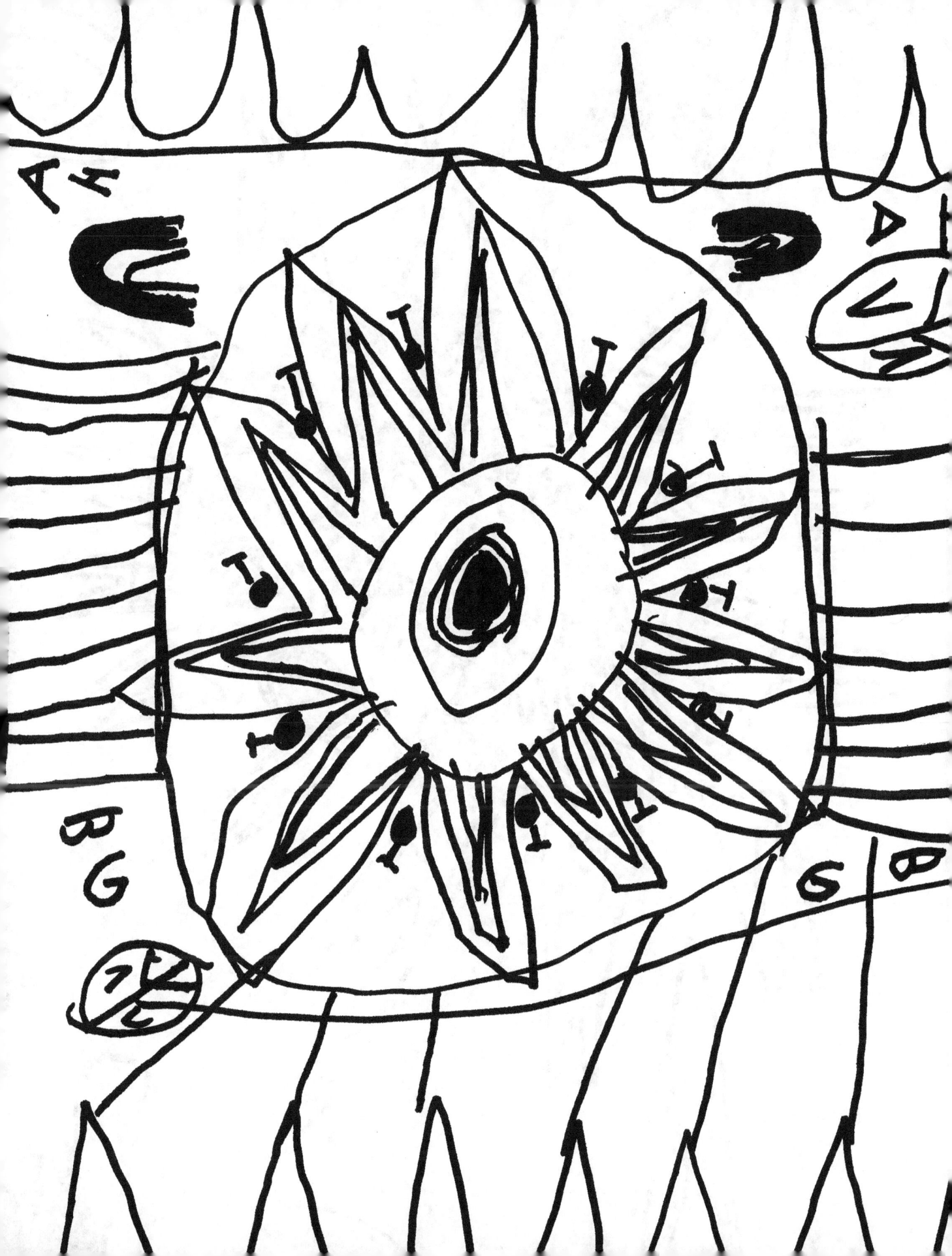

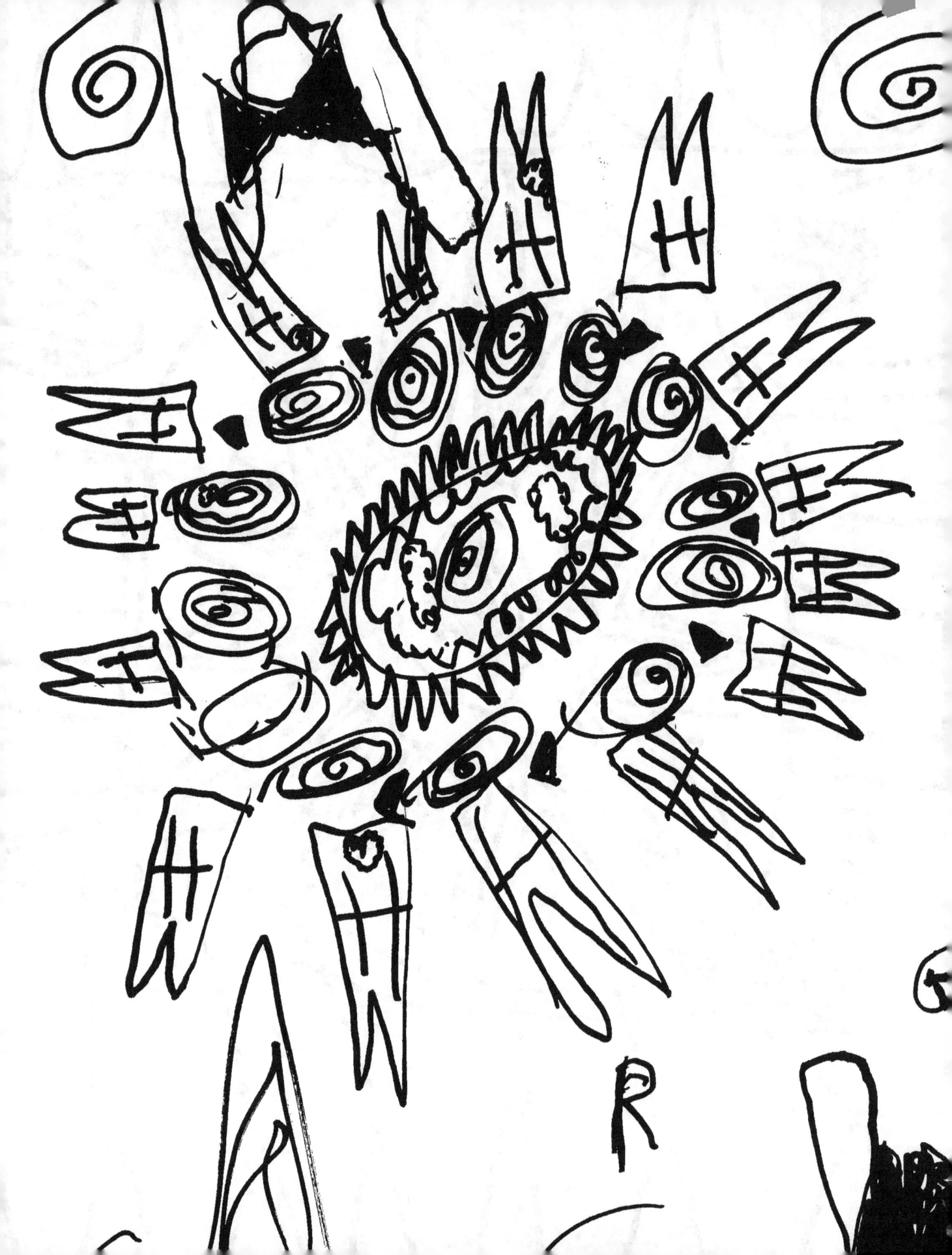

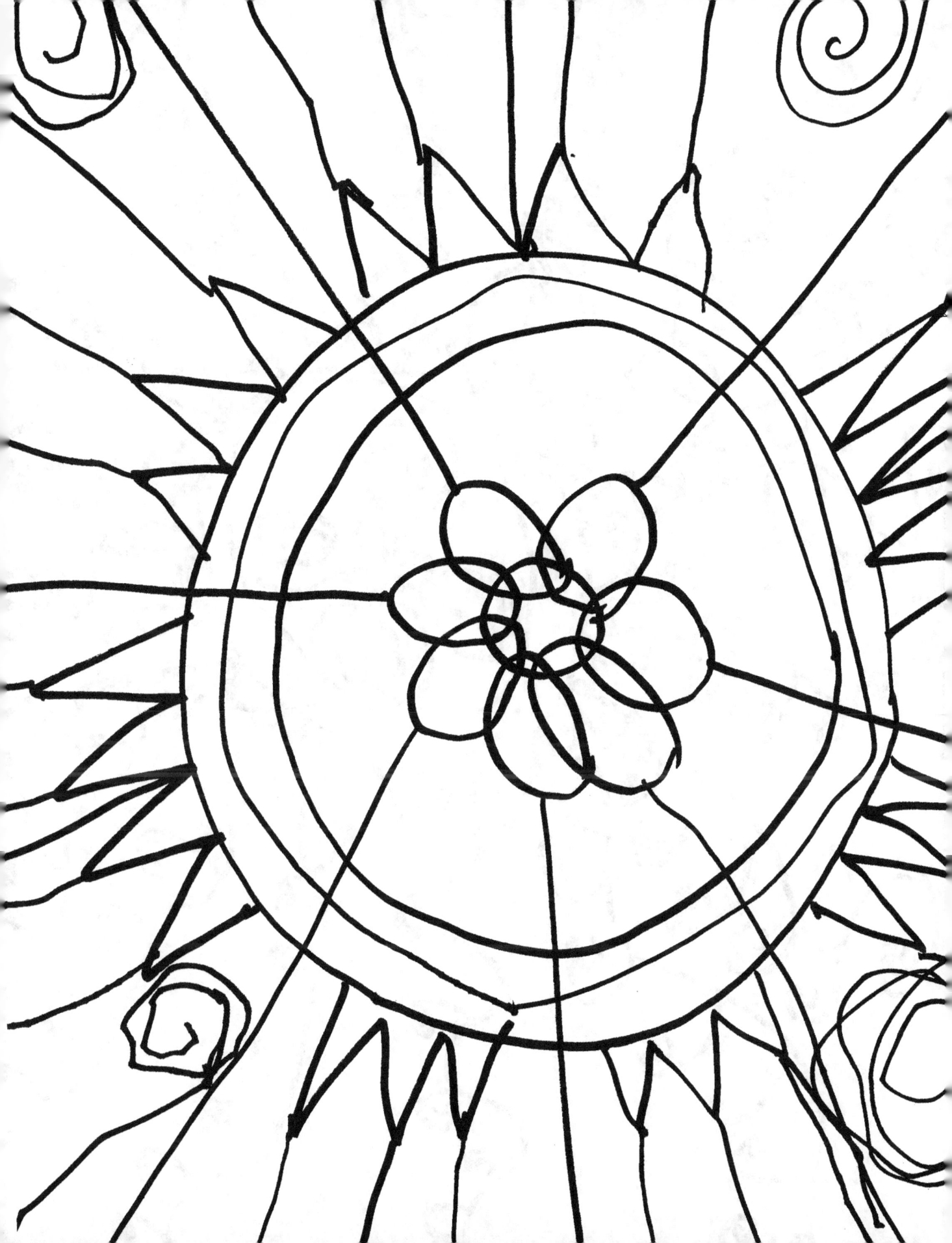

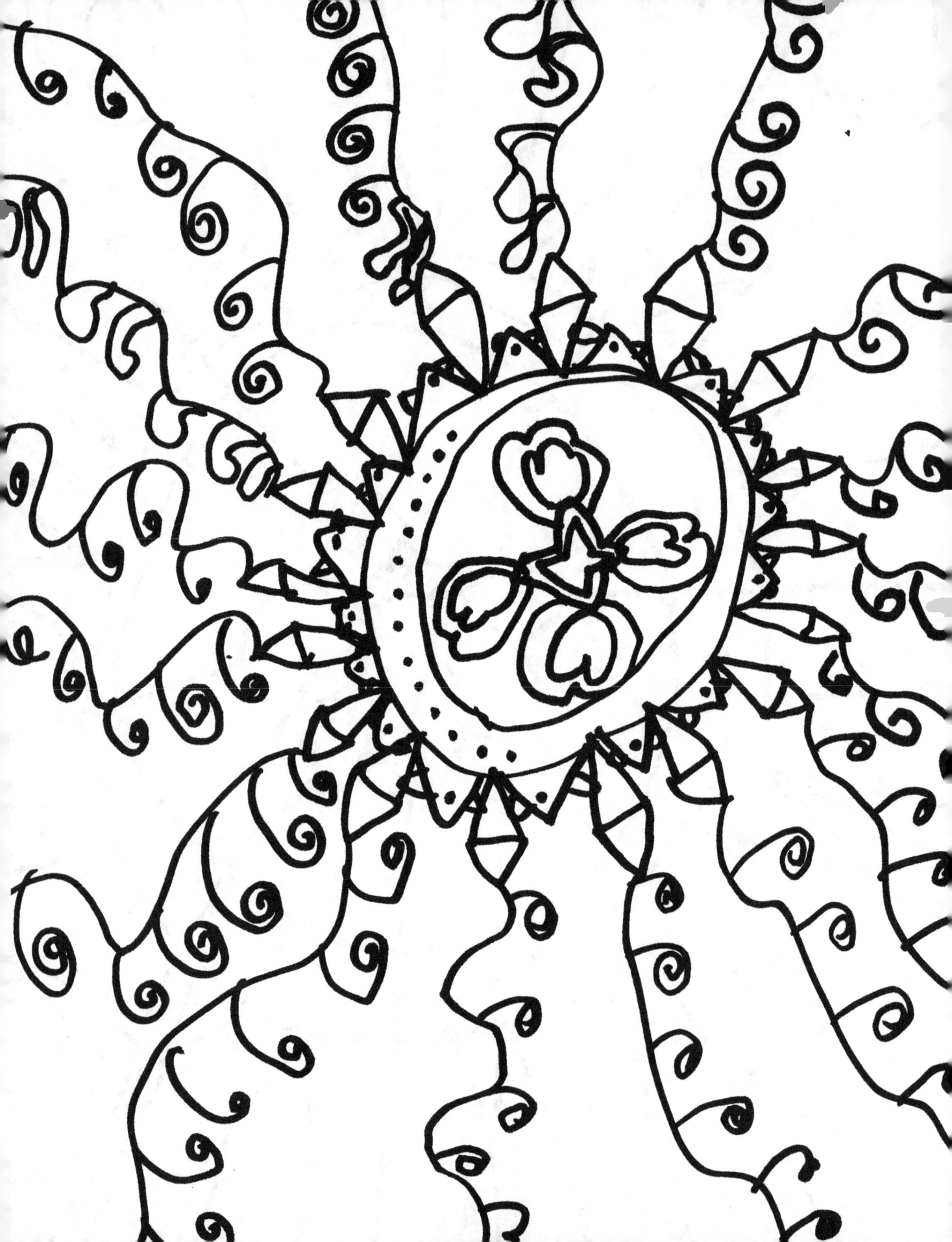

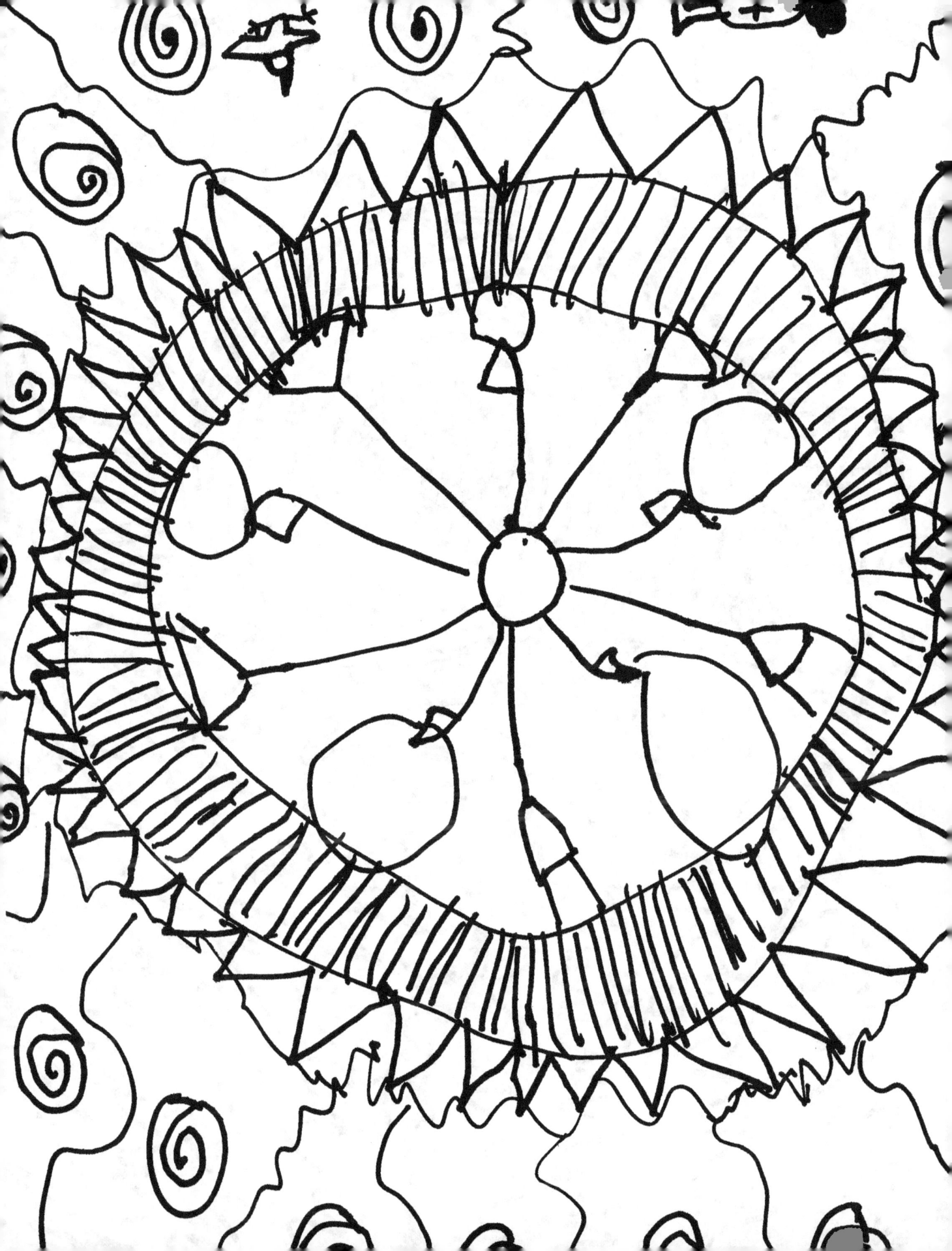

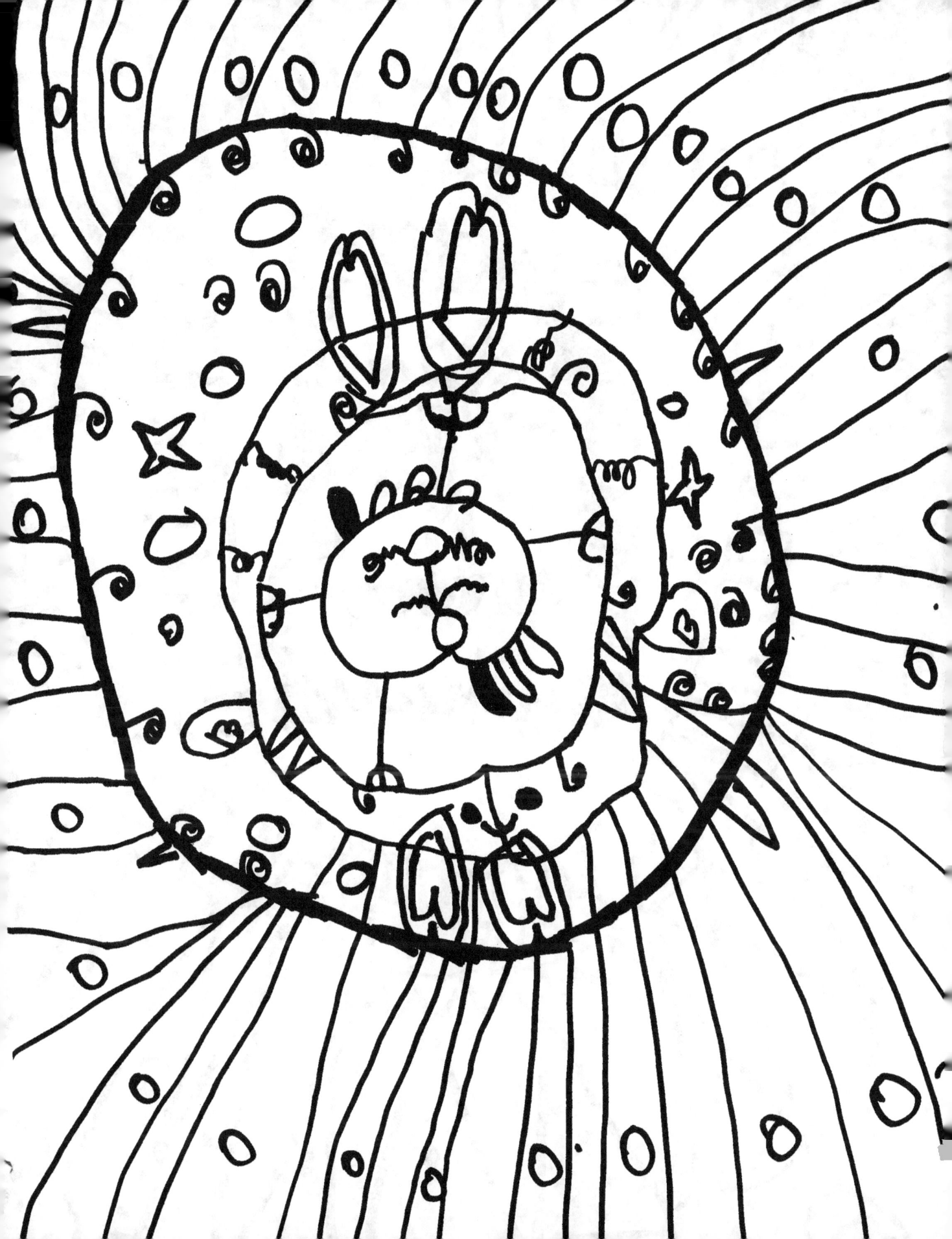

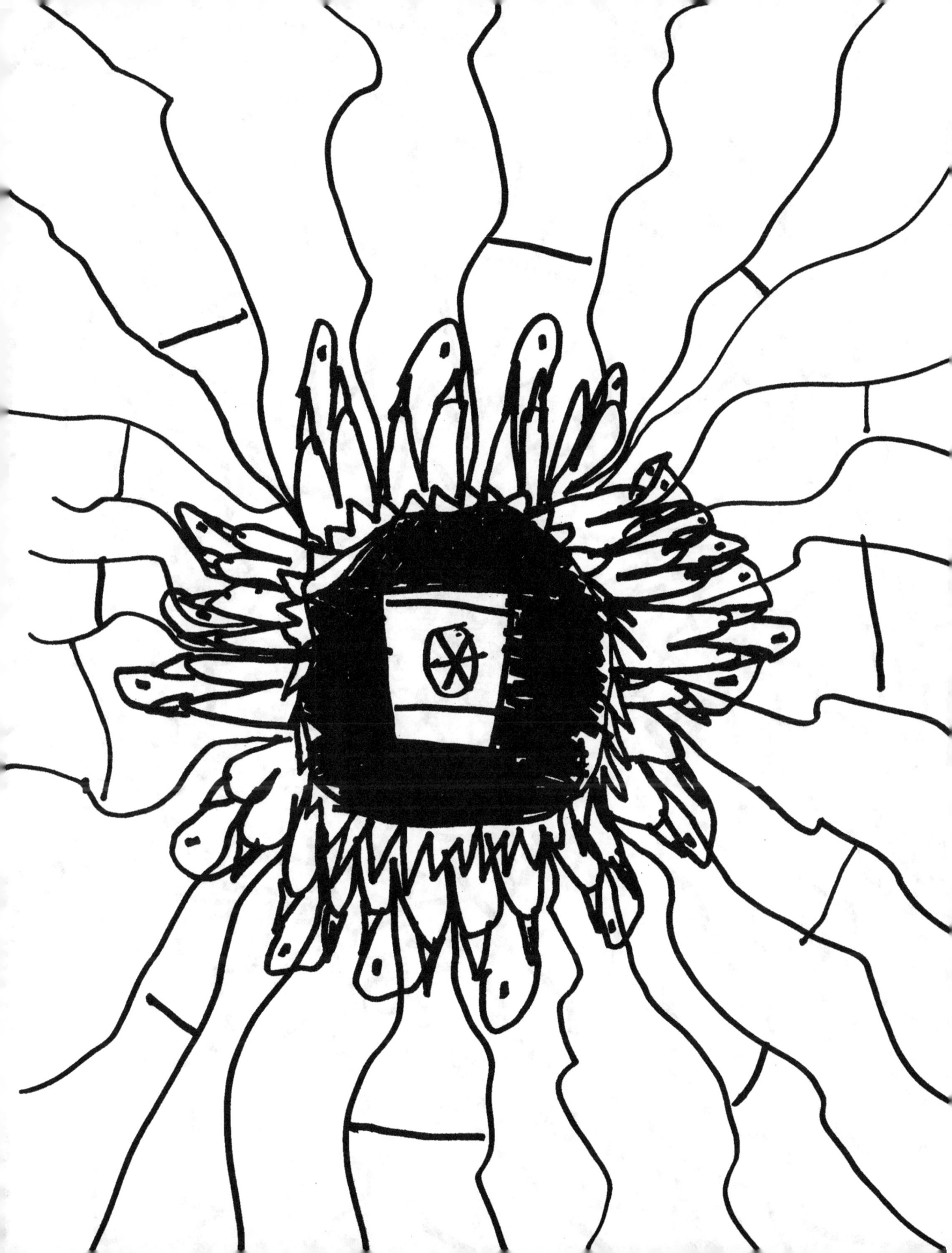

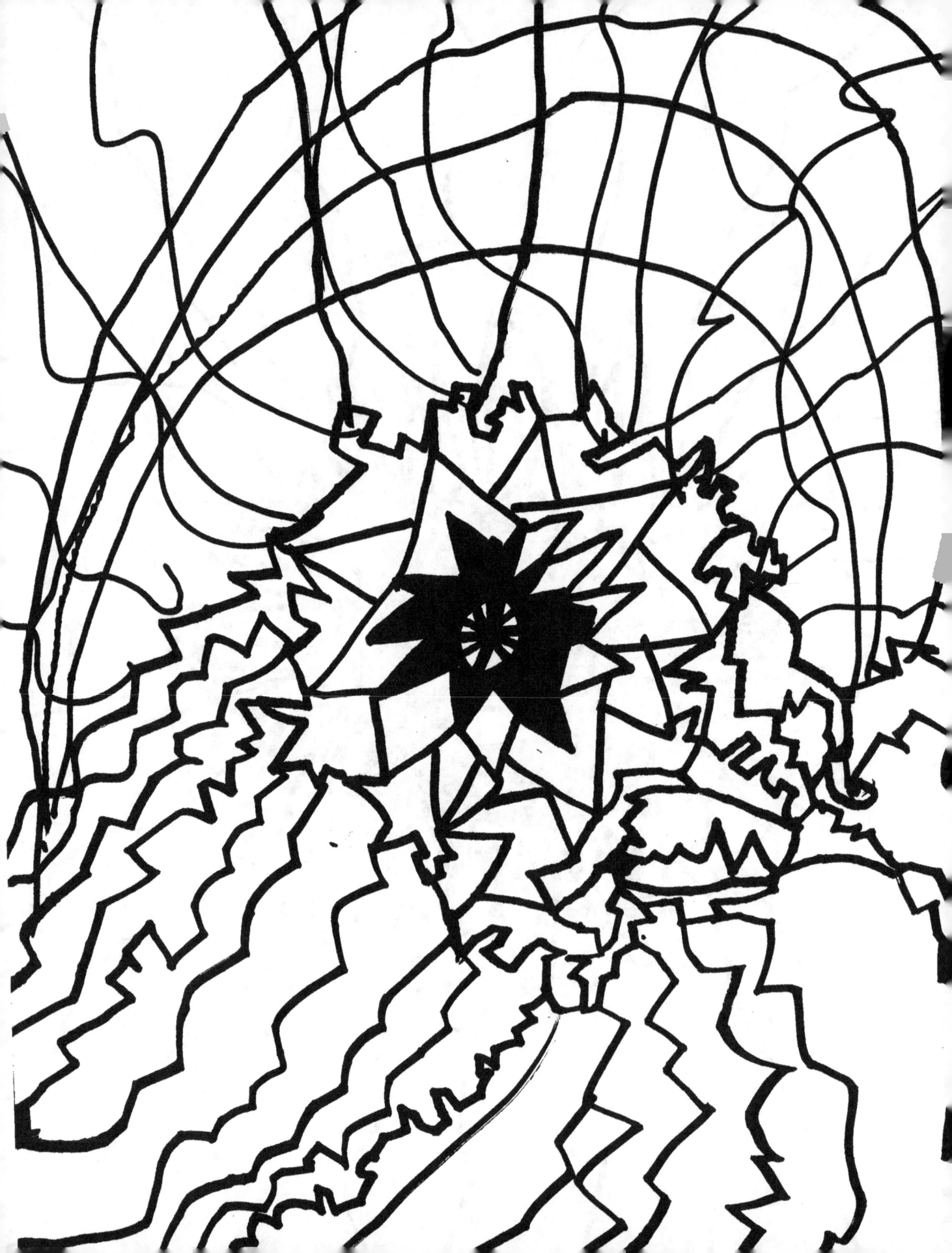

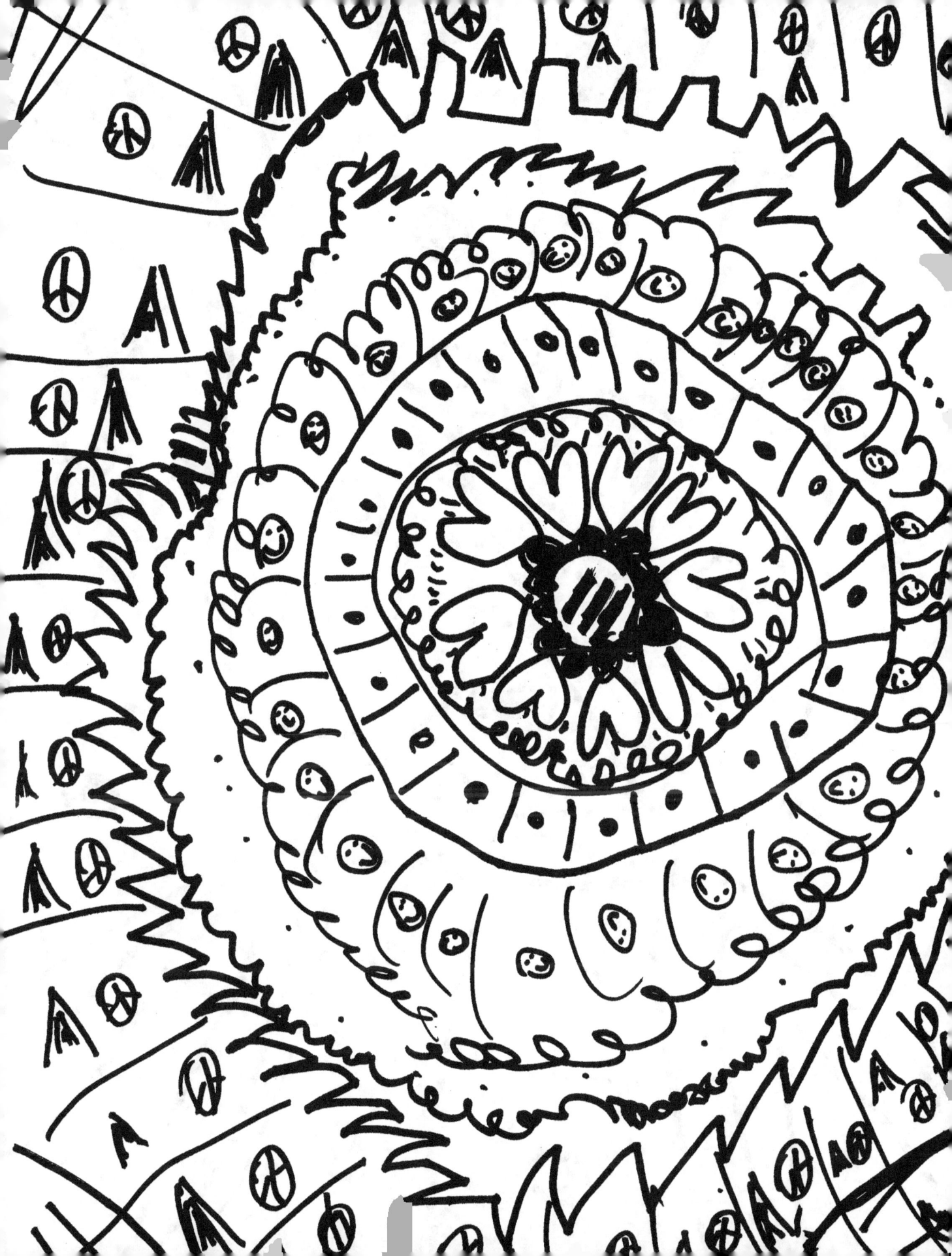

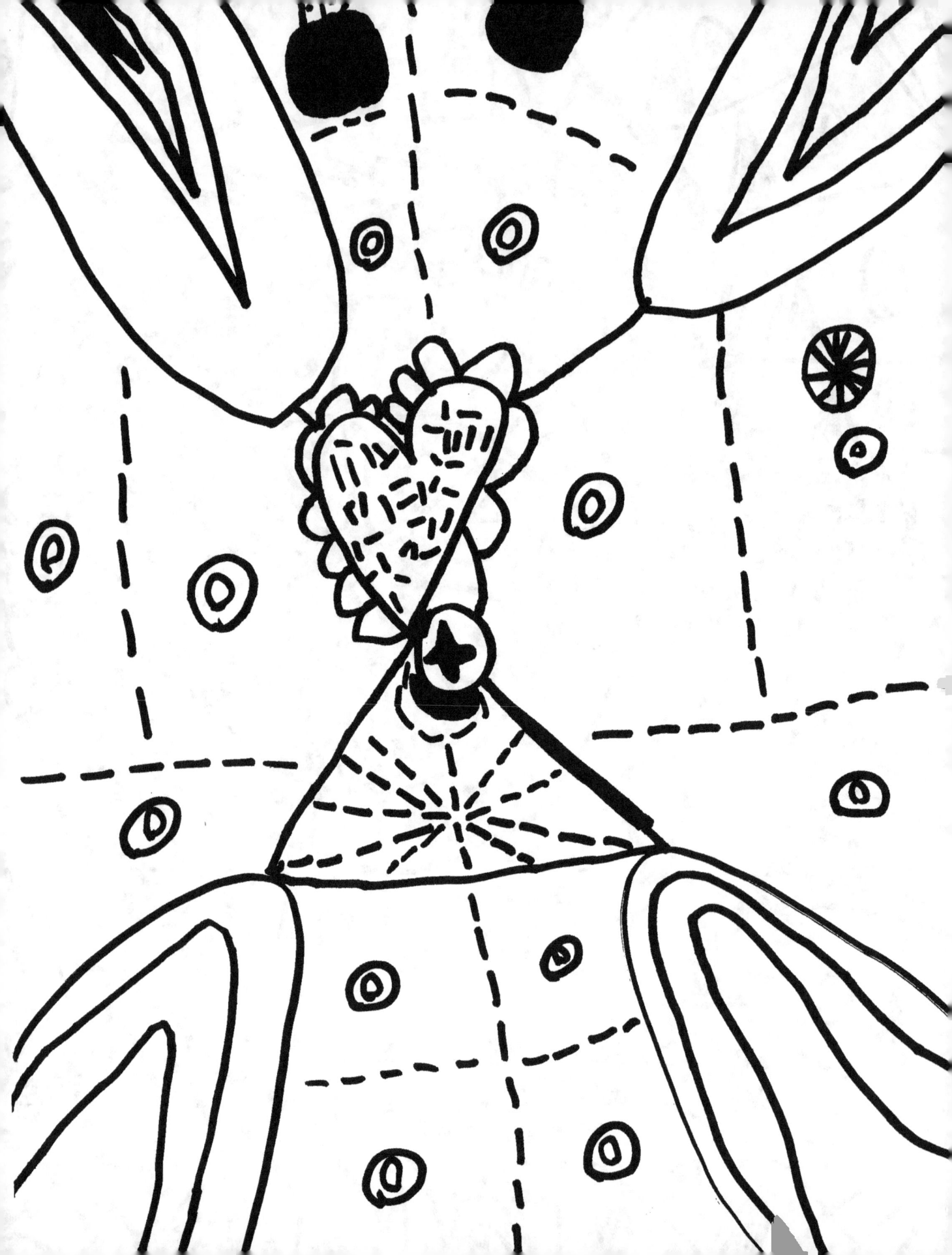

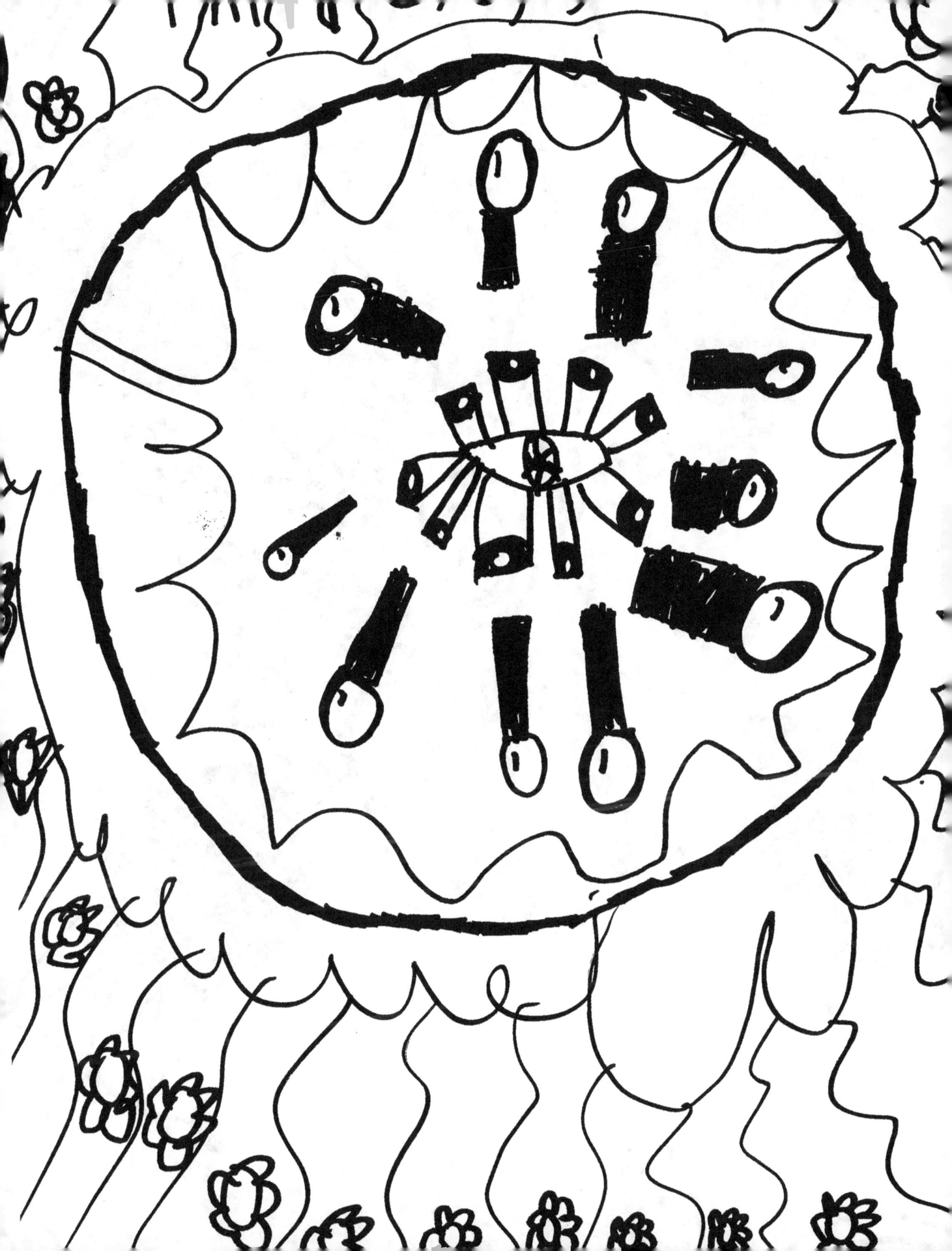

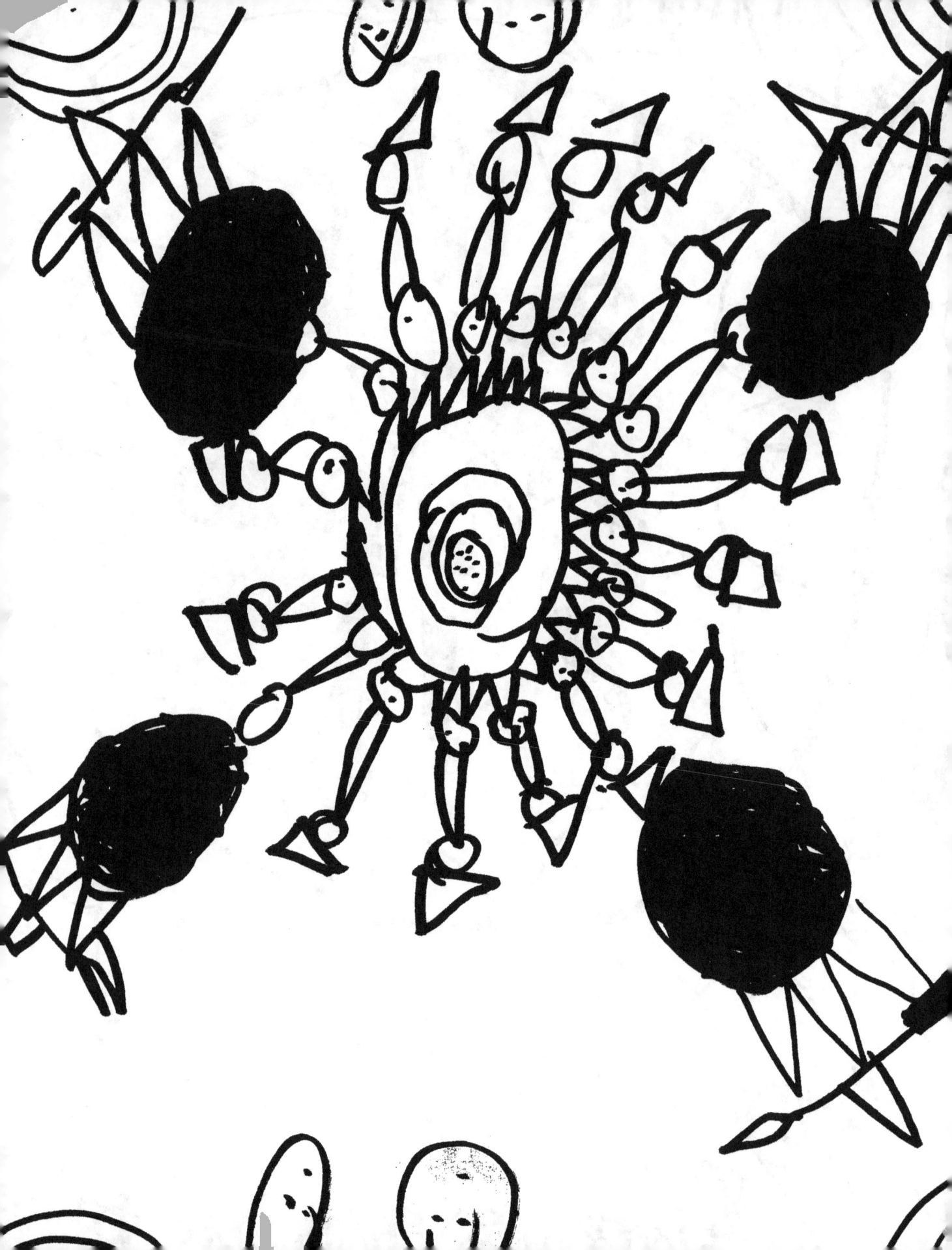

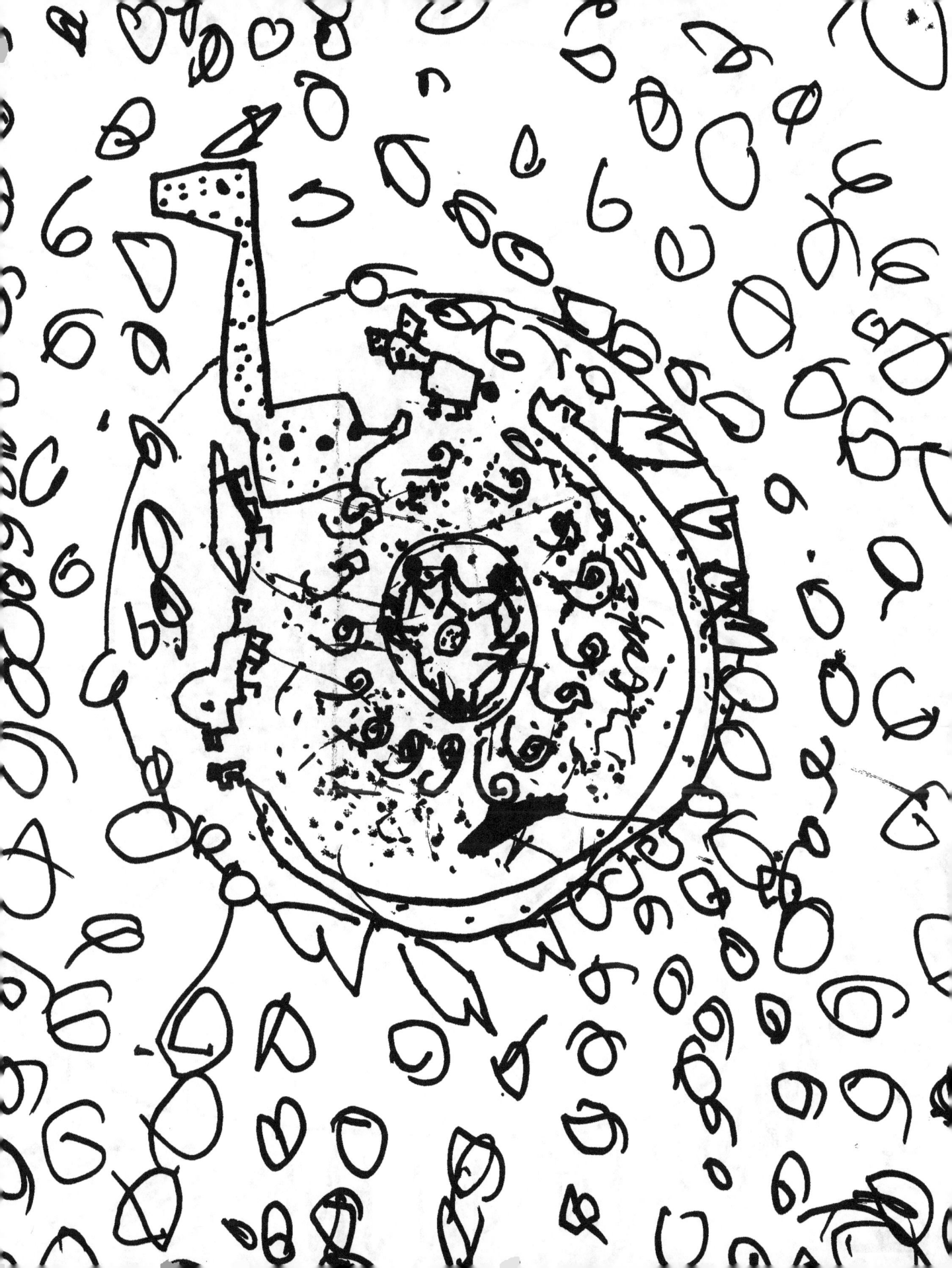

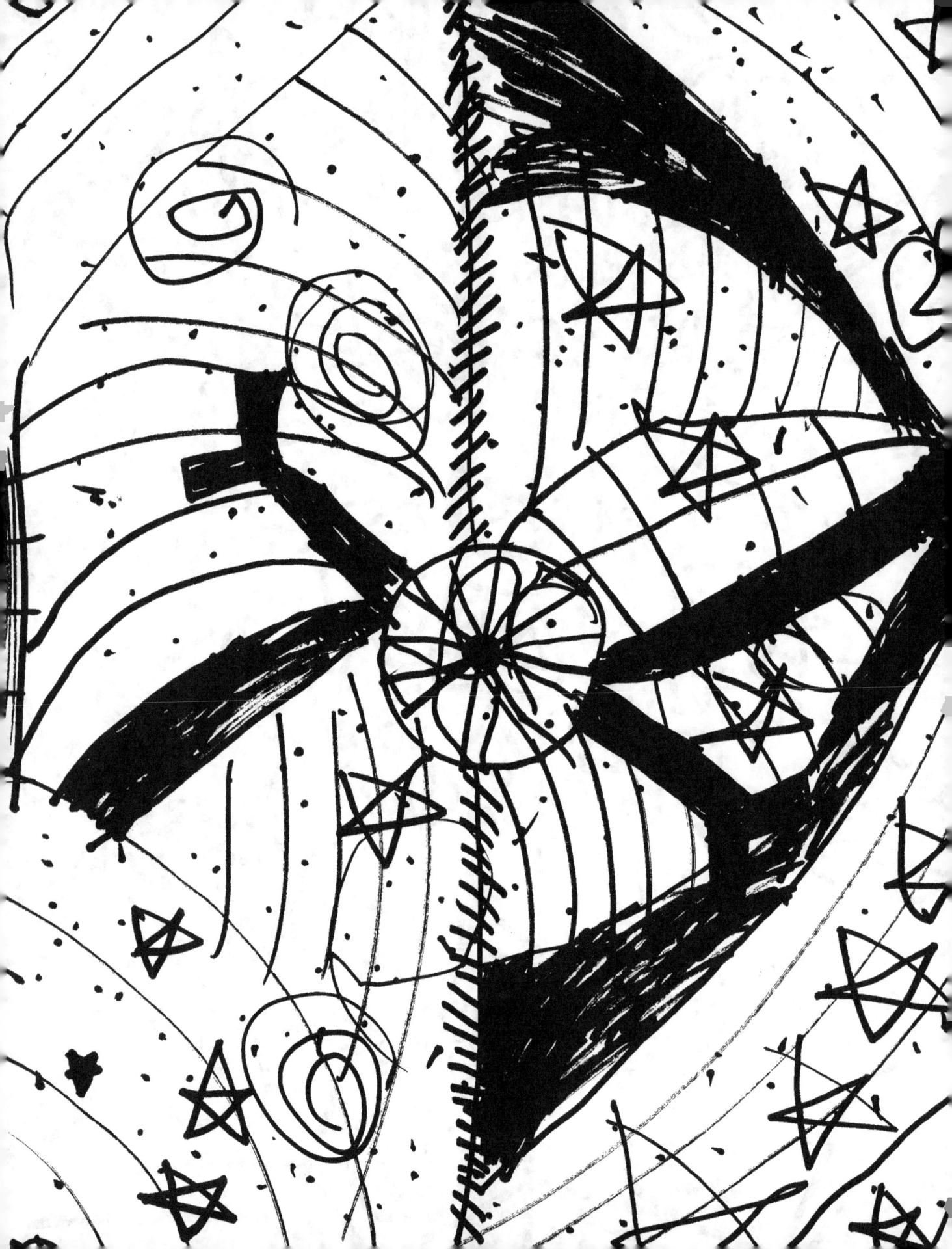

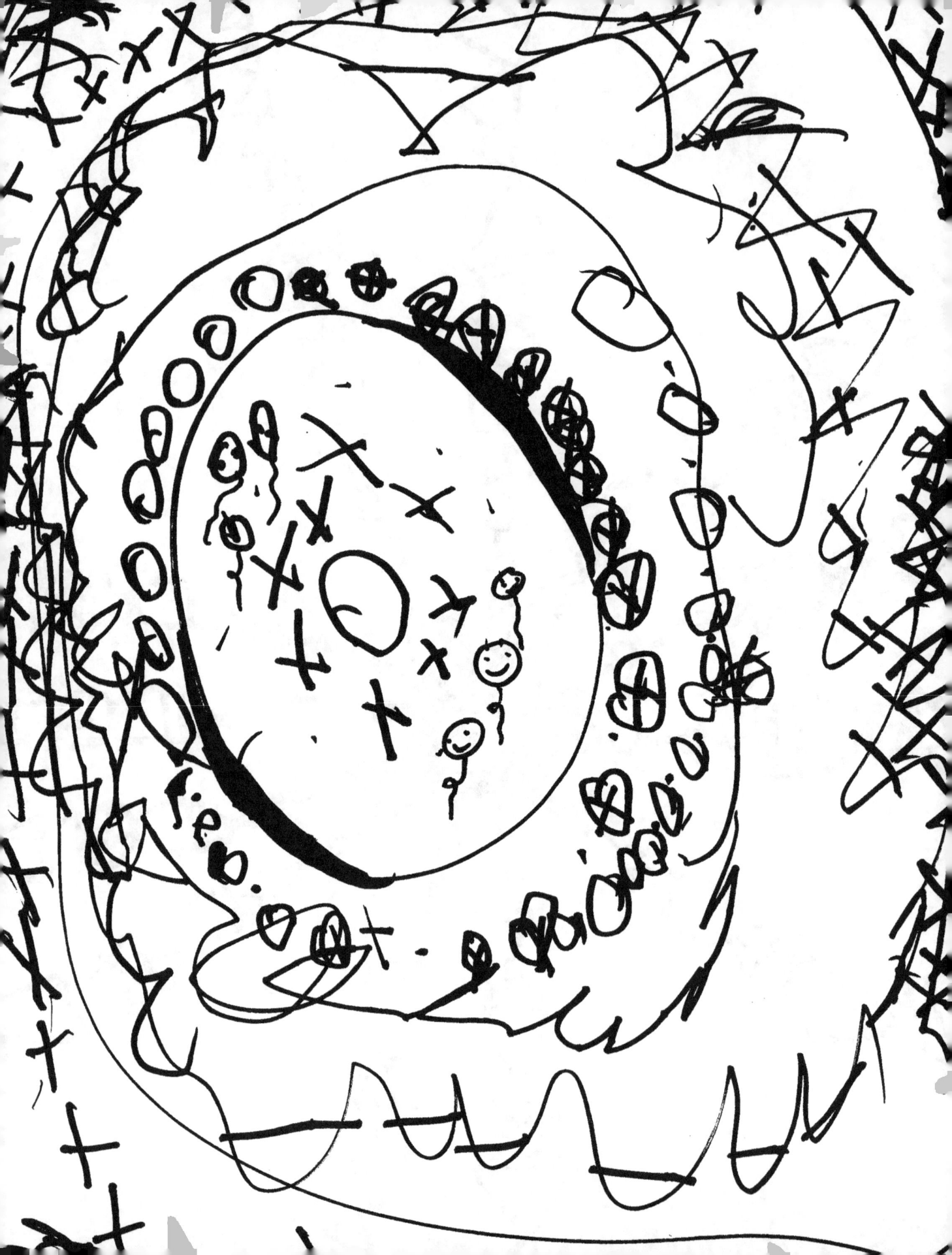

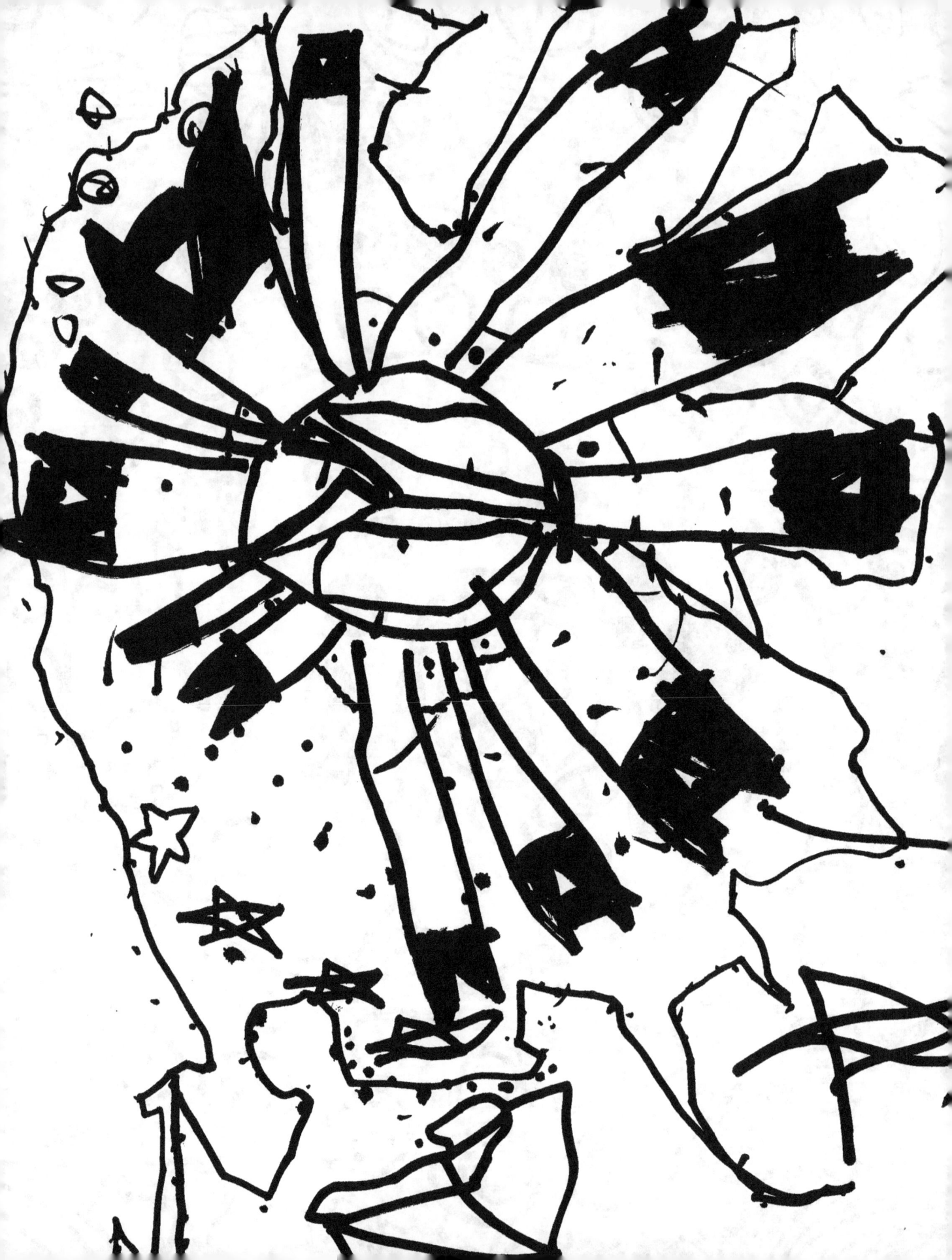

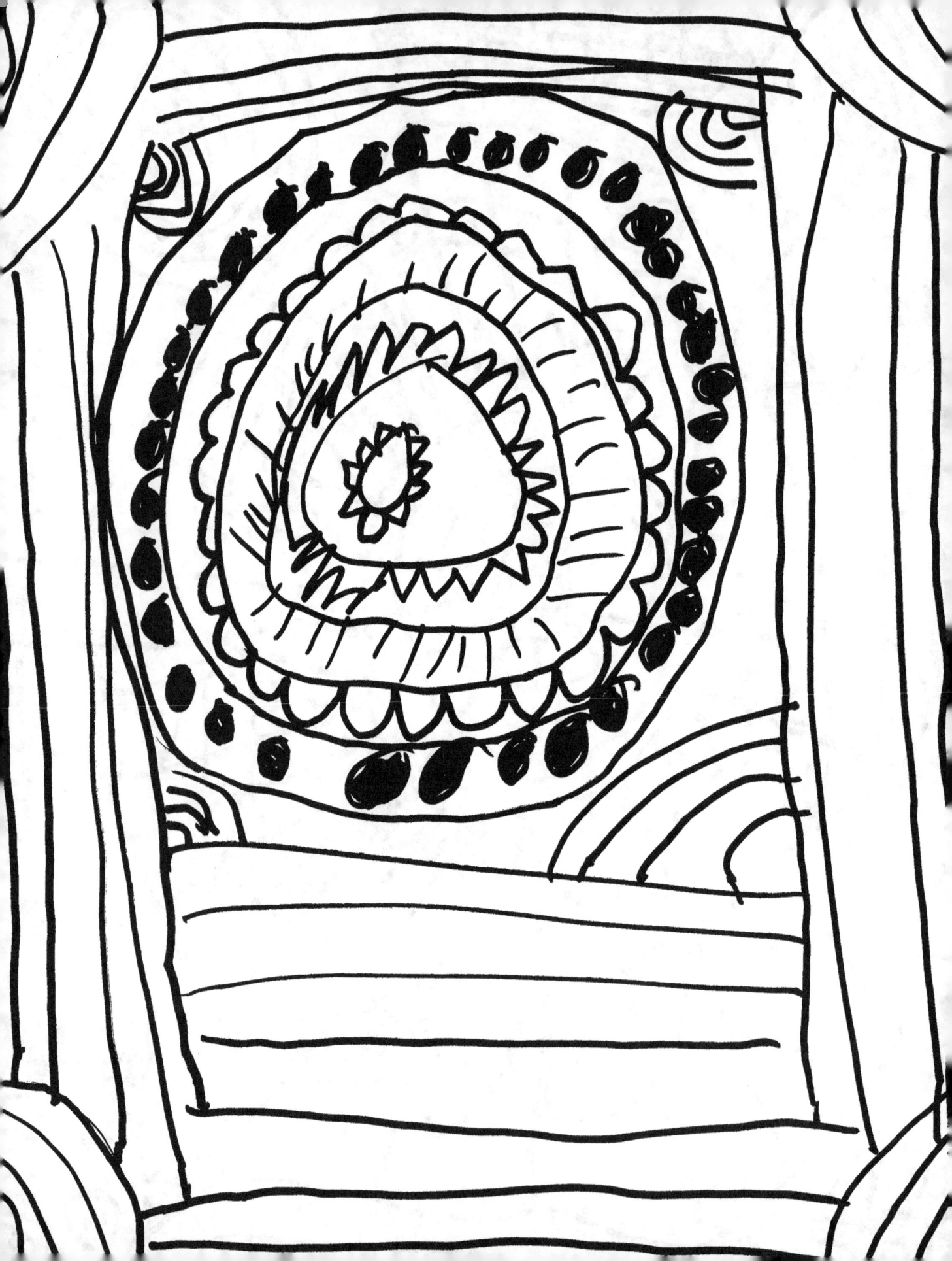

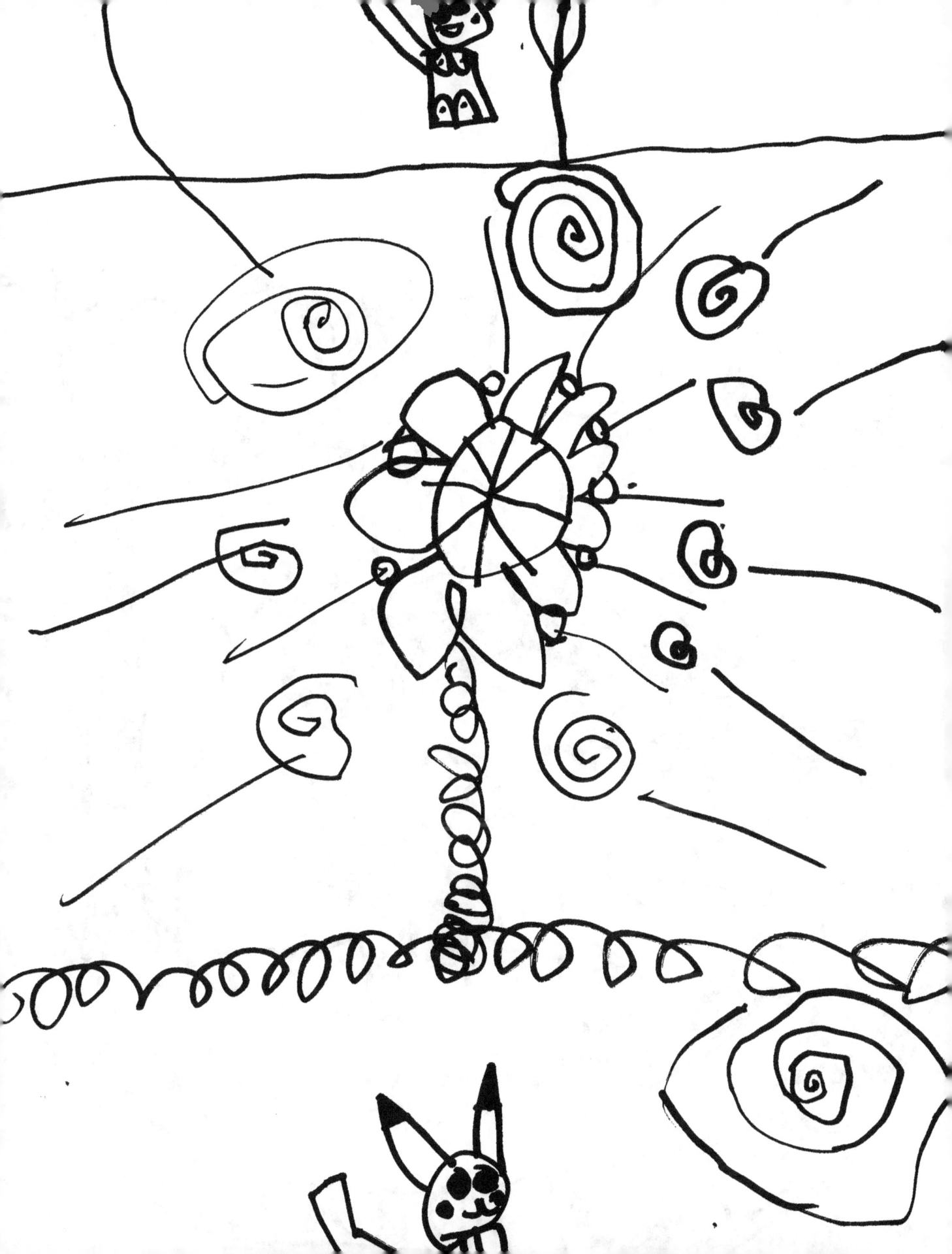

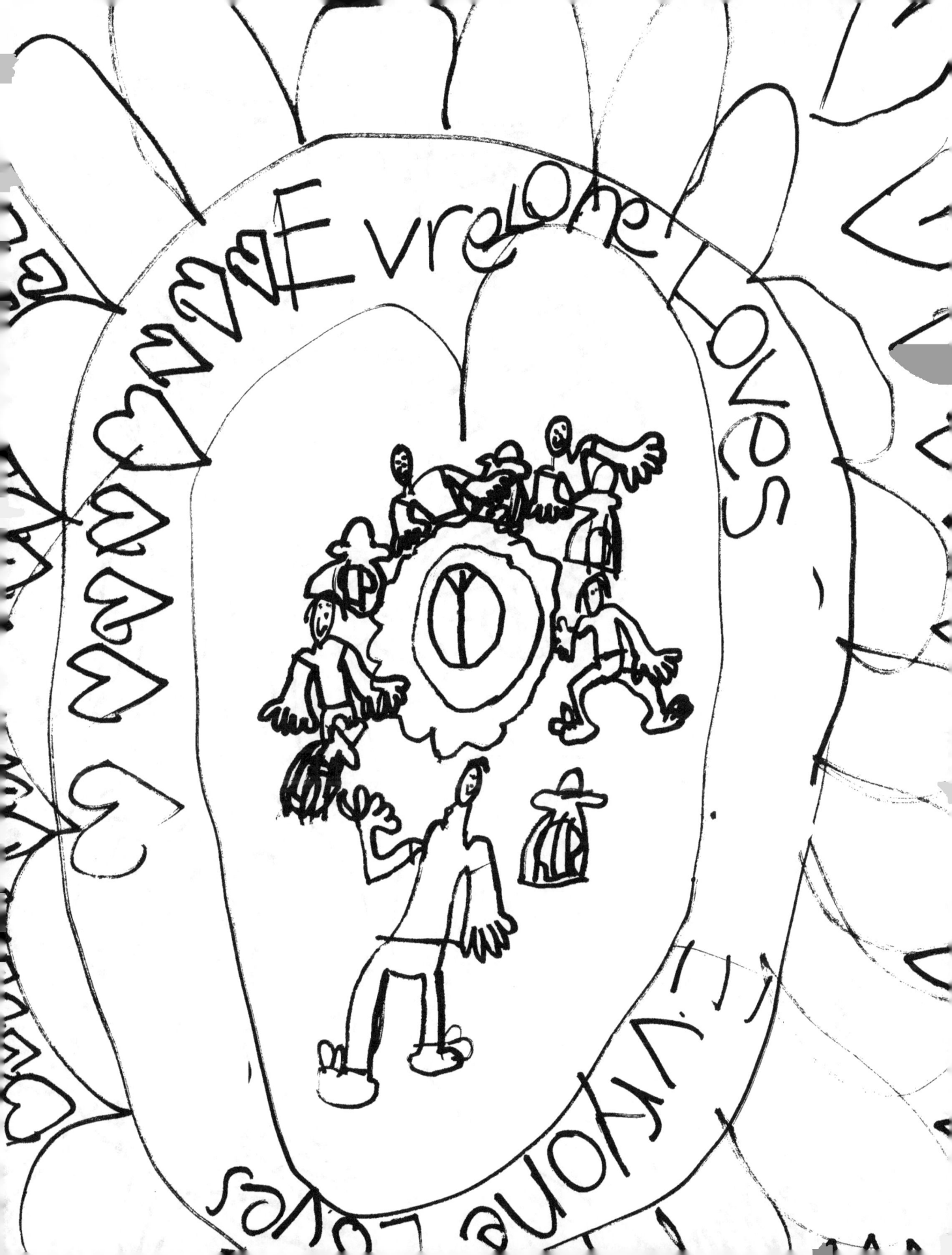

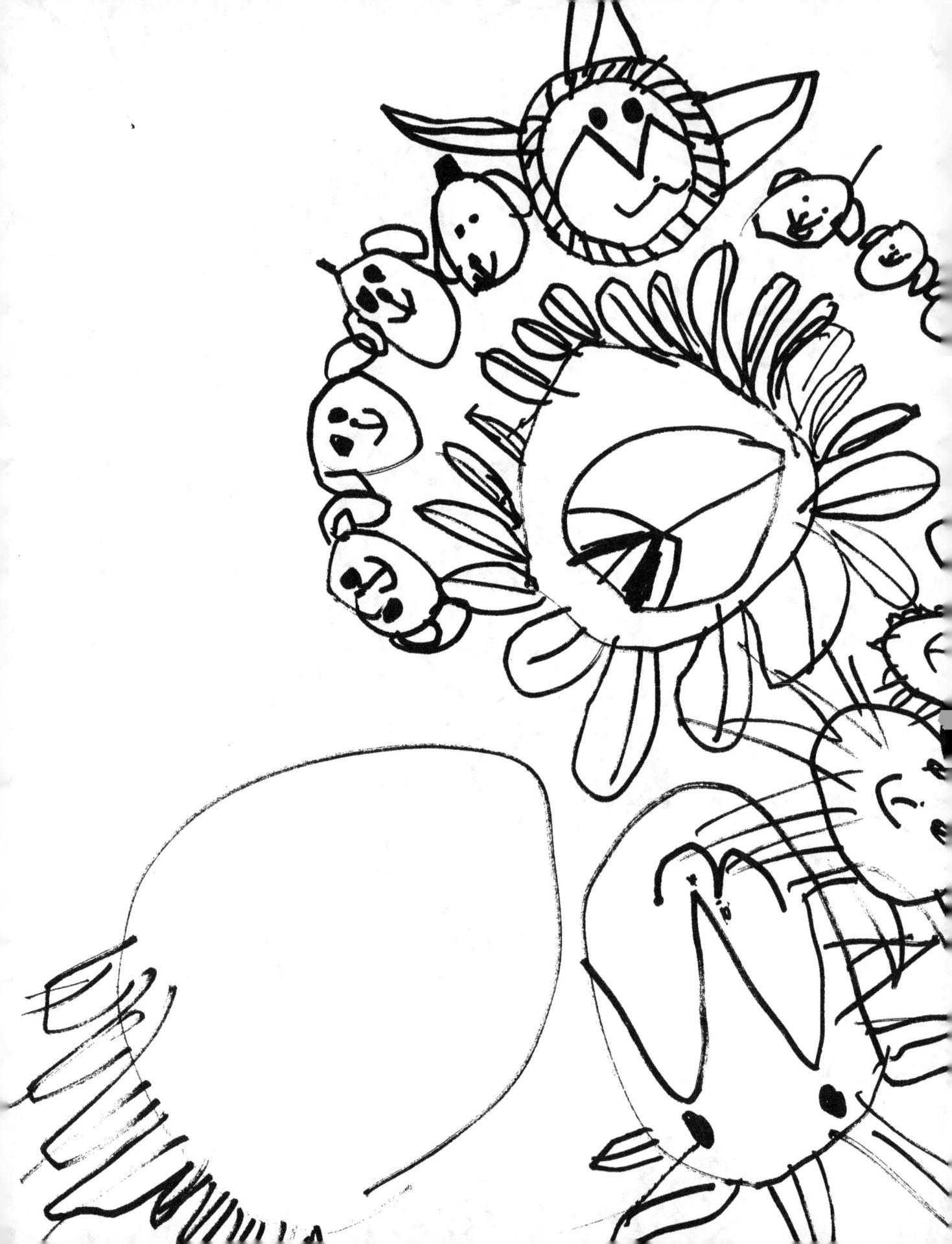

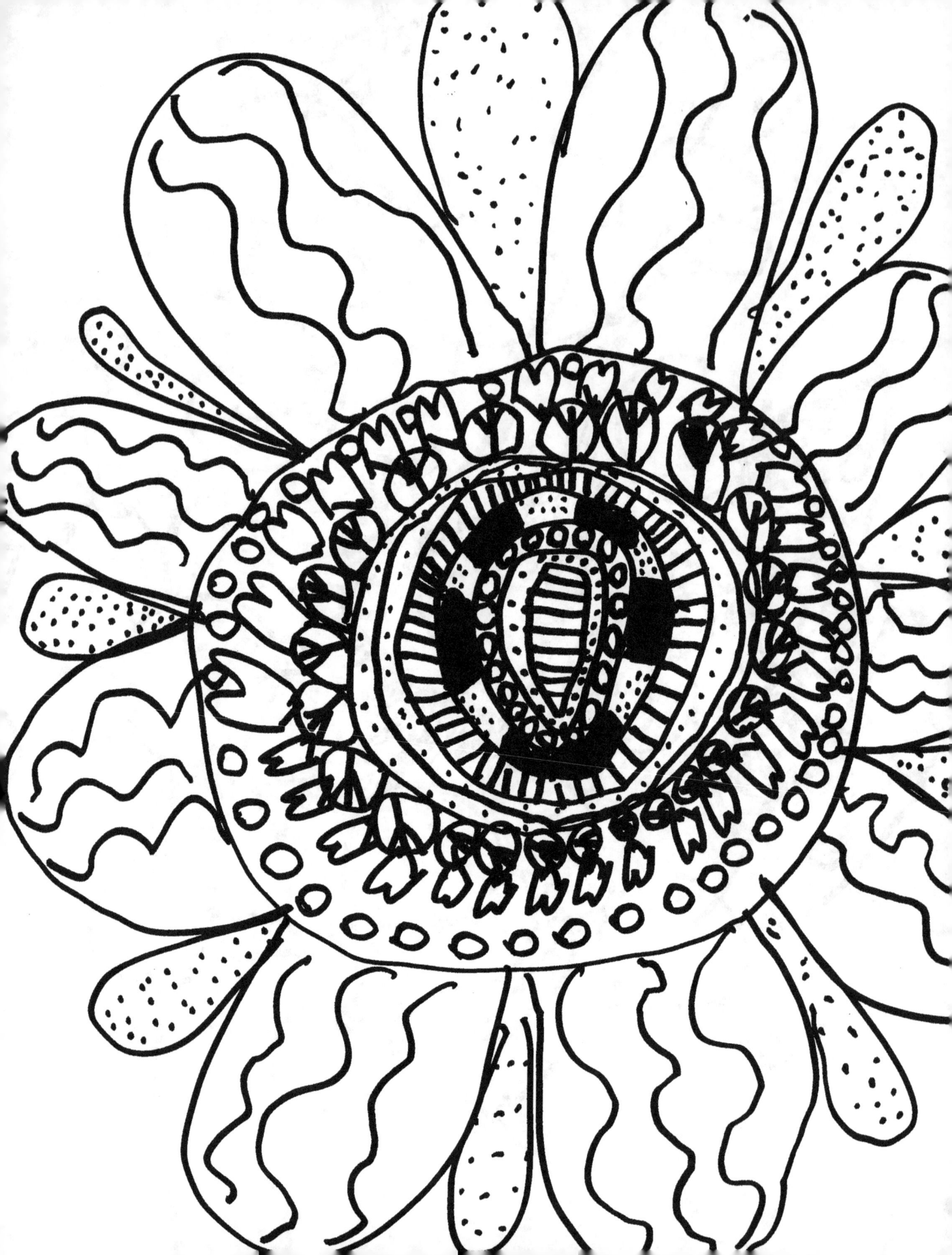

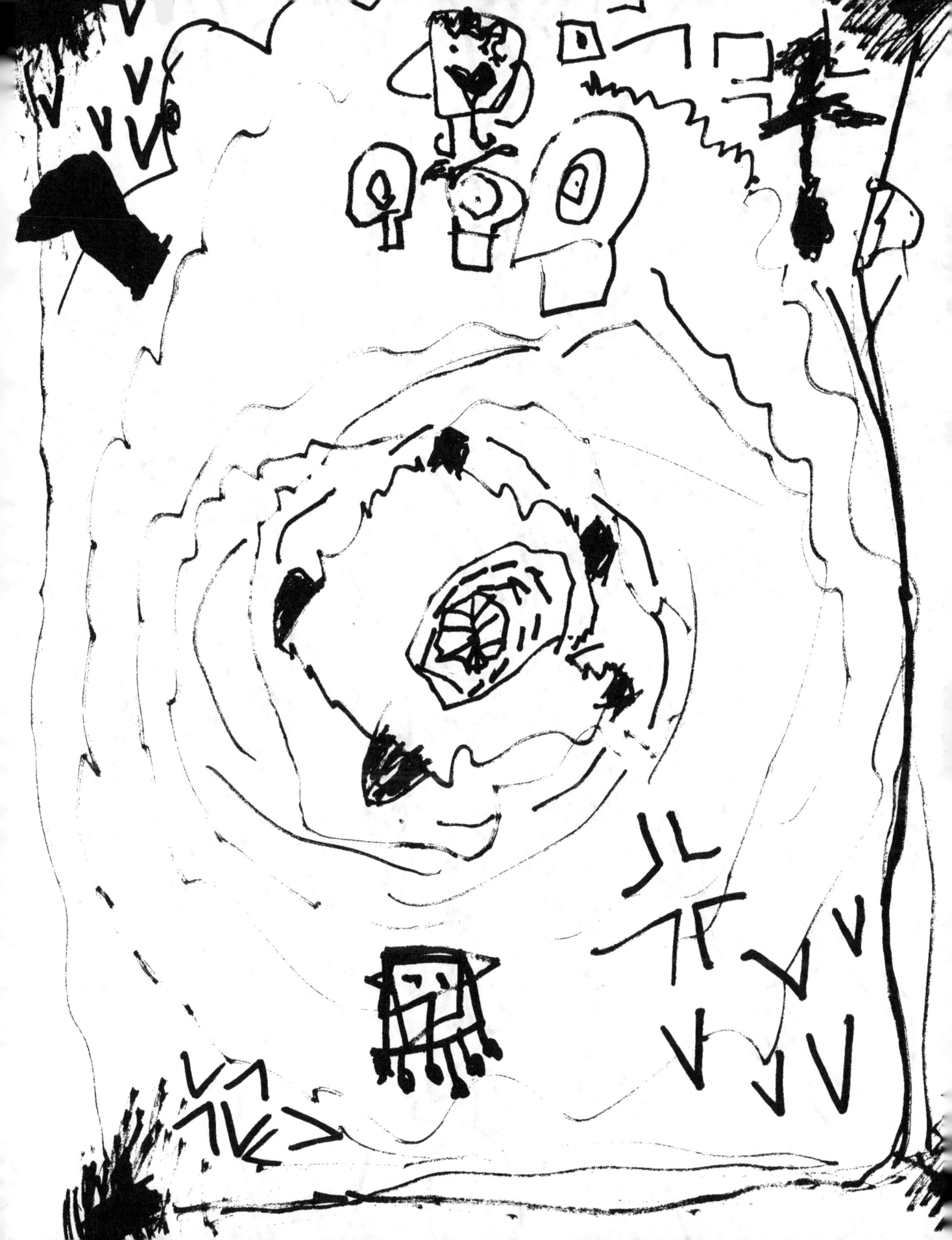

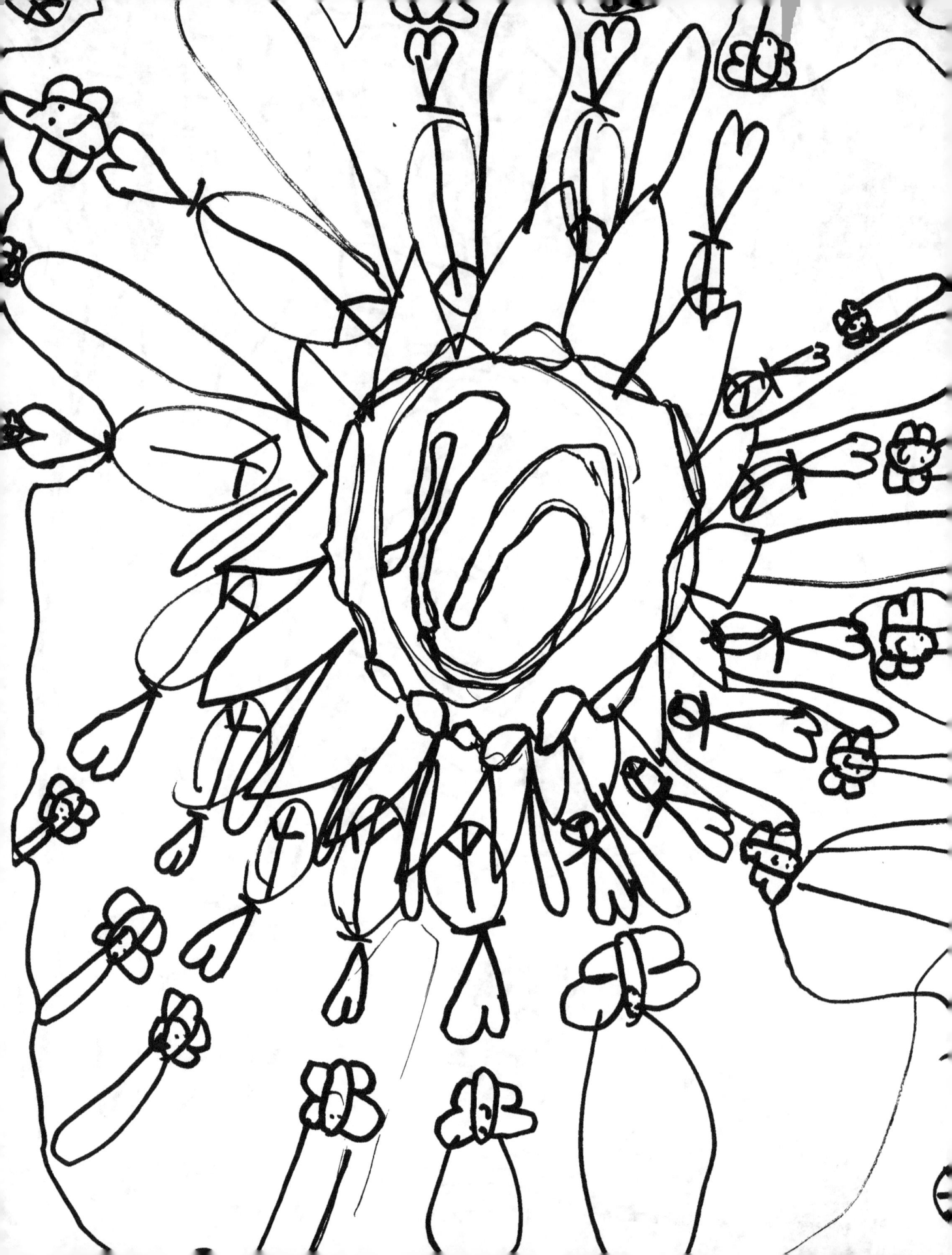

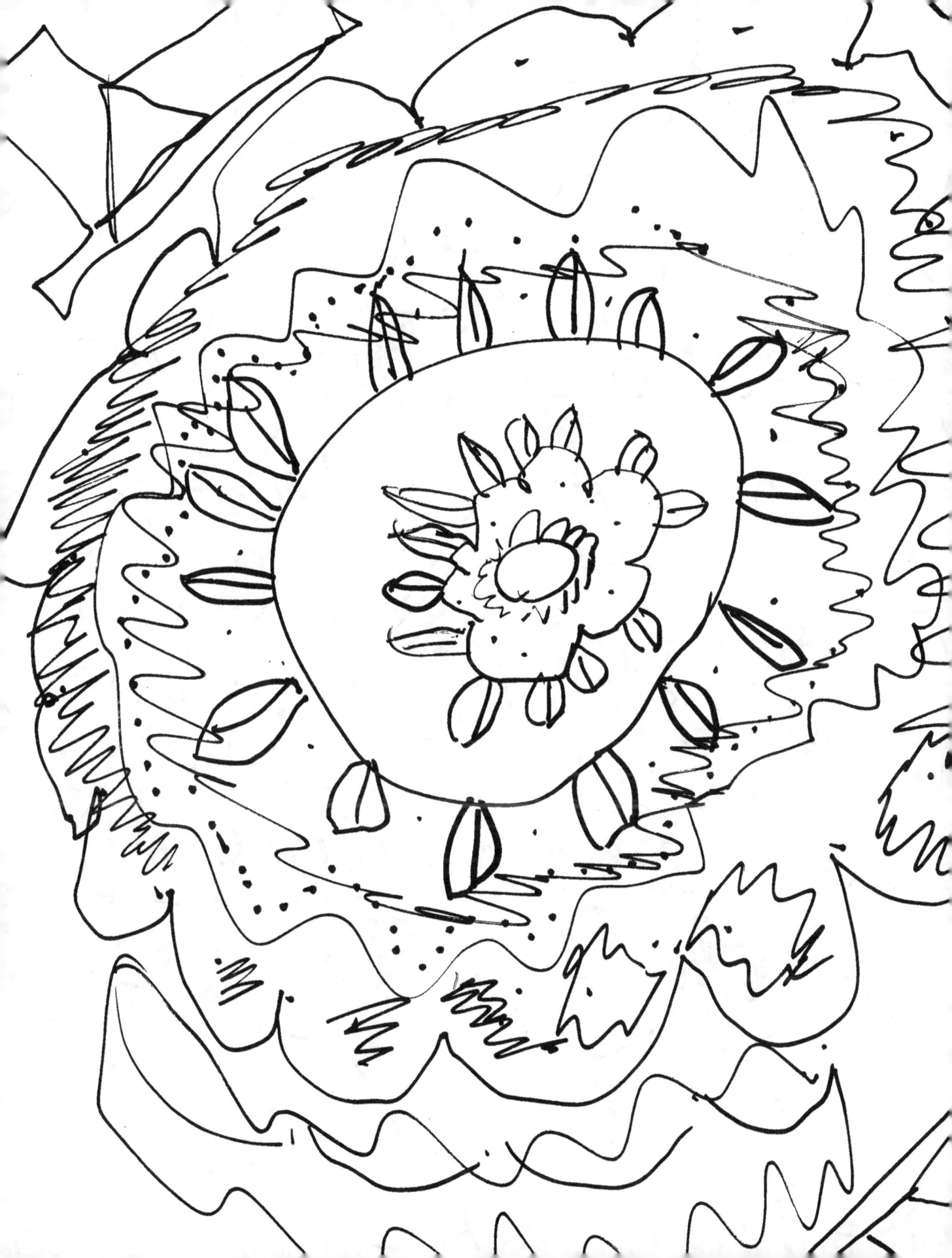

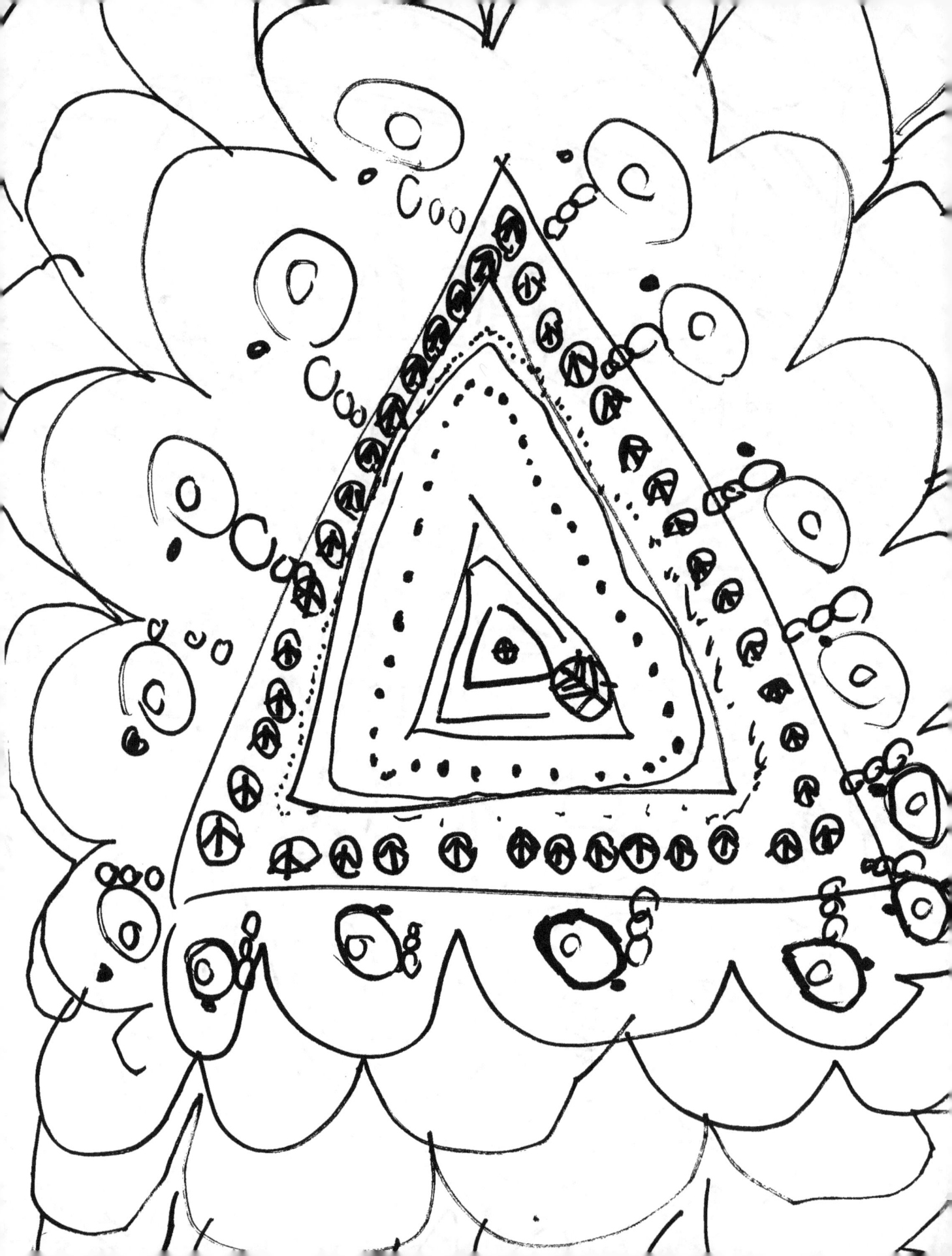

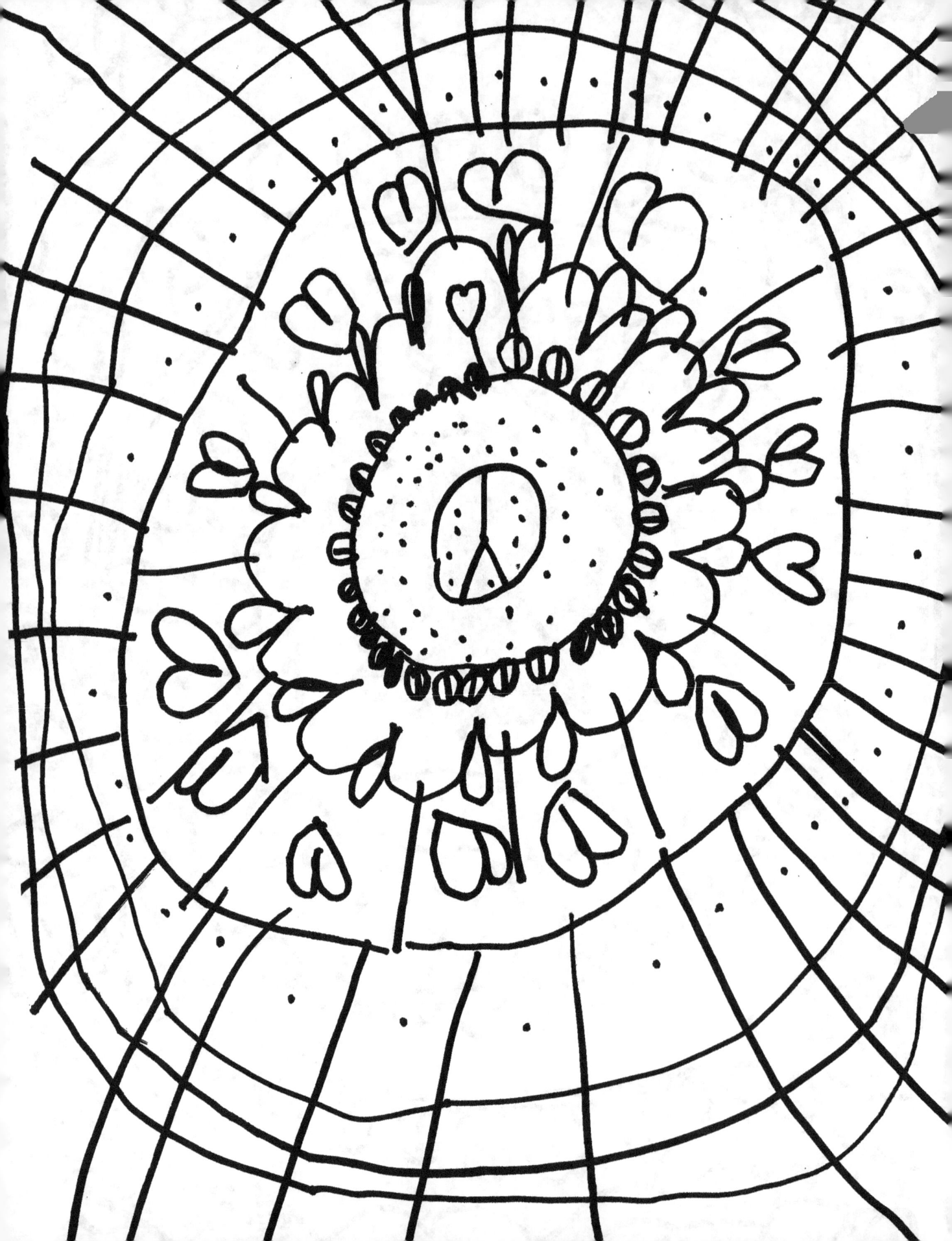

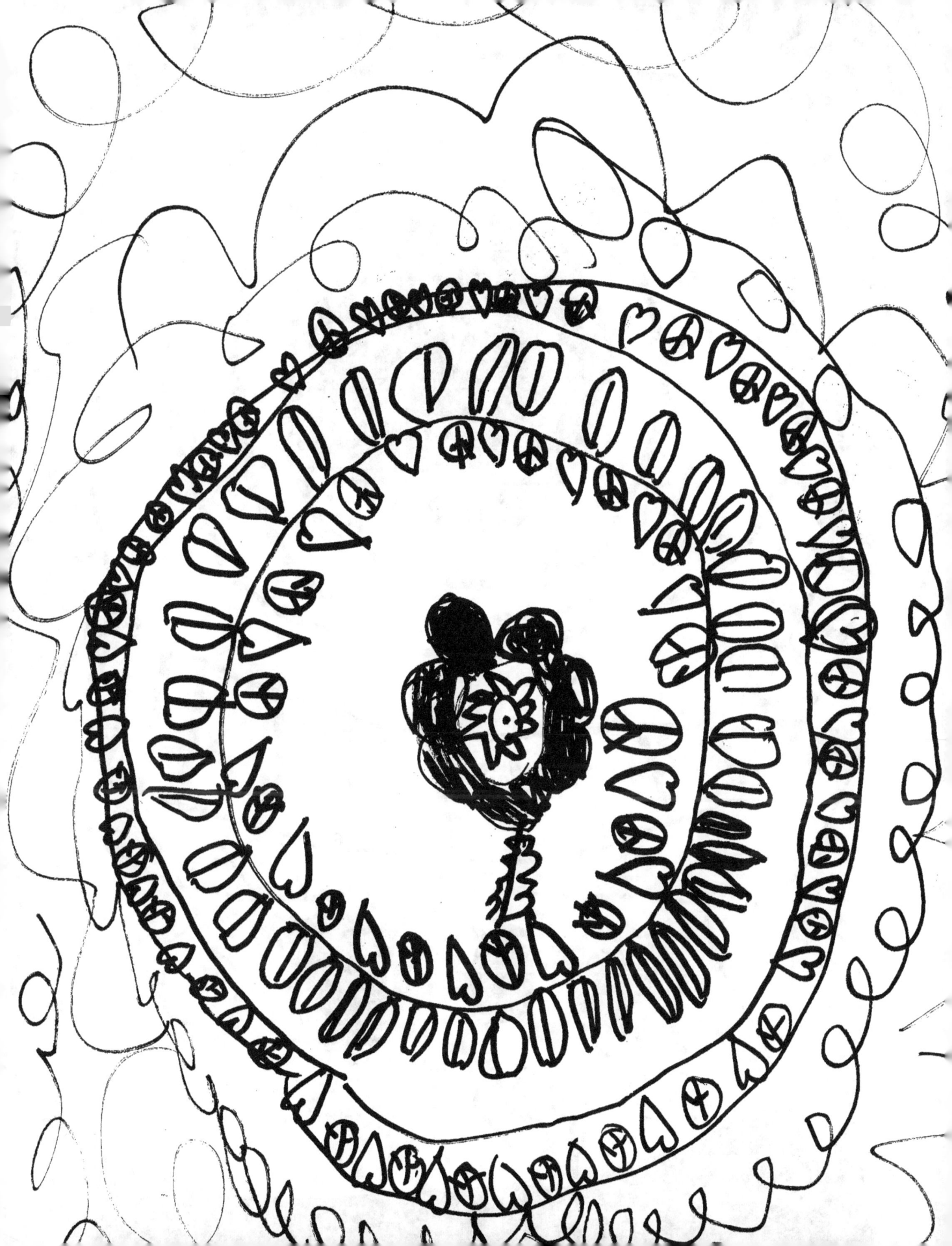

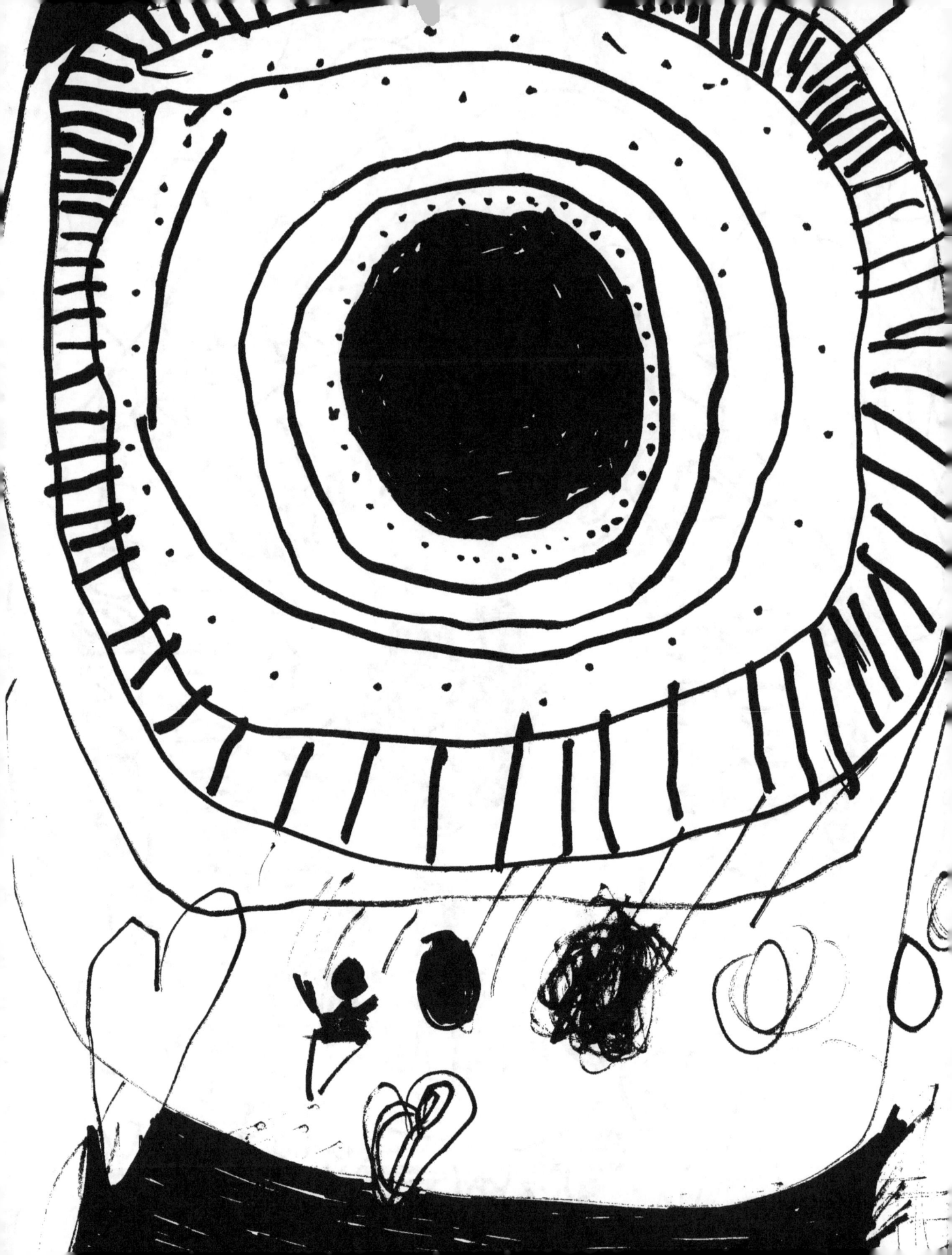

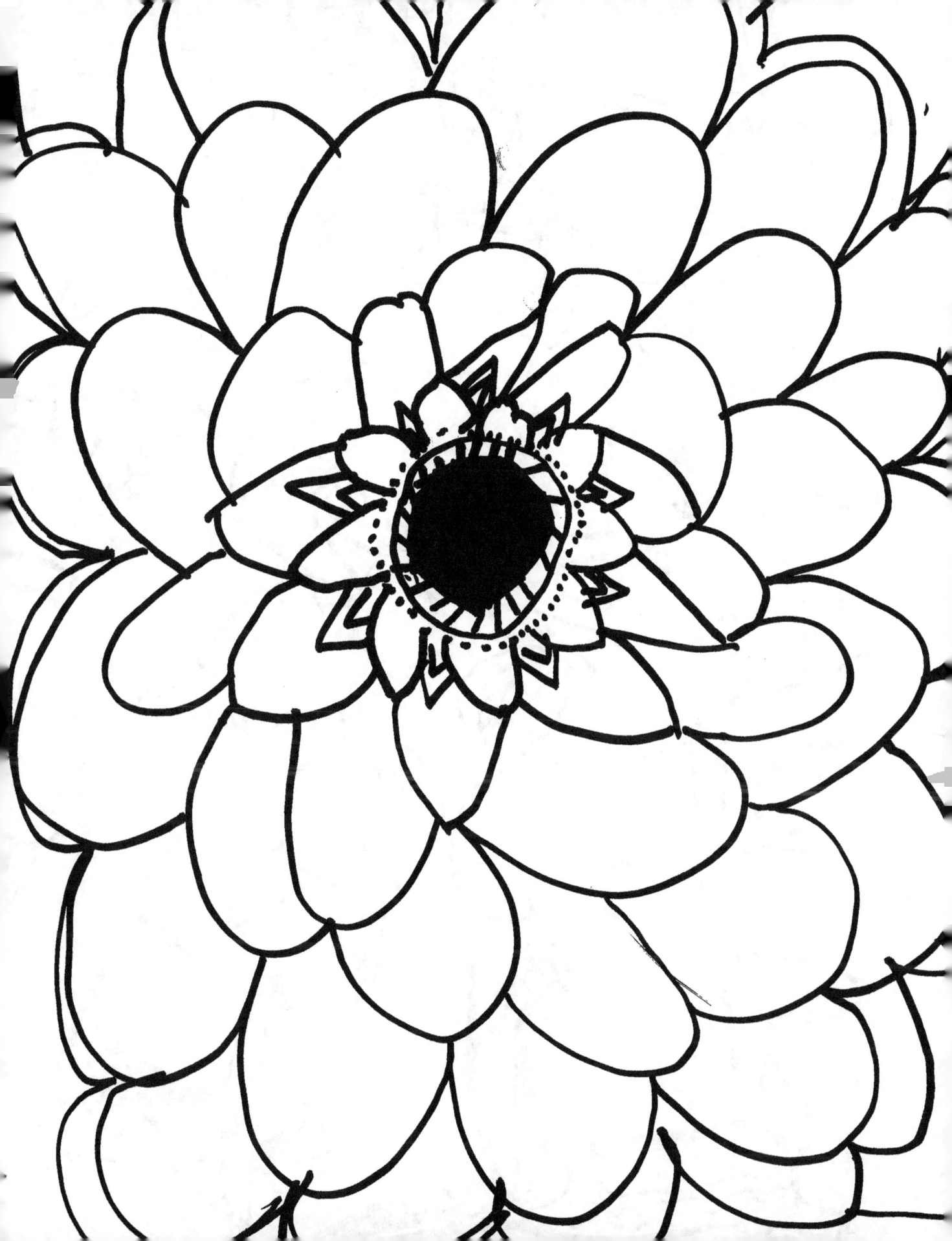

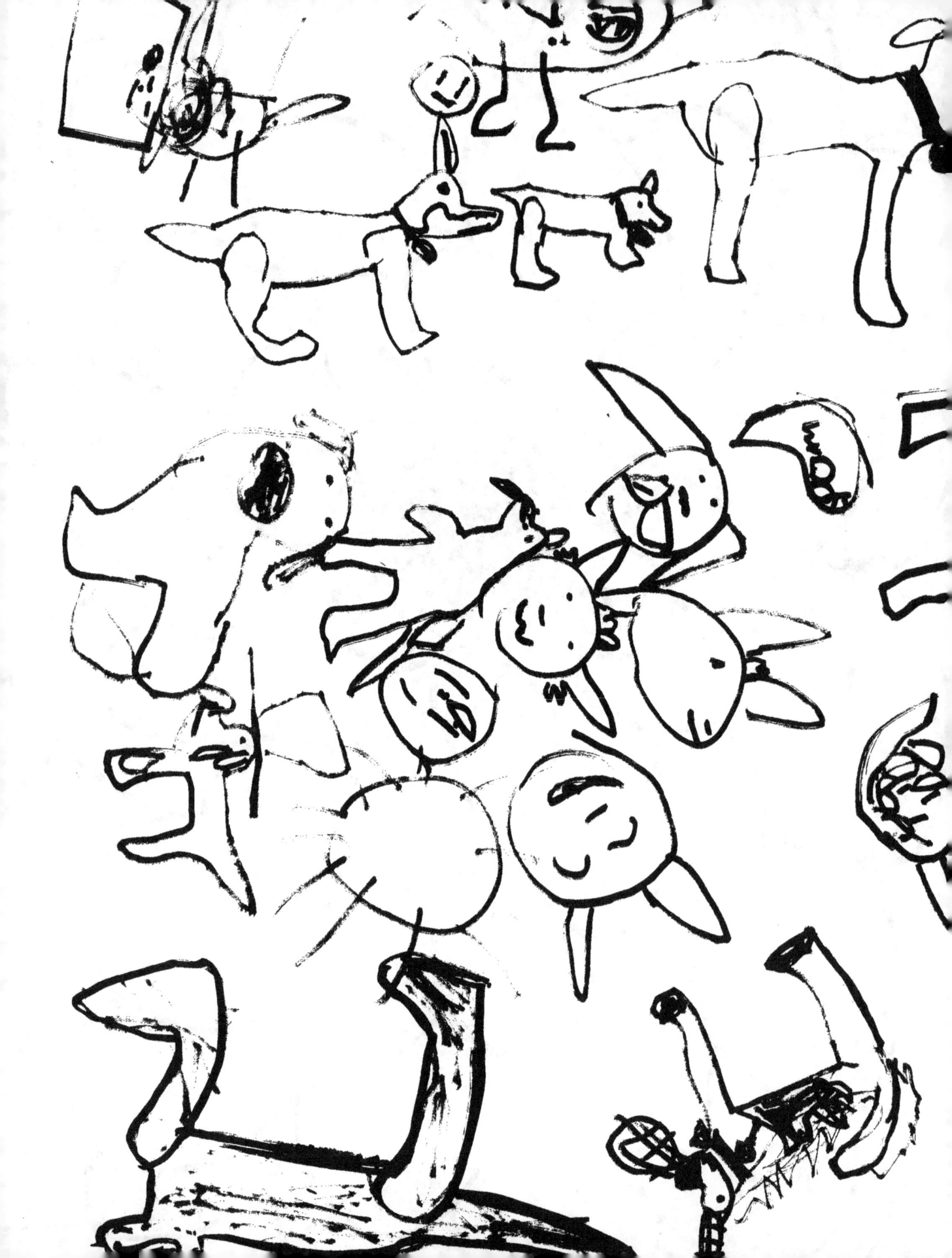

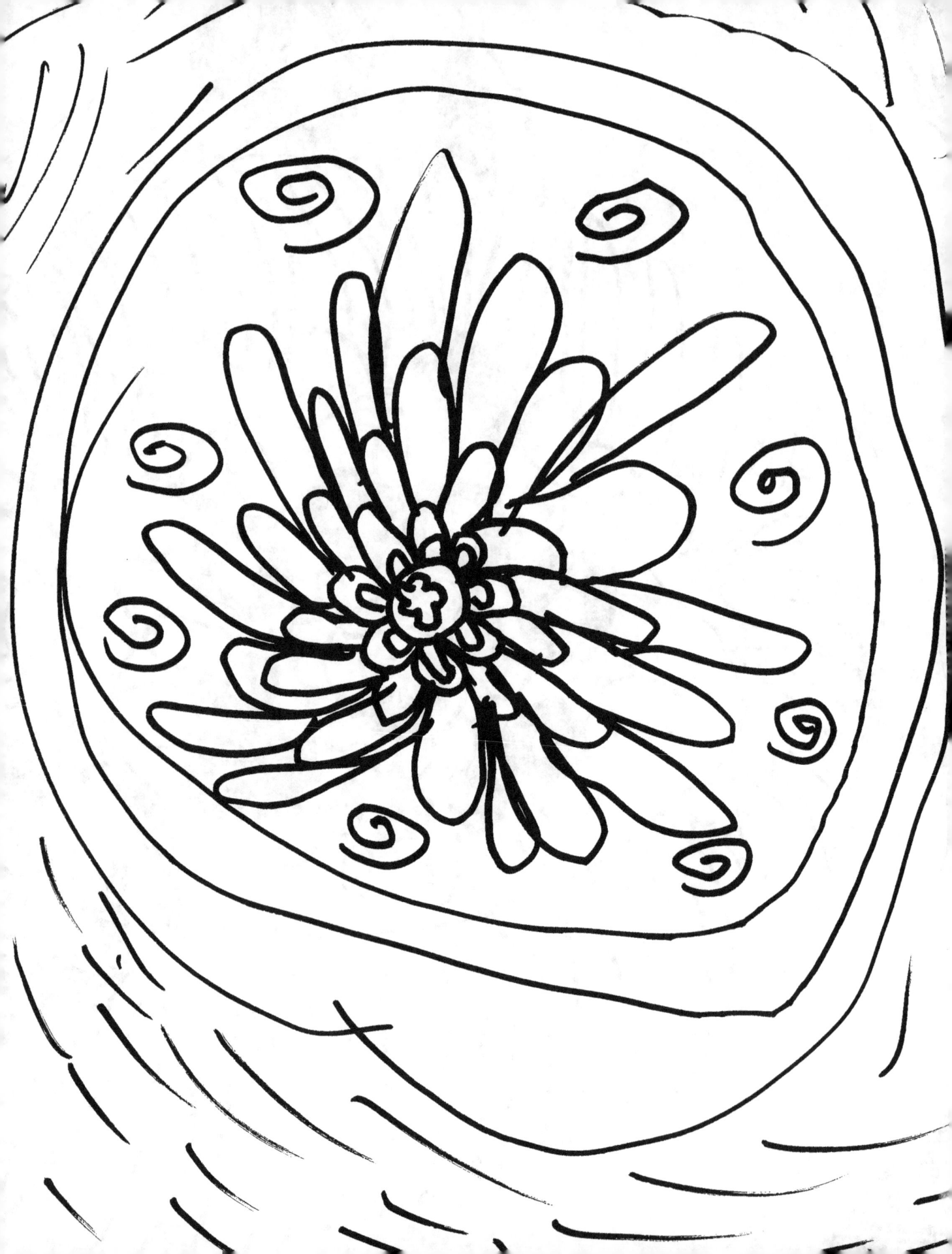

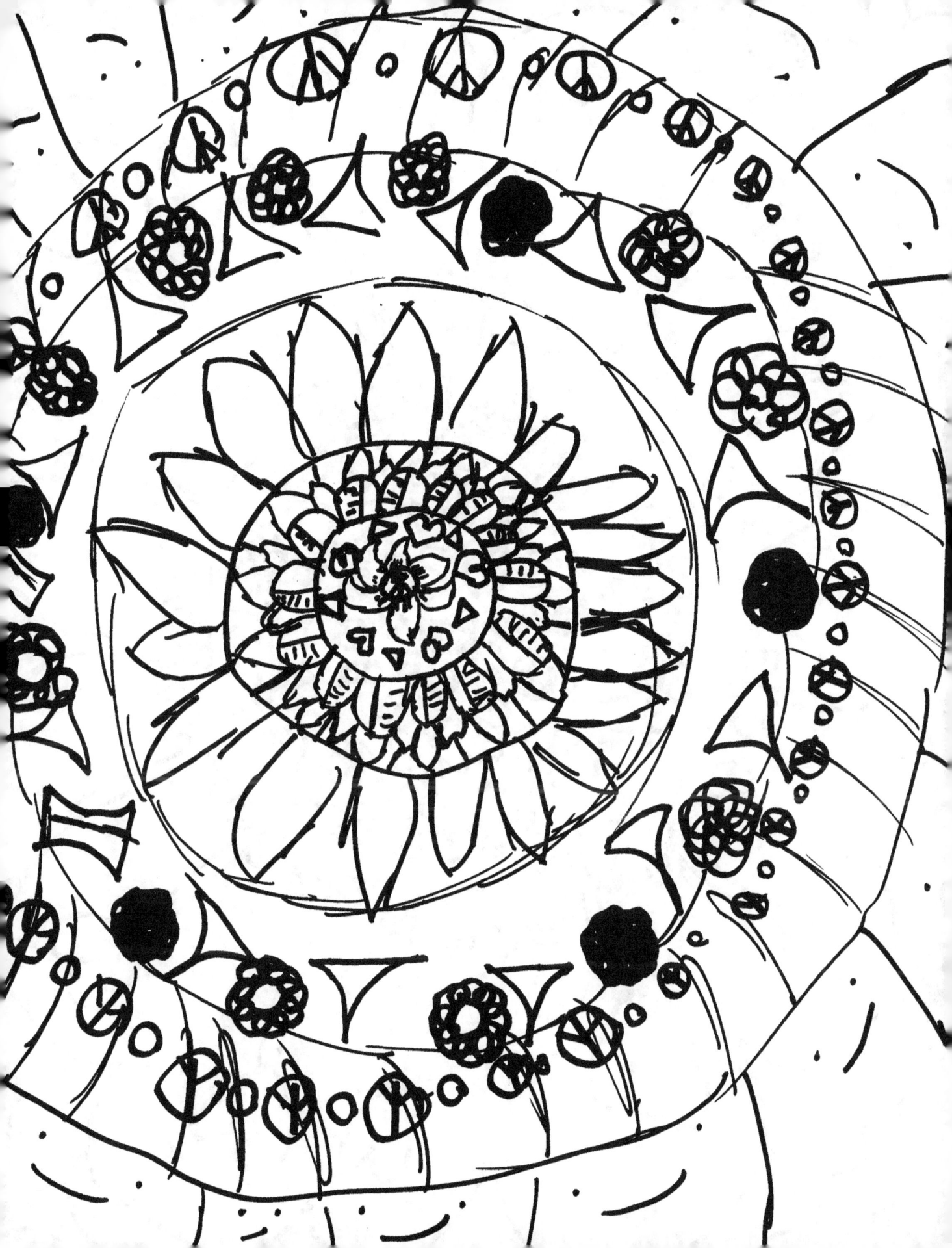

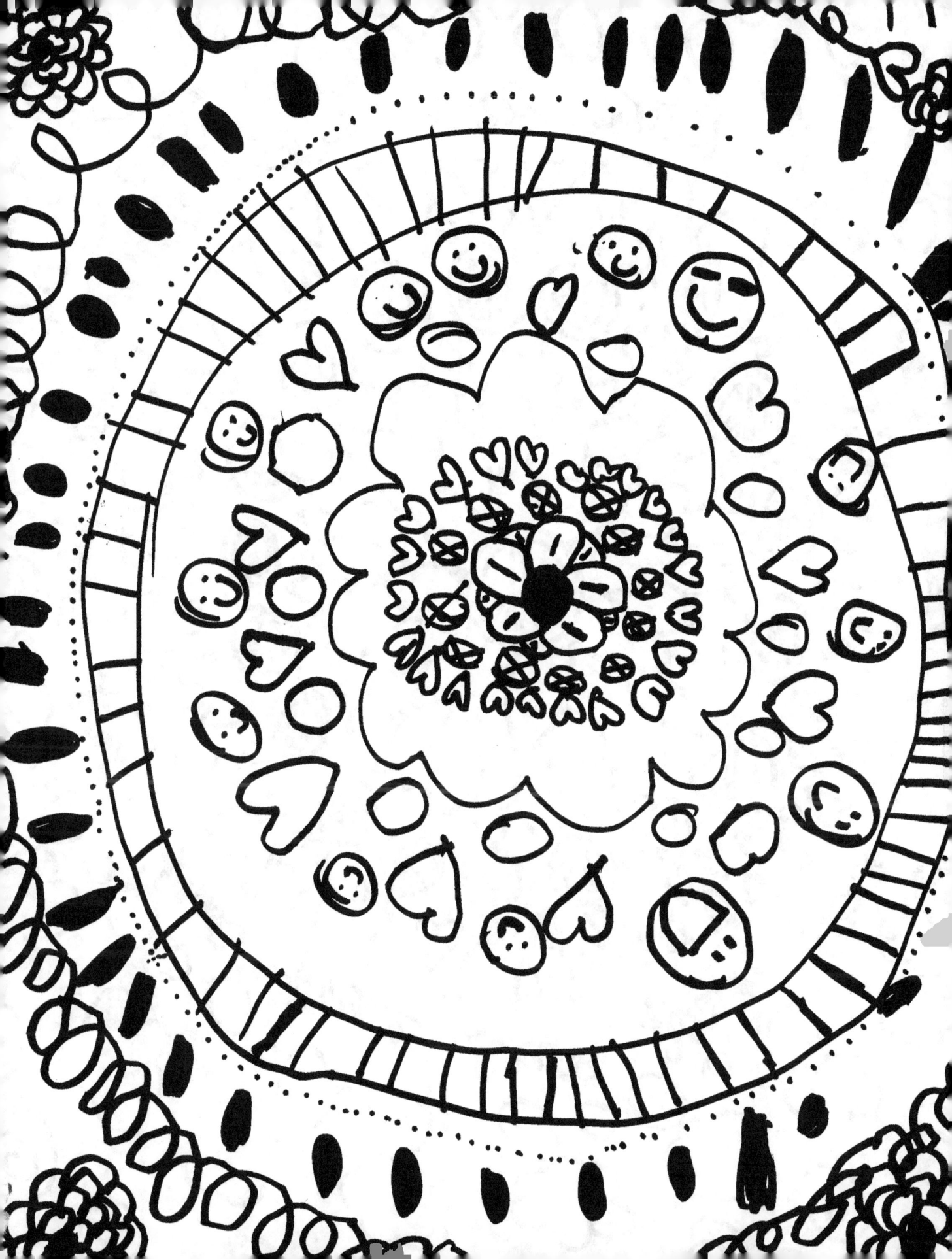

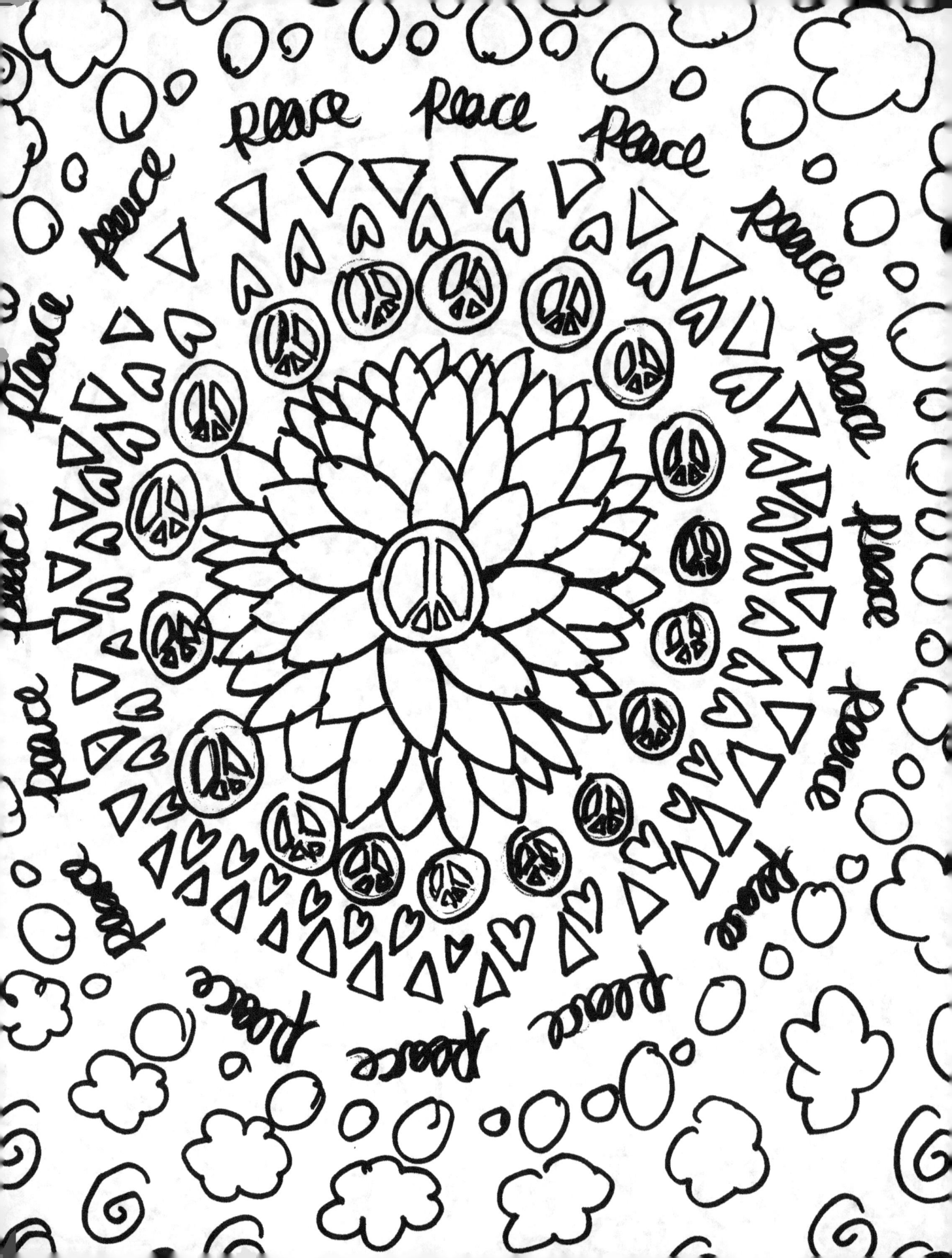

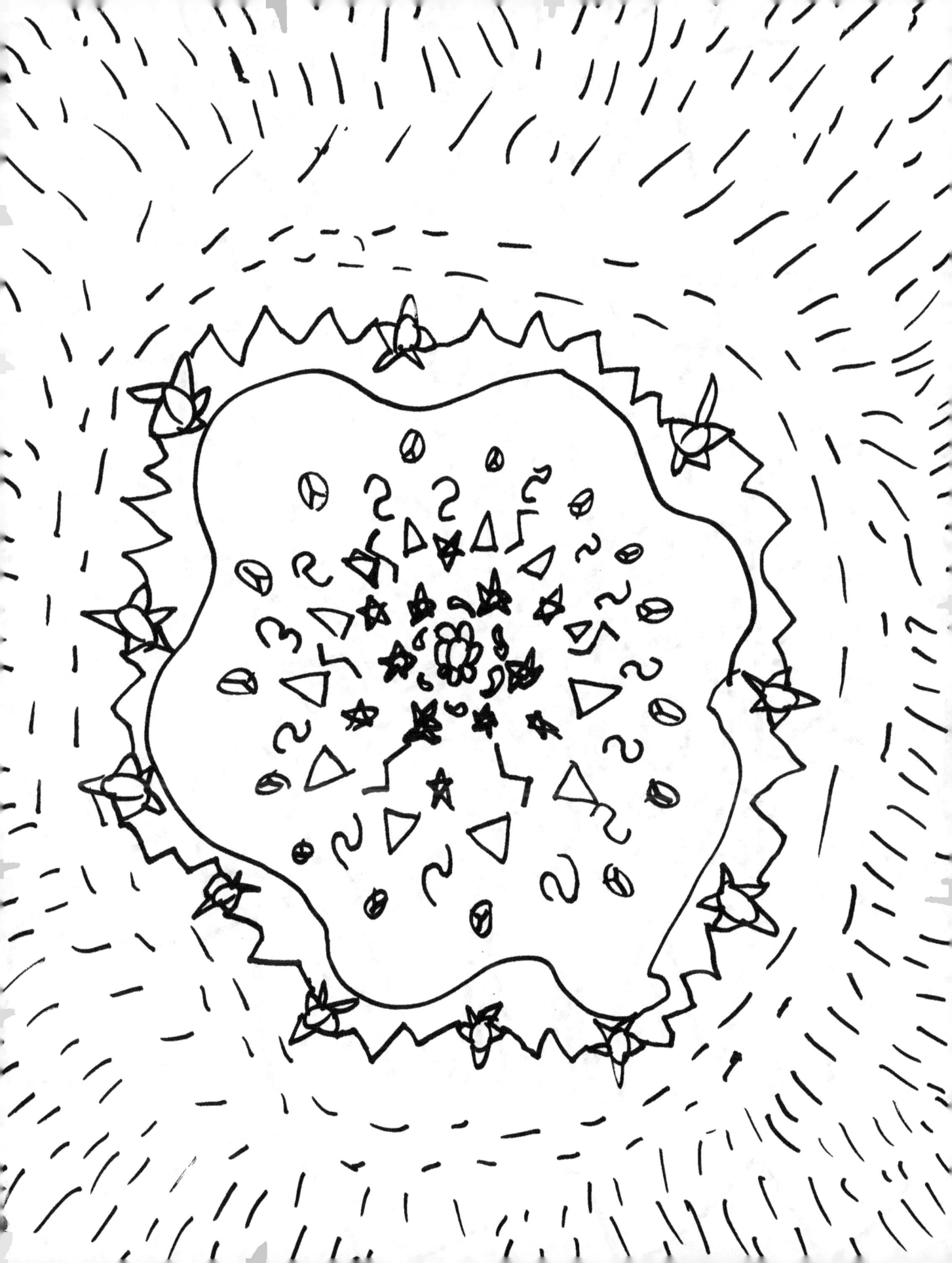

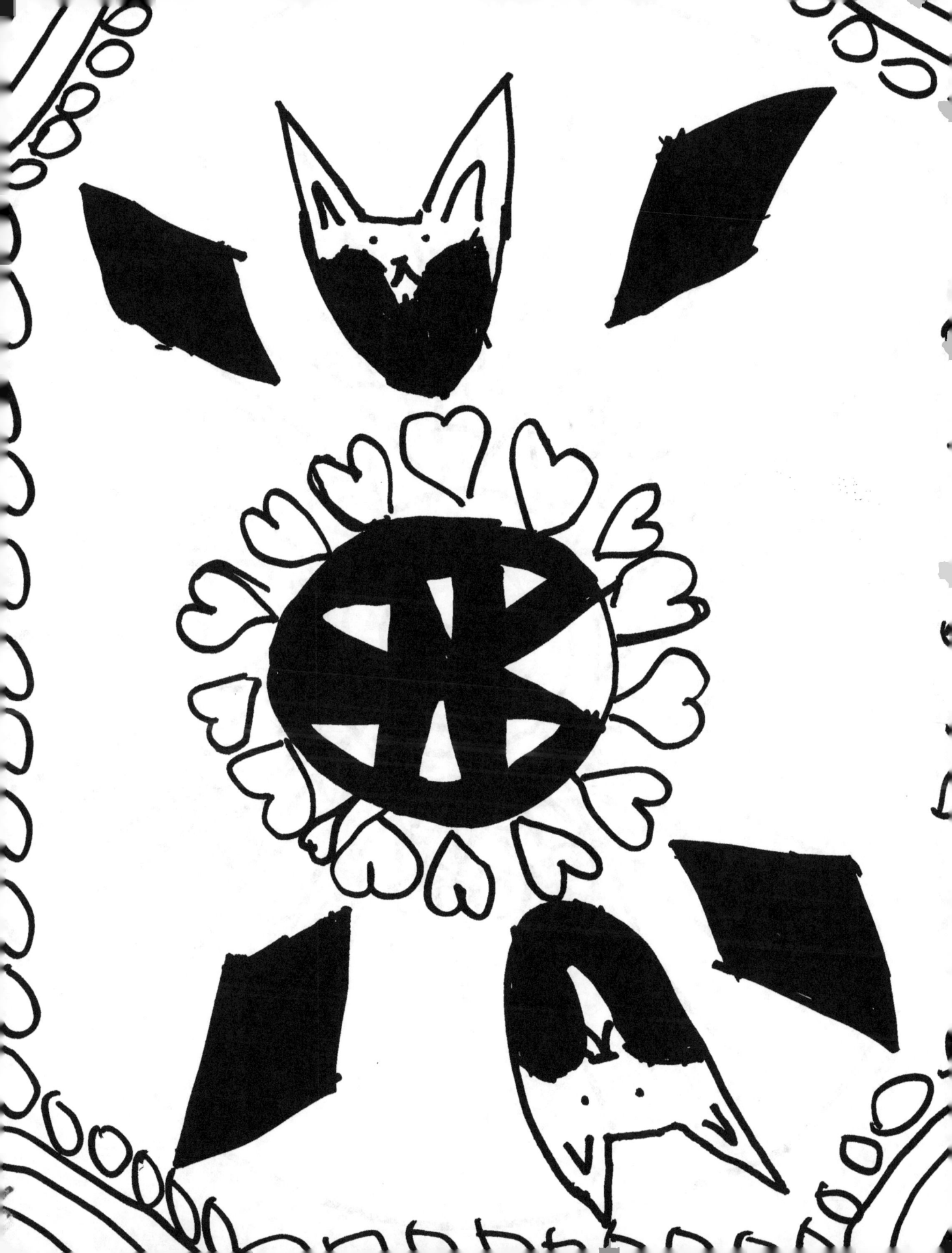

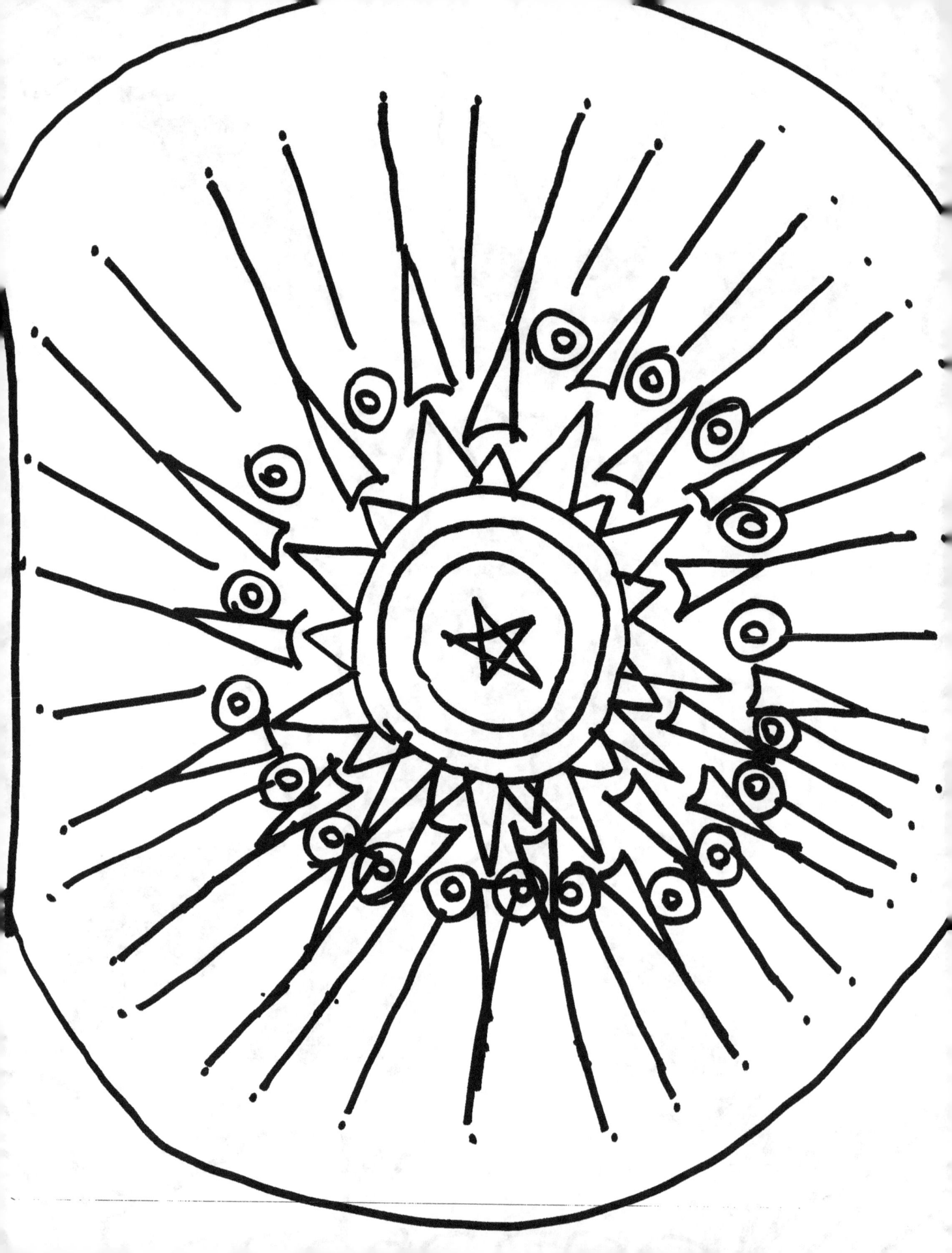

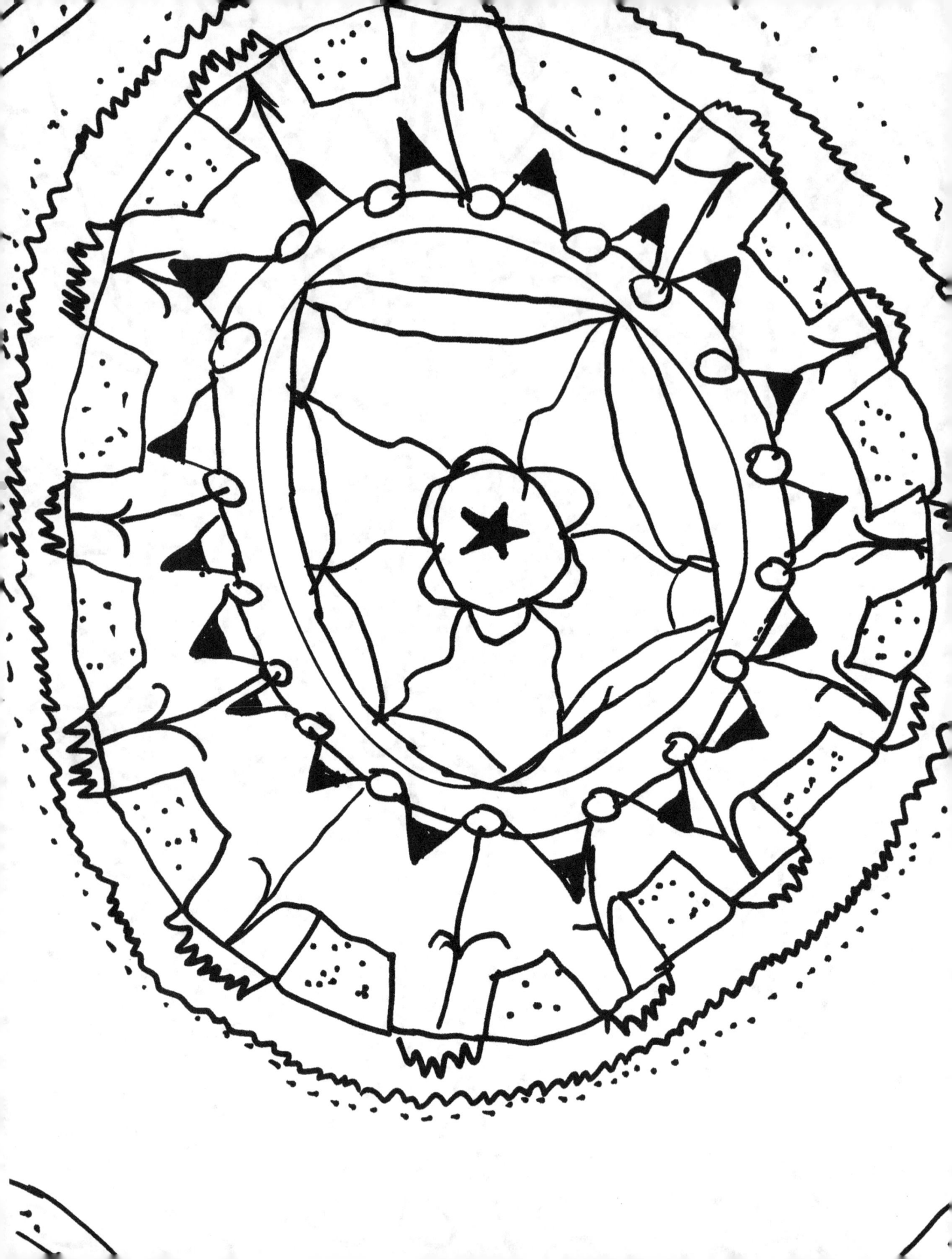

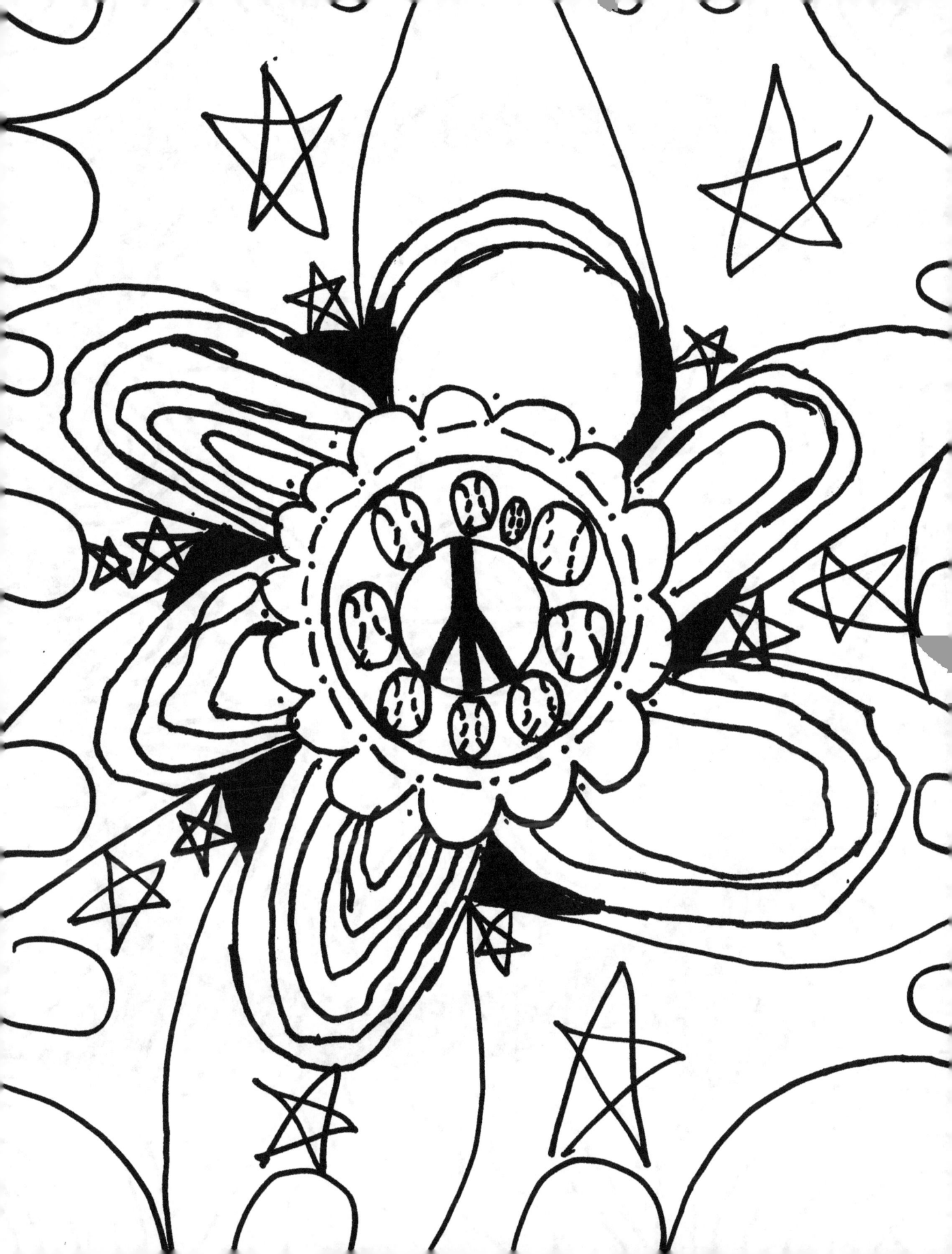

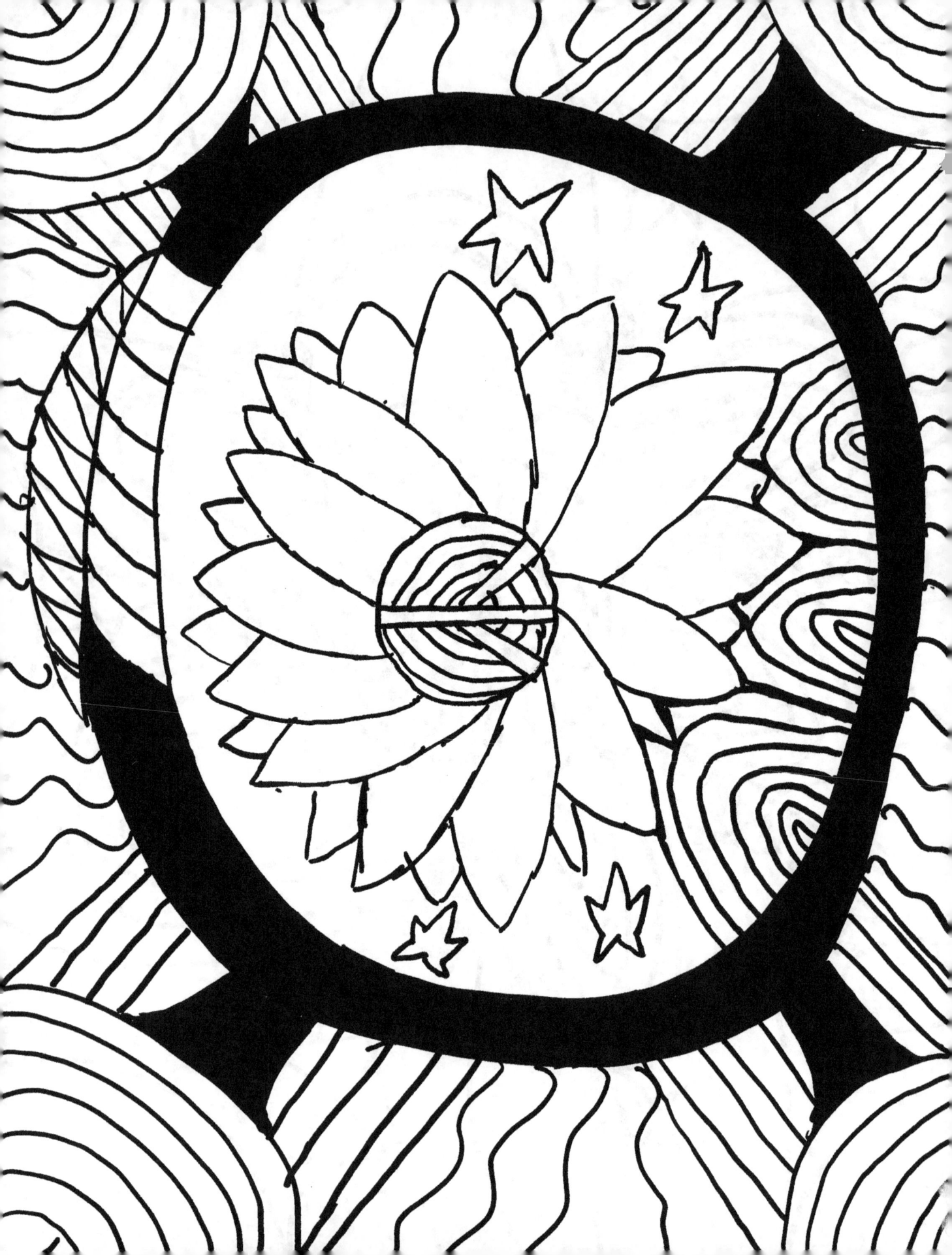

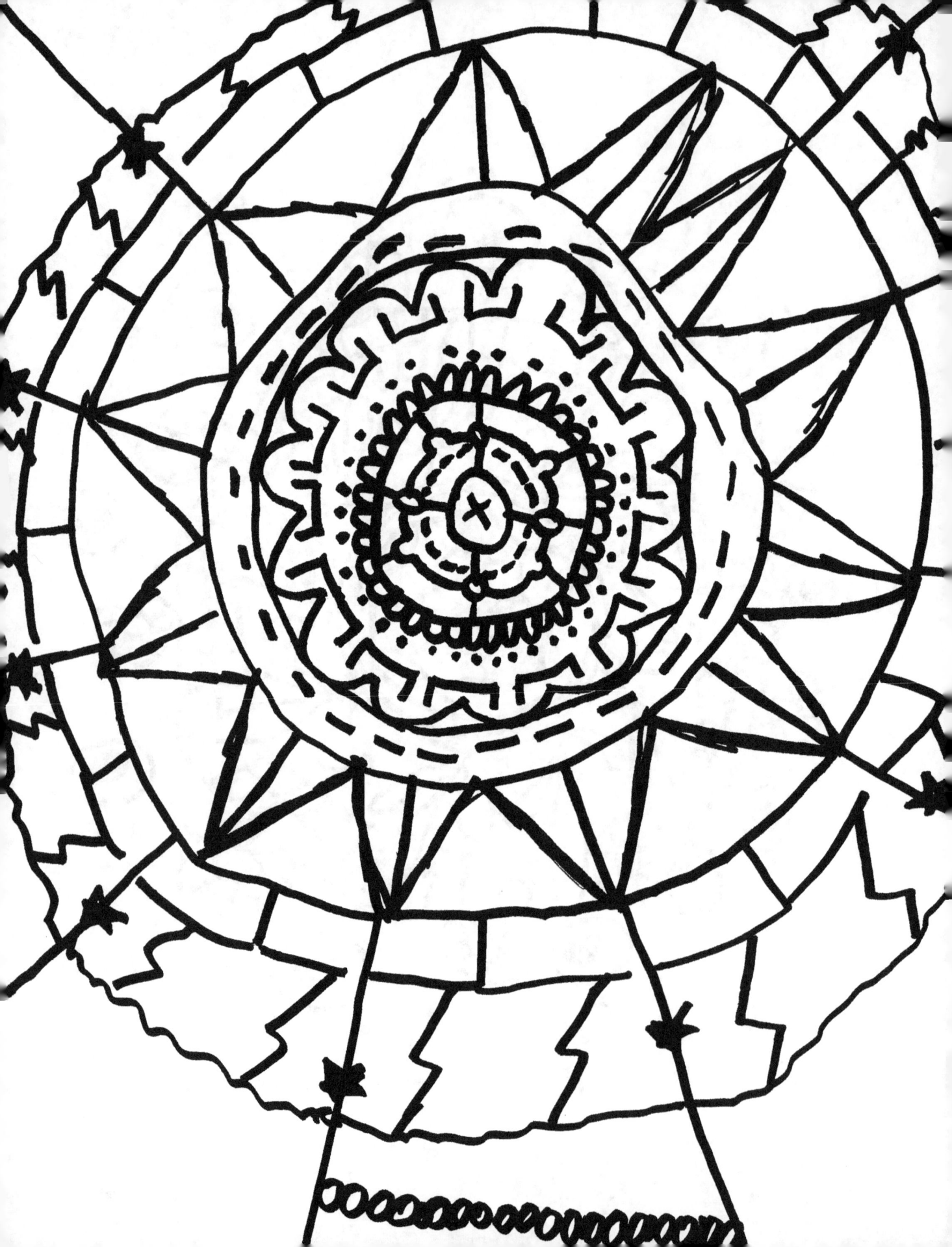

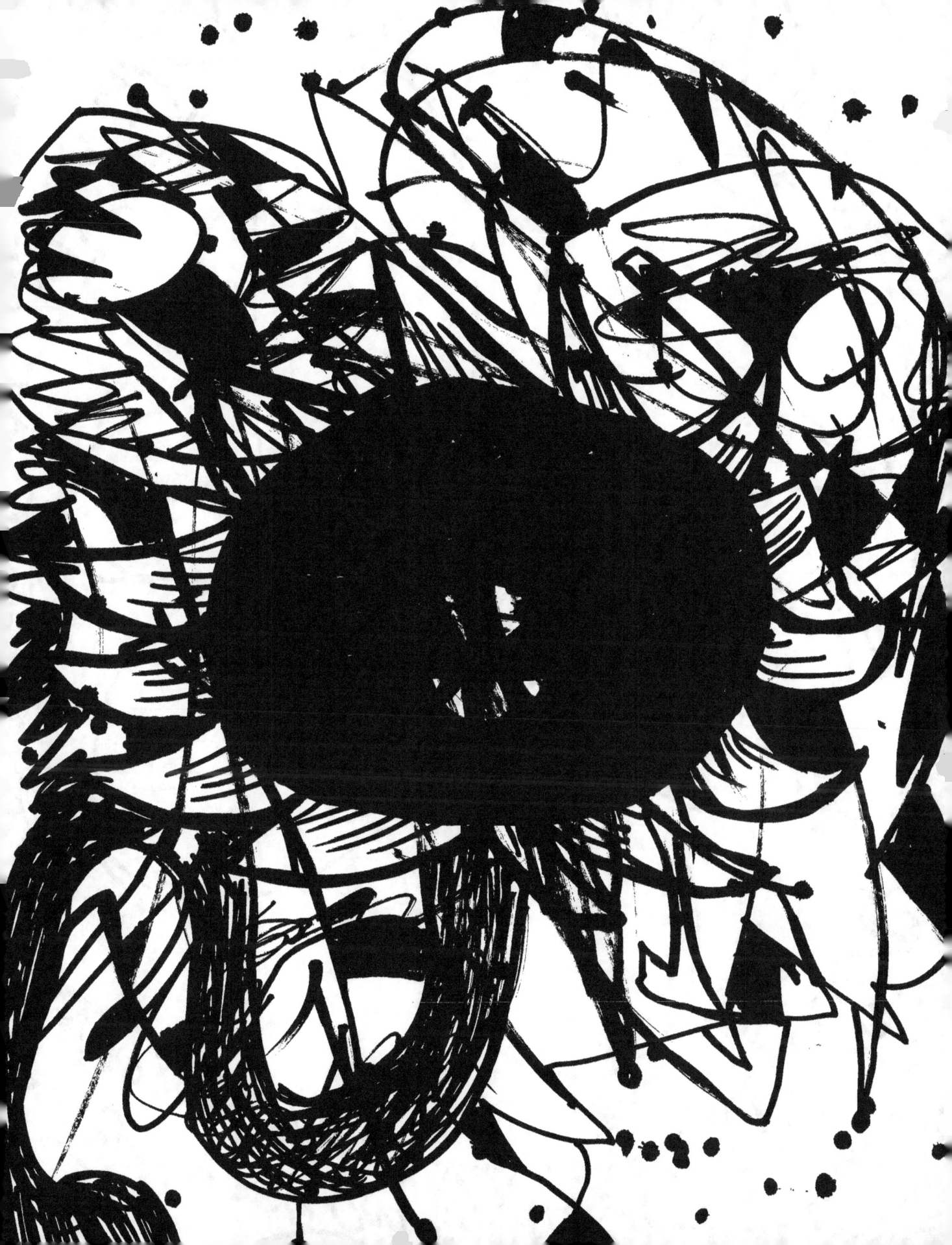

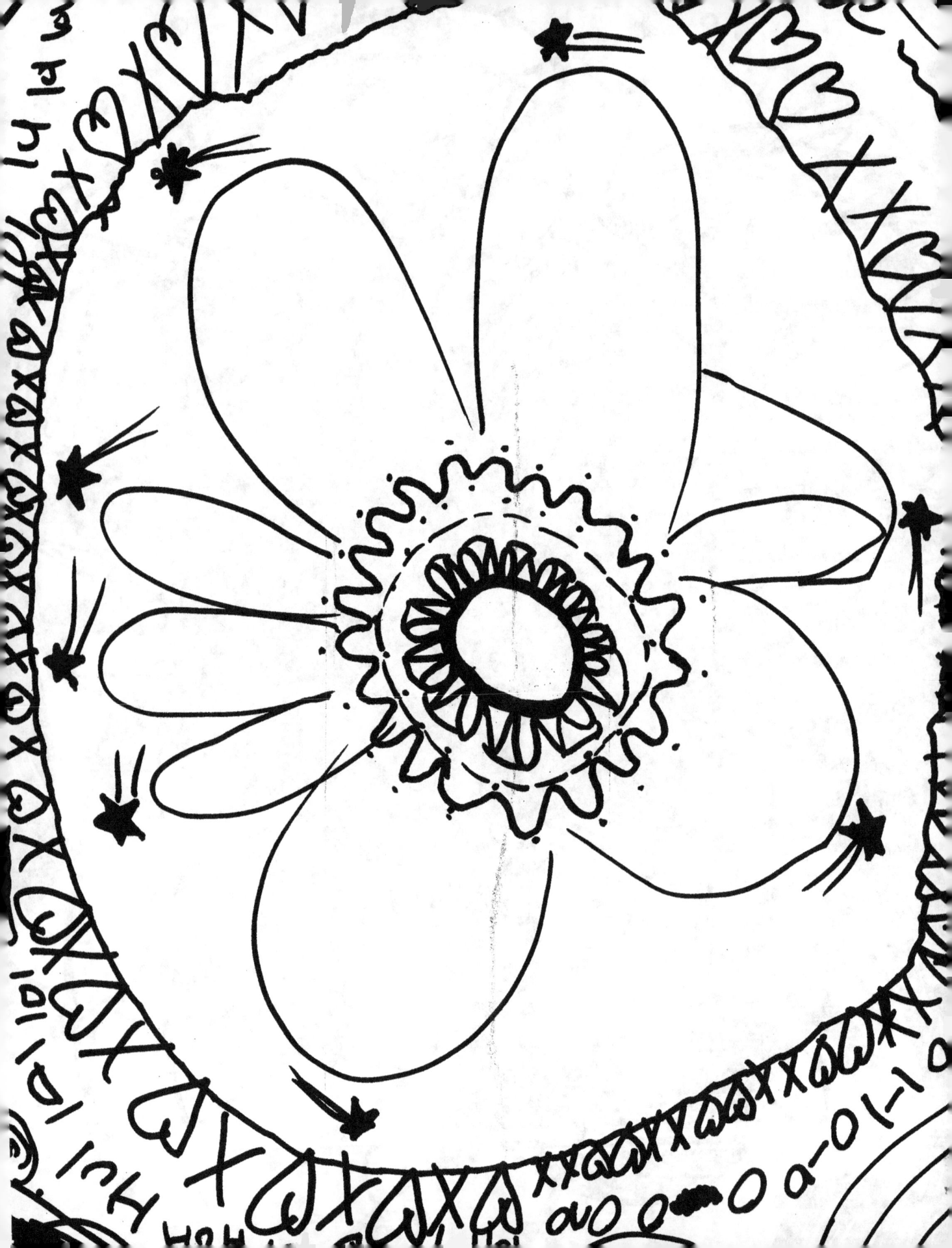

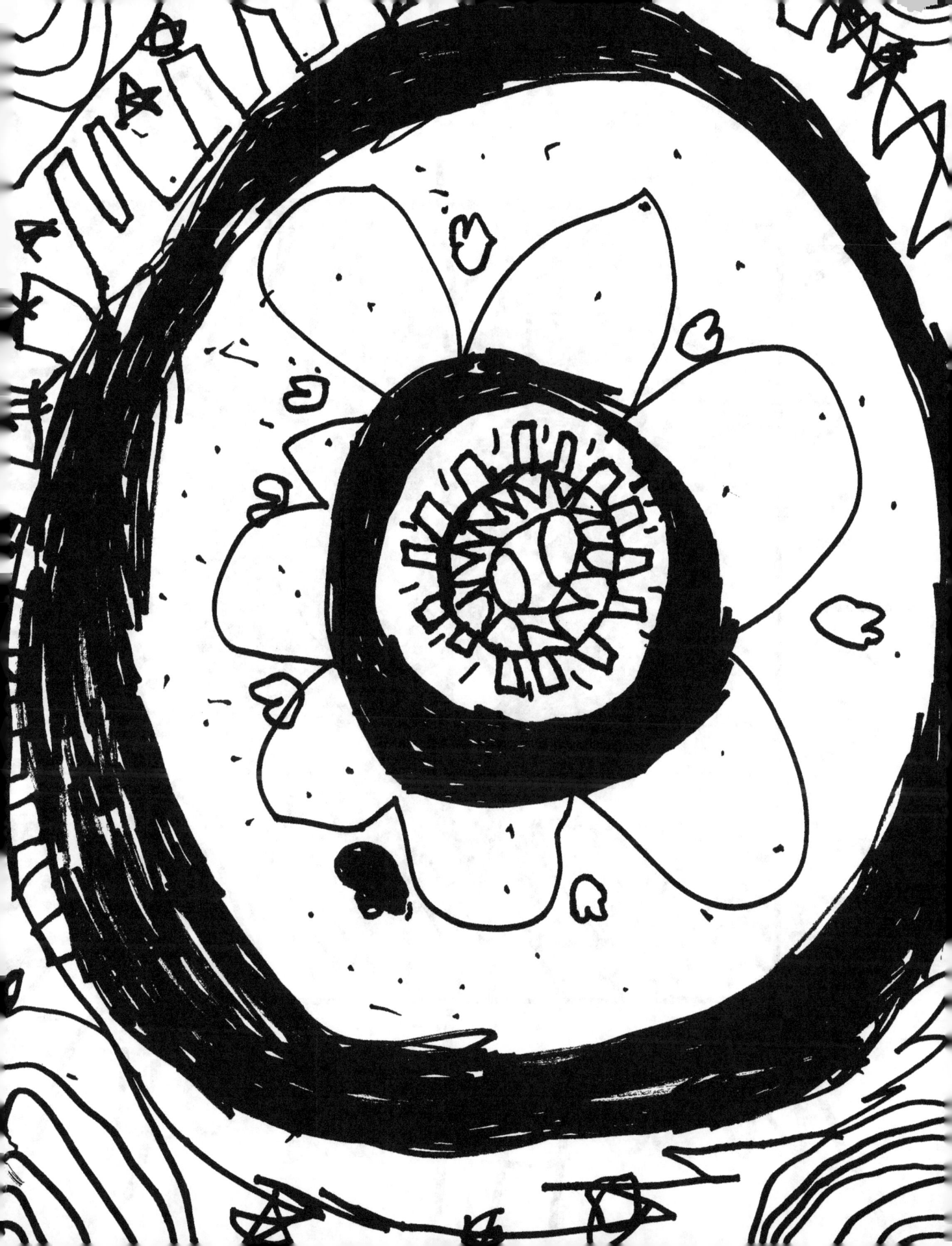

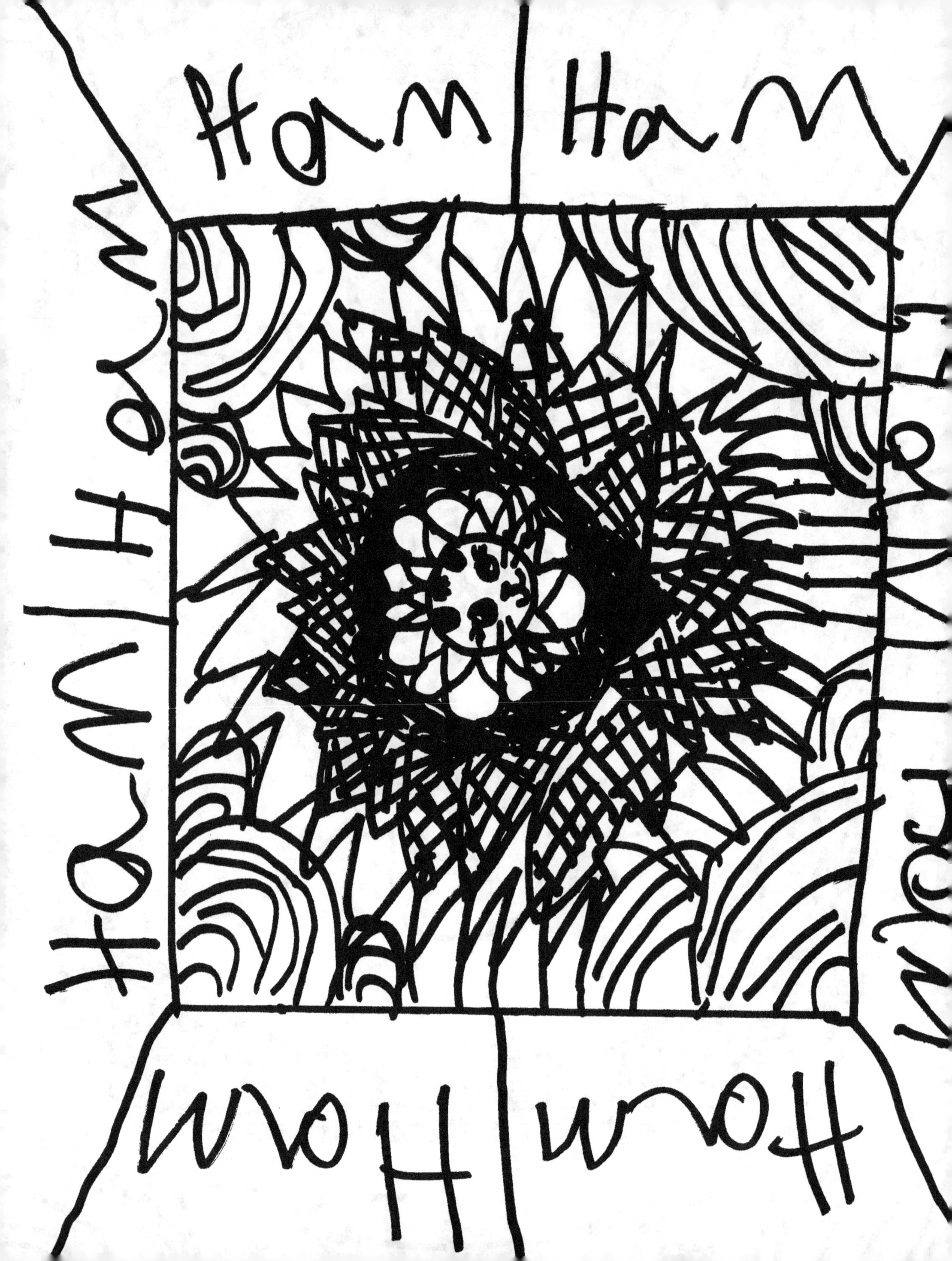

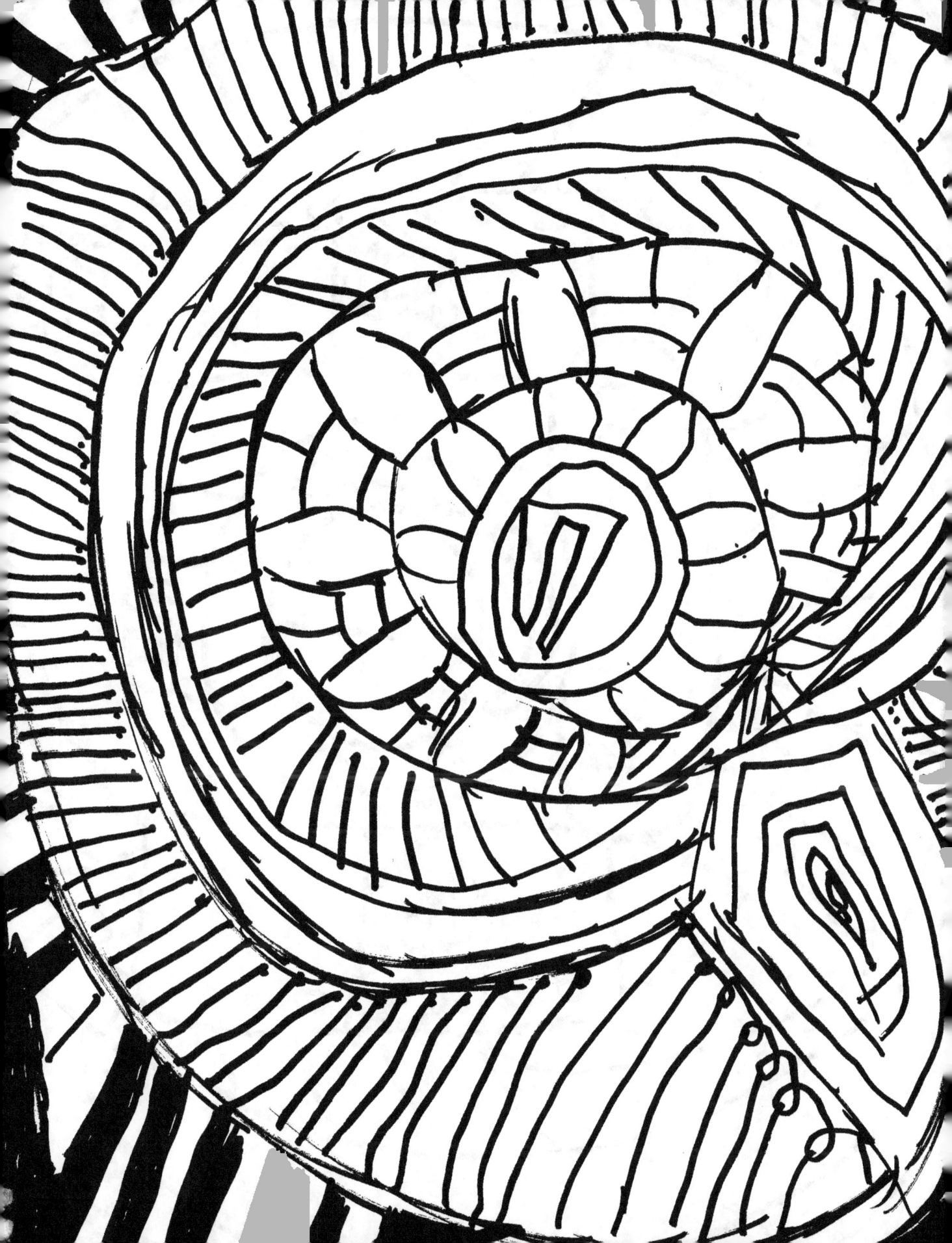

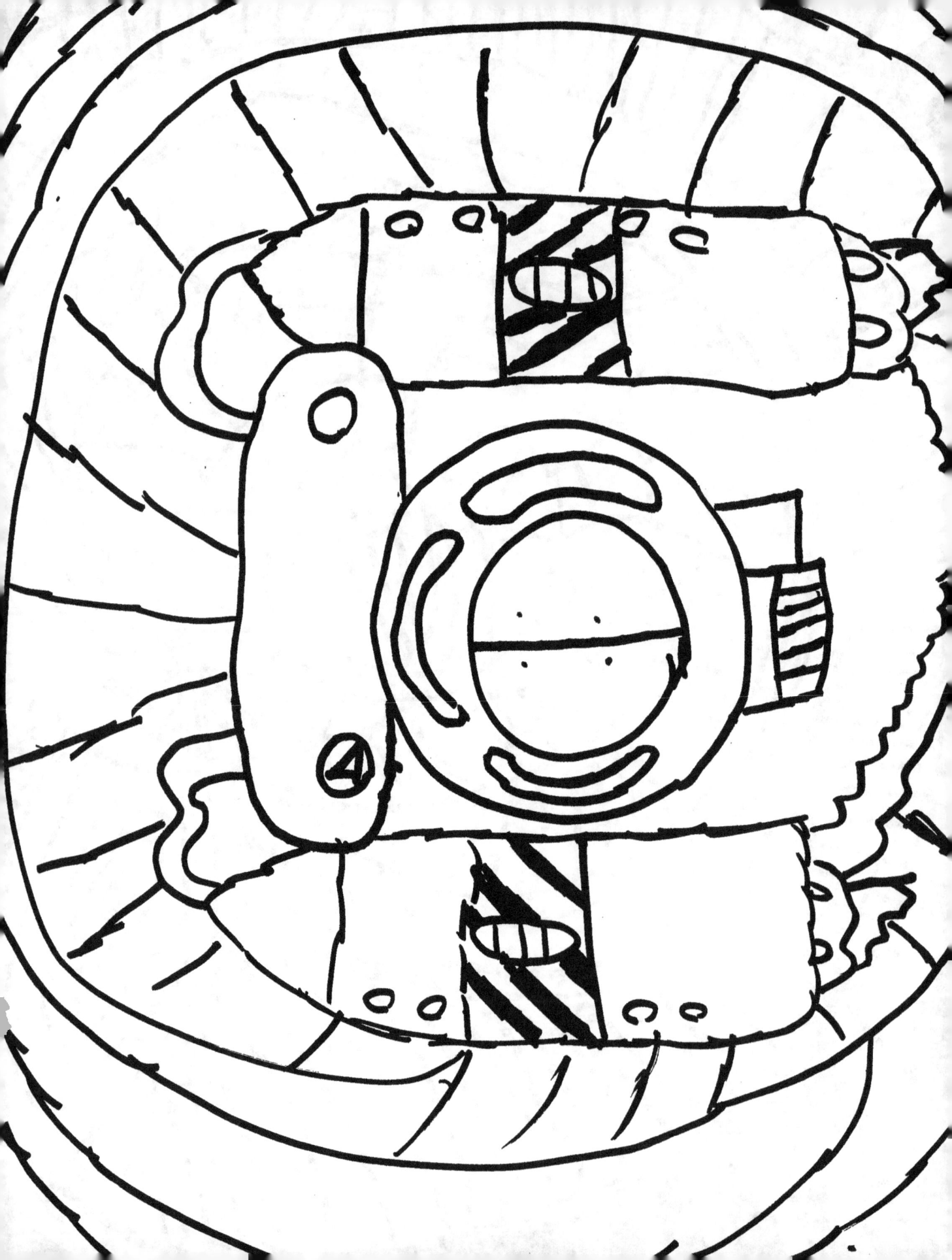

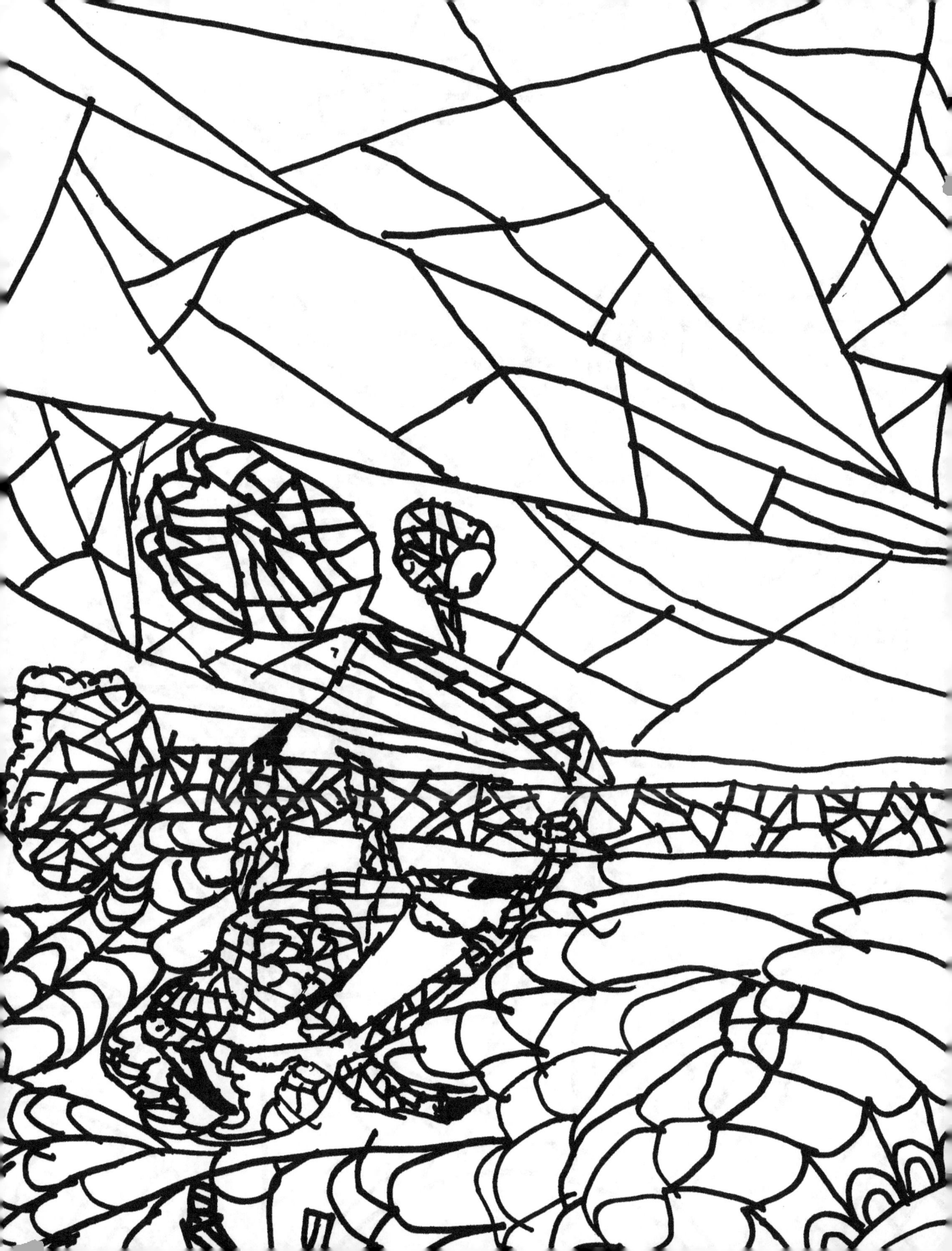

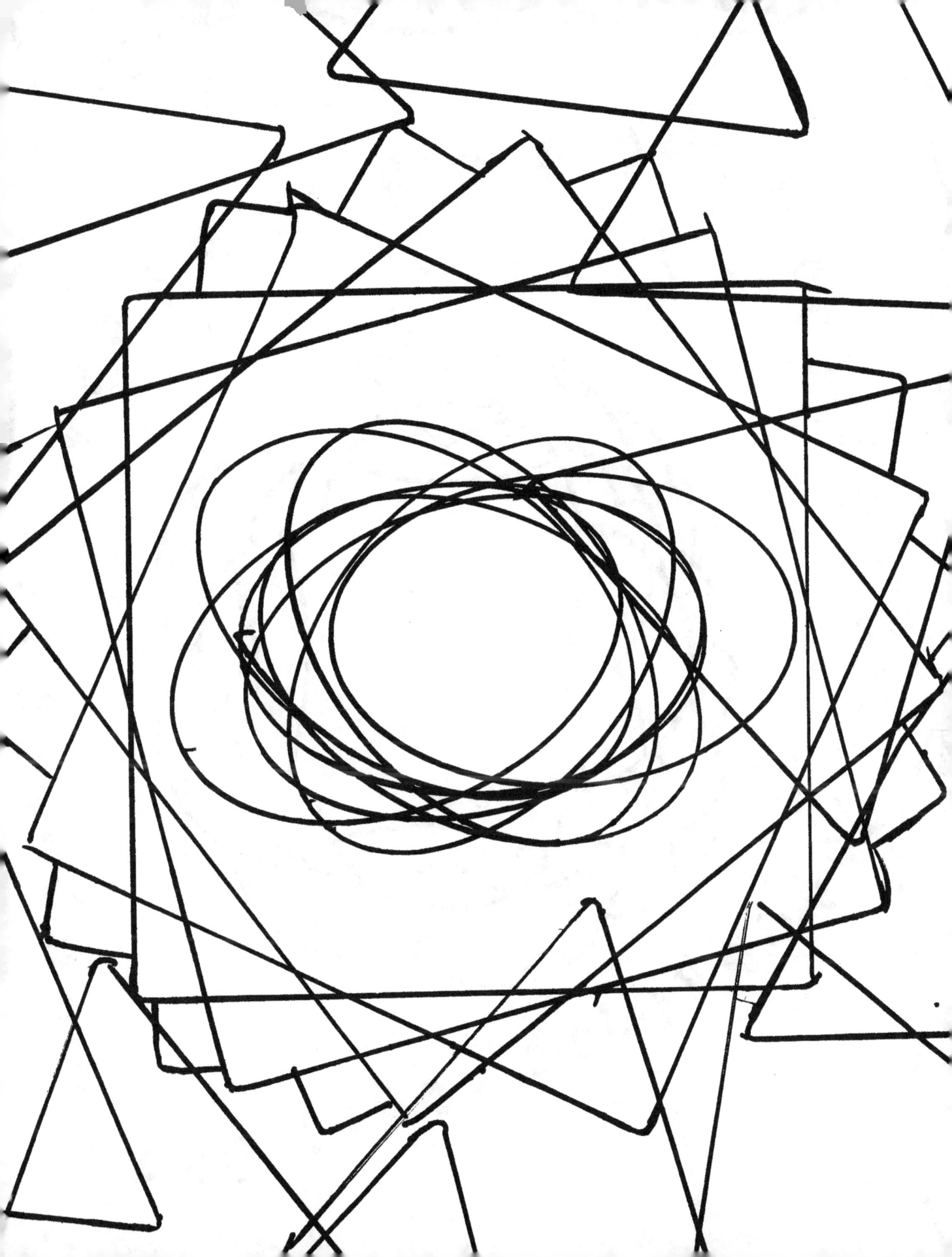

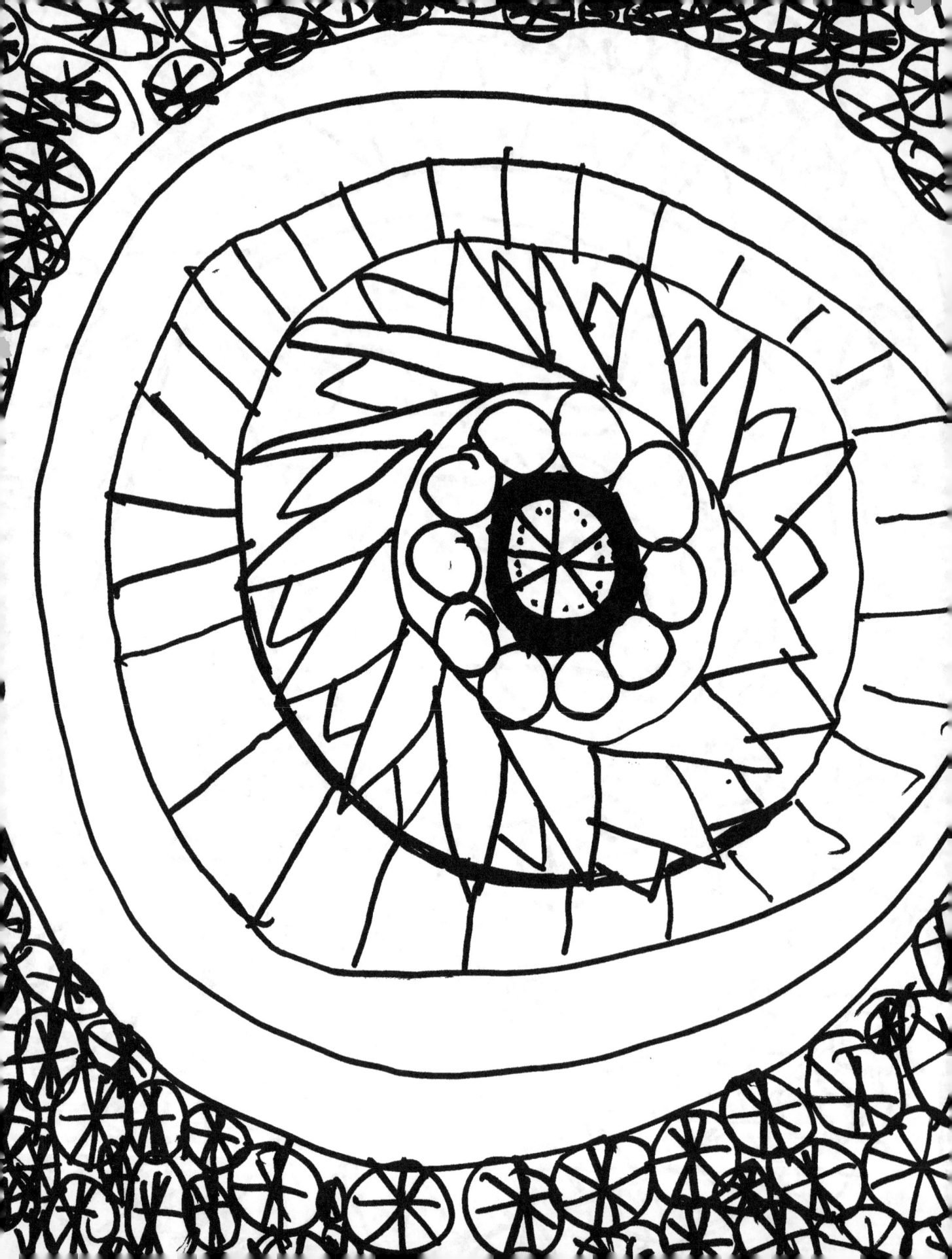

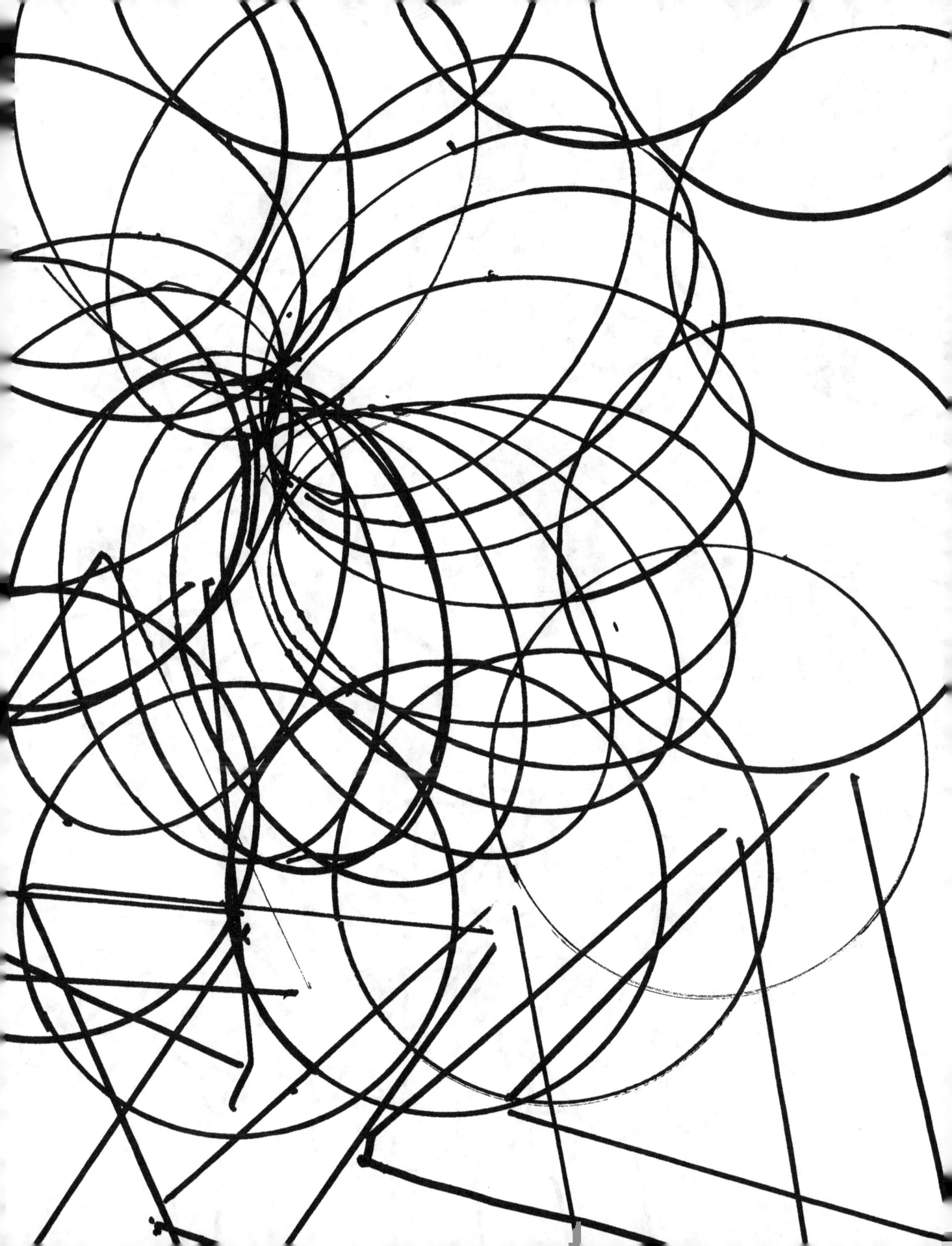

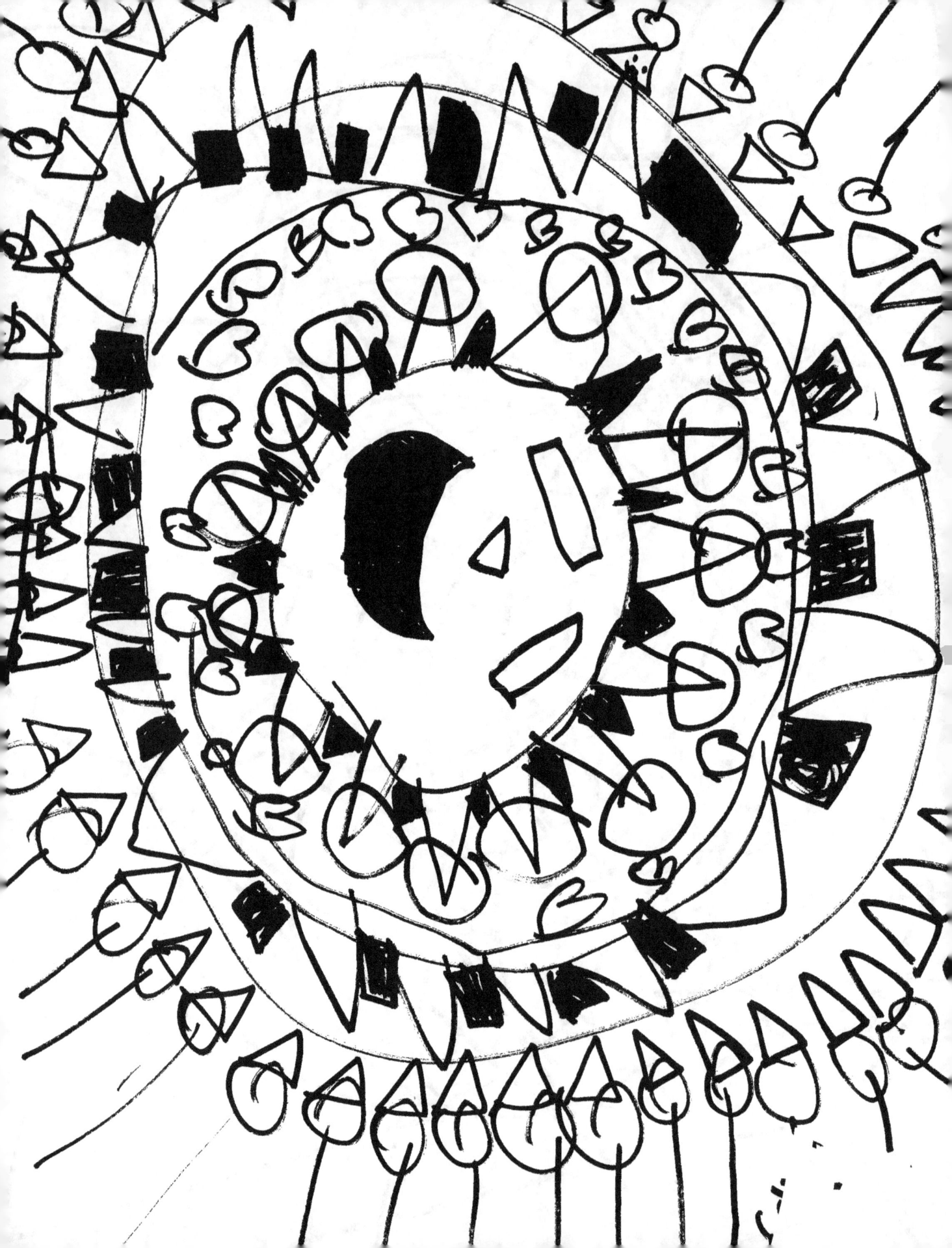

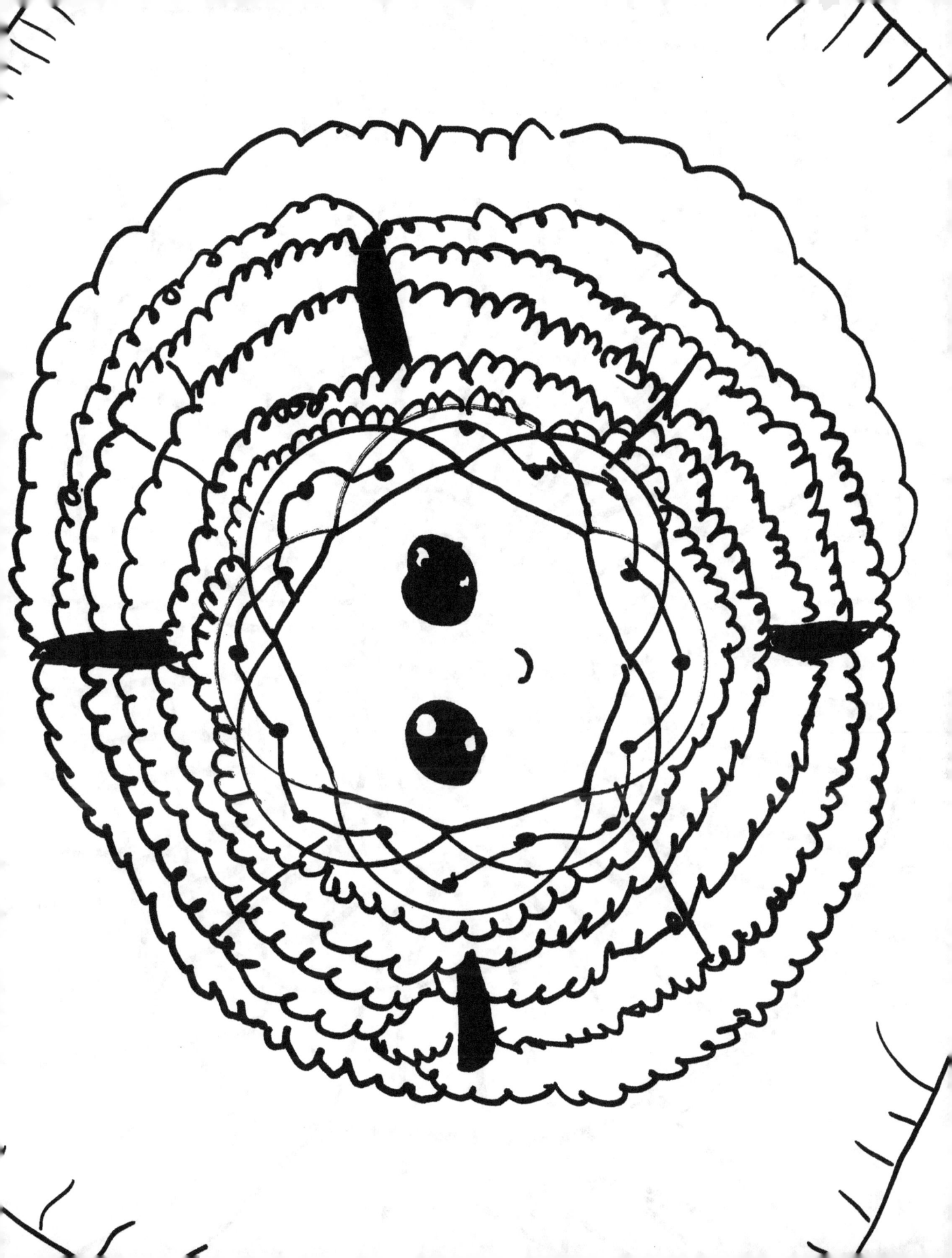

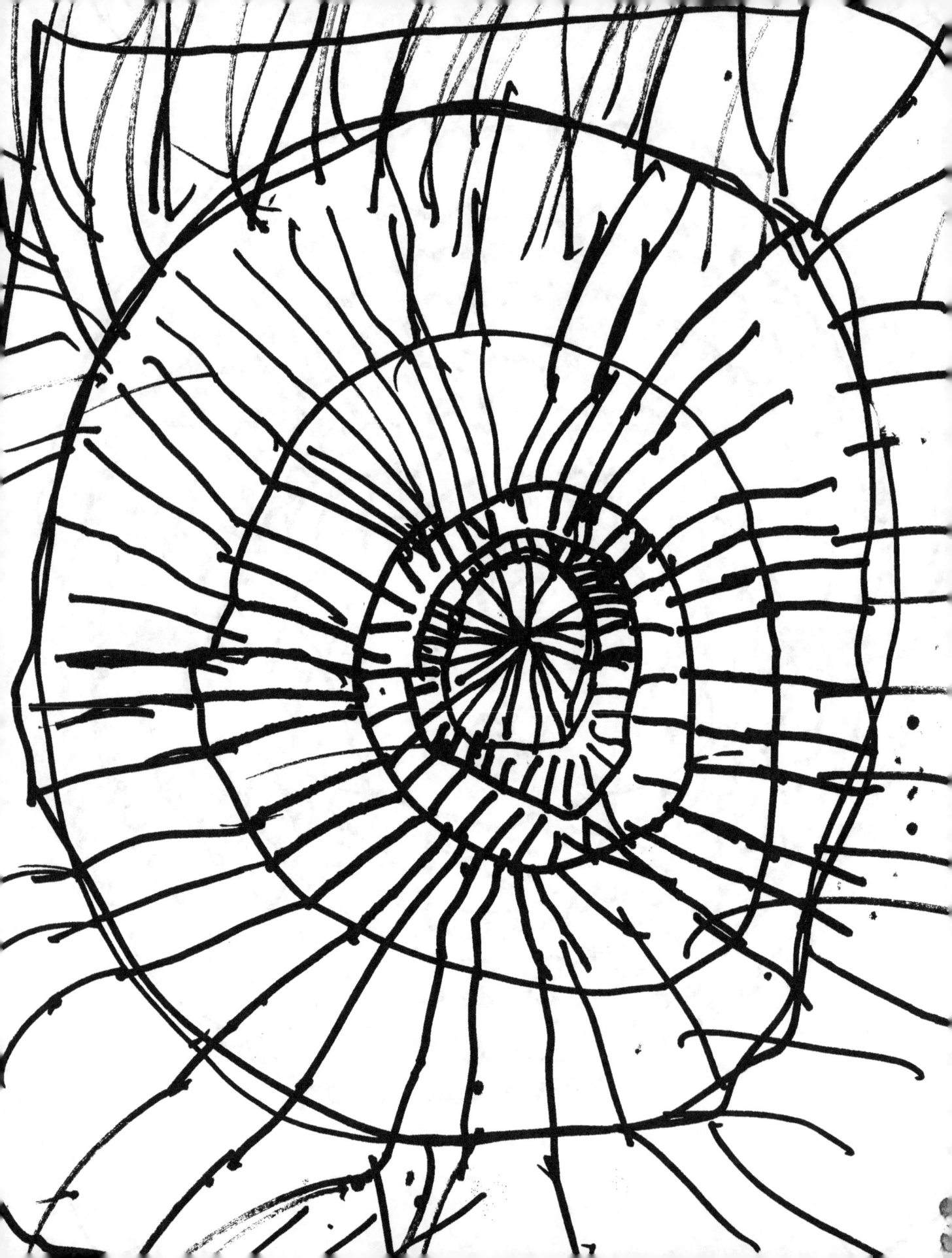

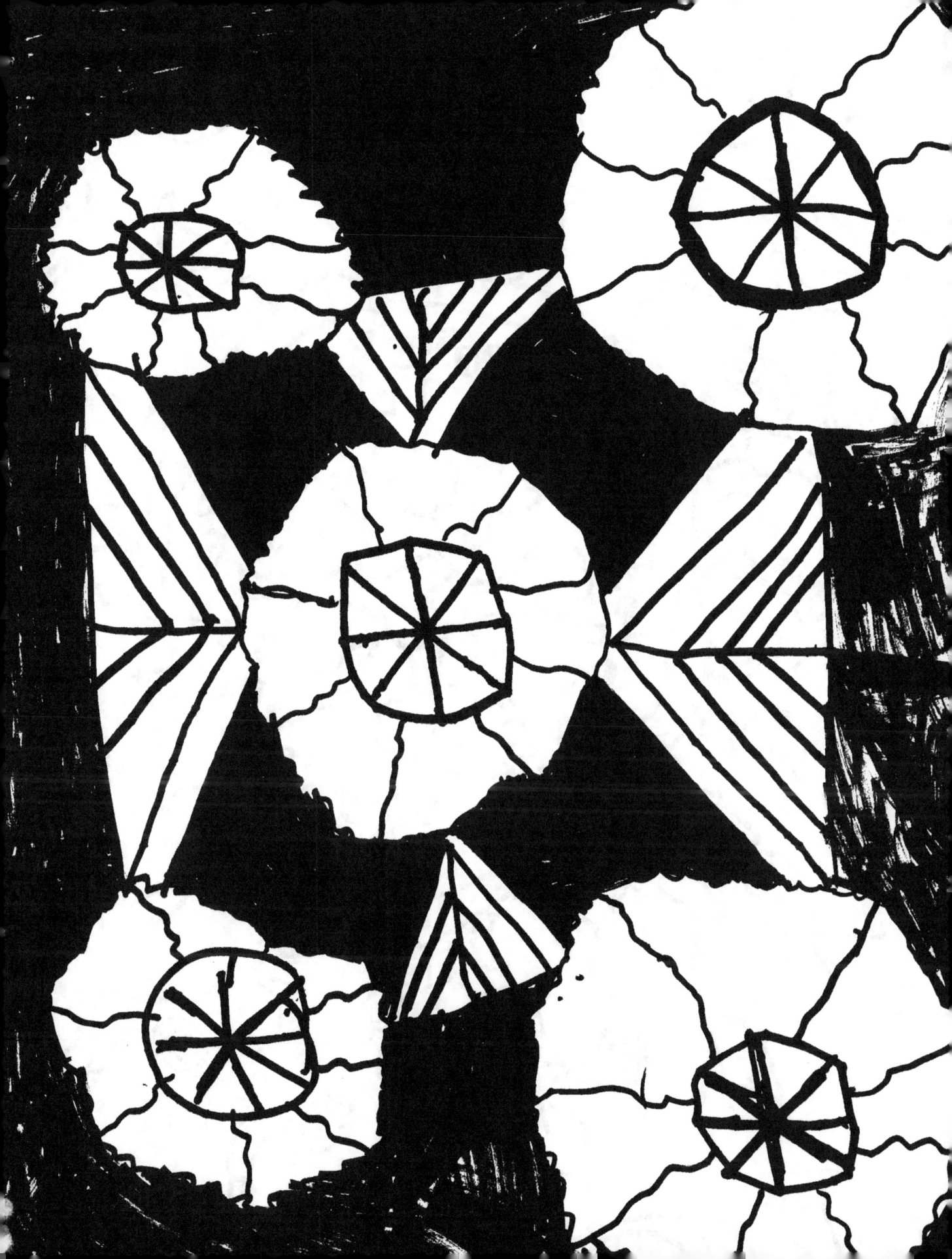

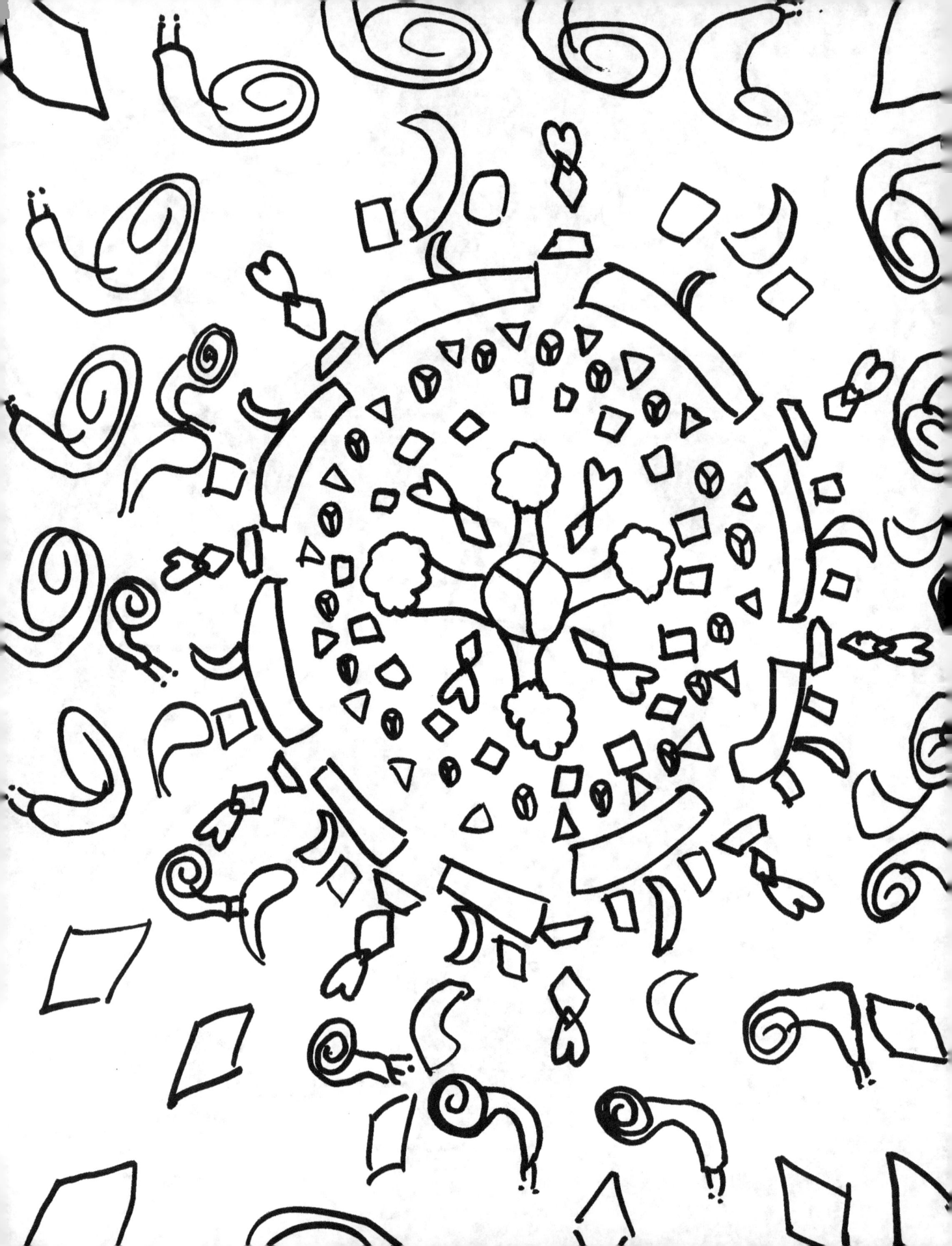

Peace

The peace pin!

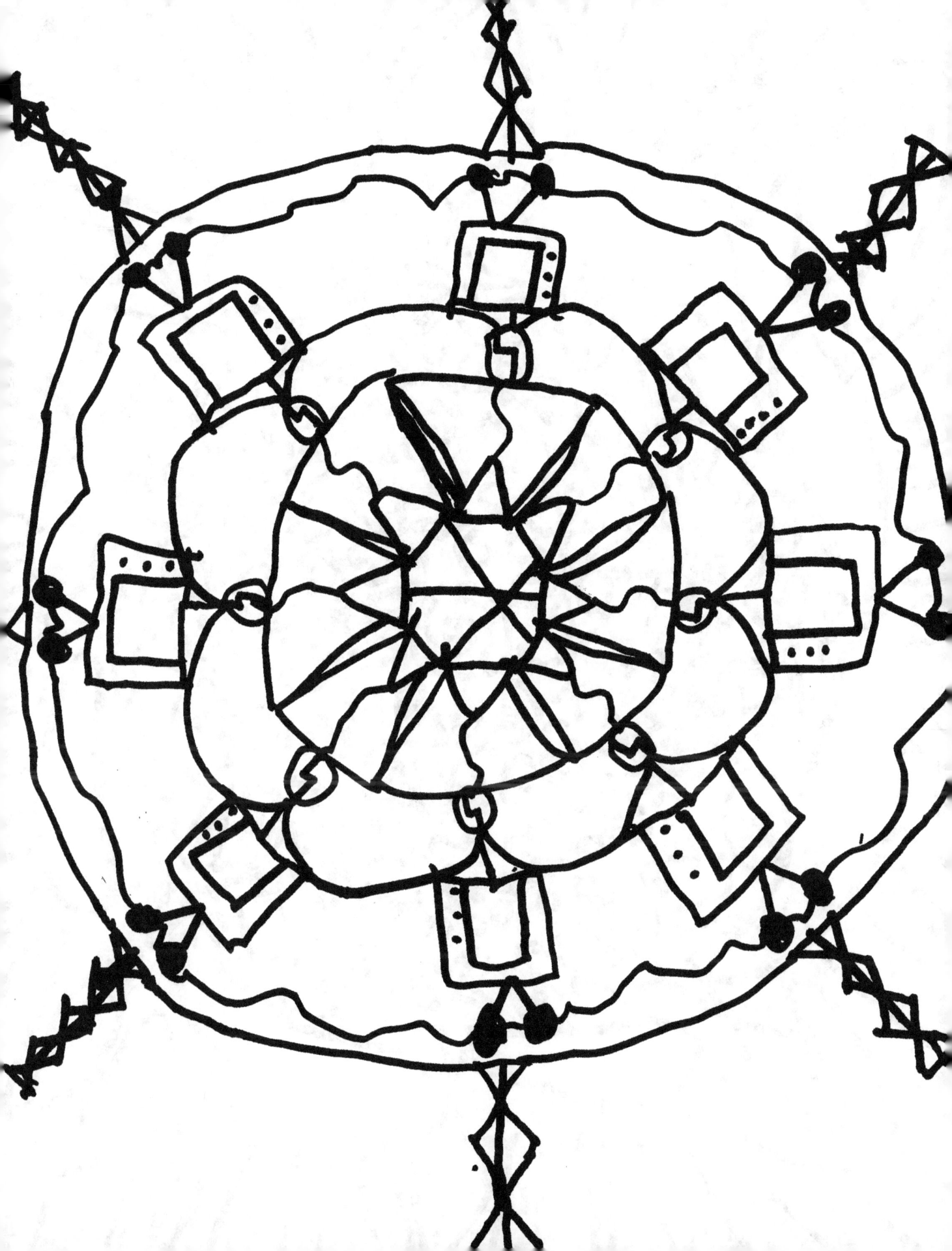

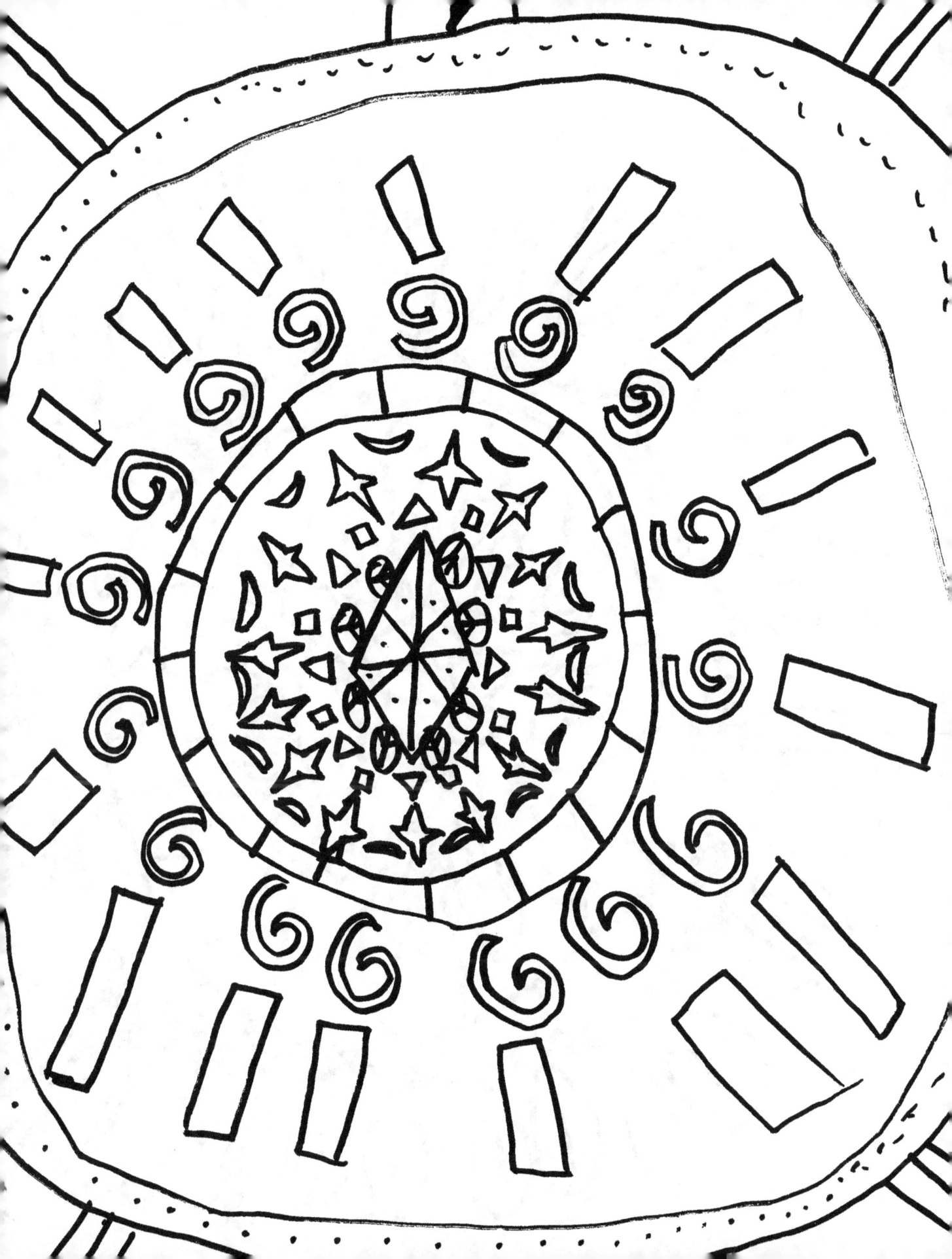

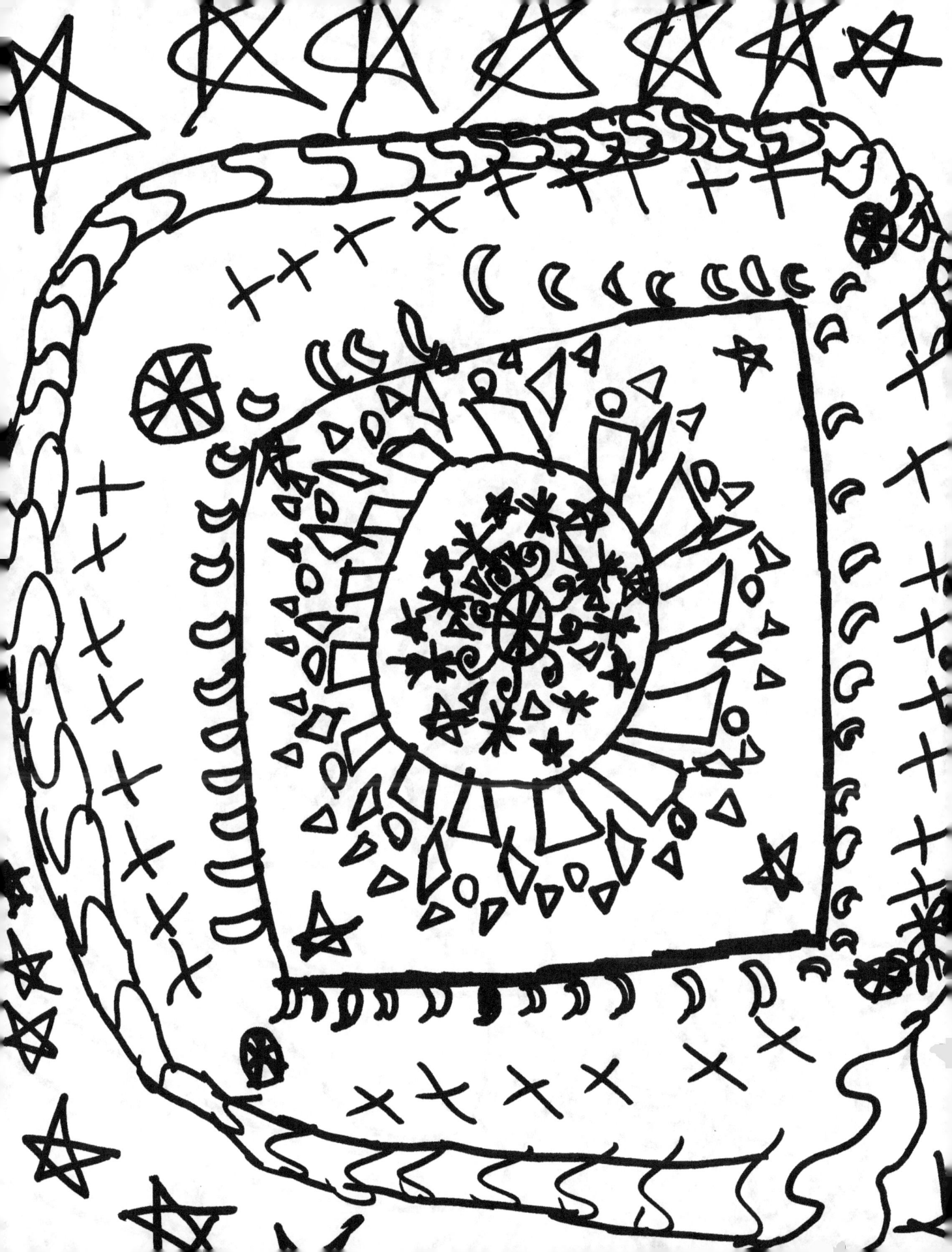

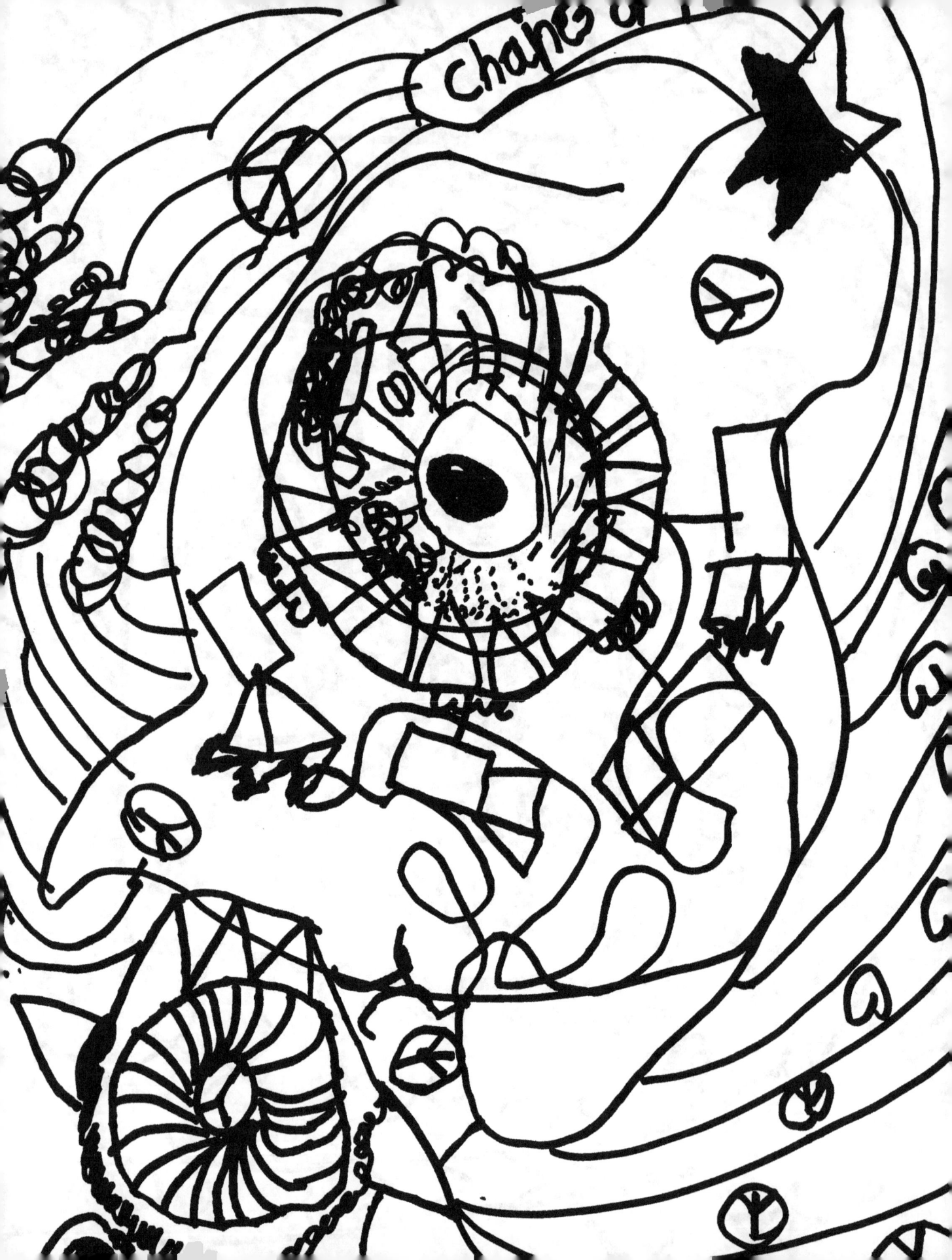

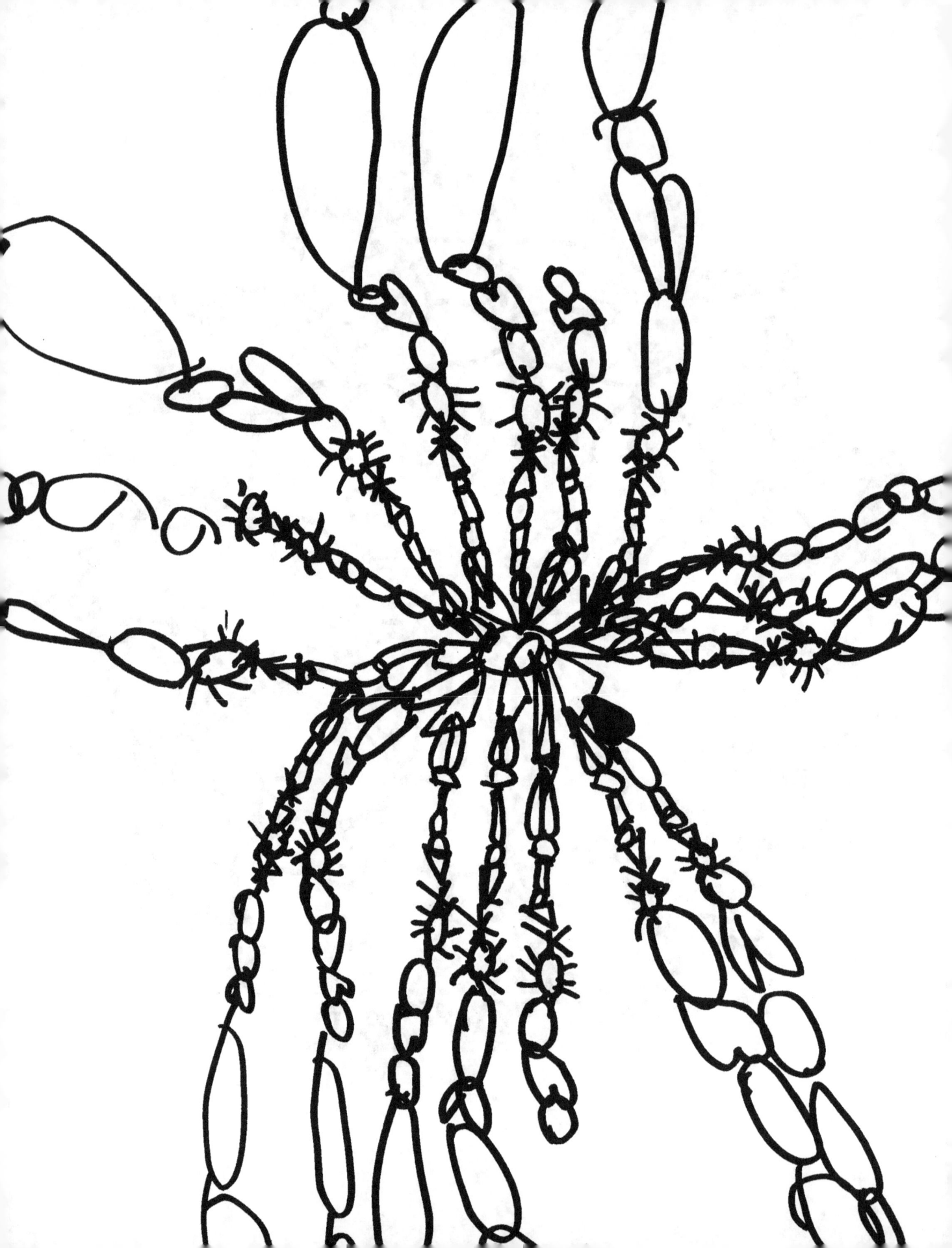

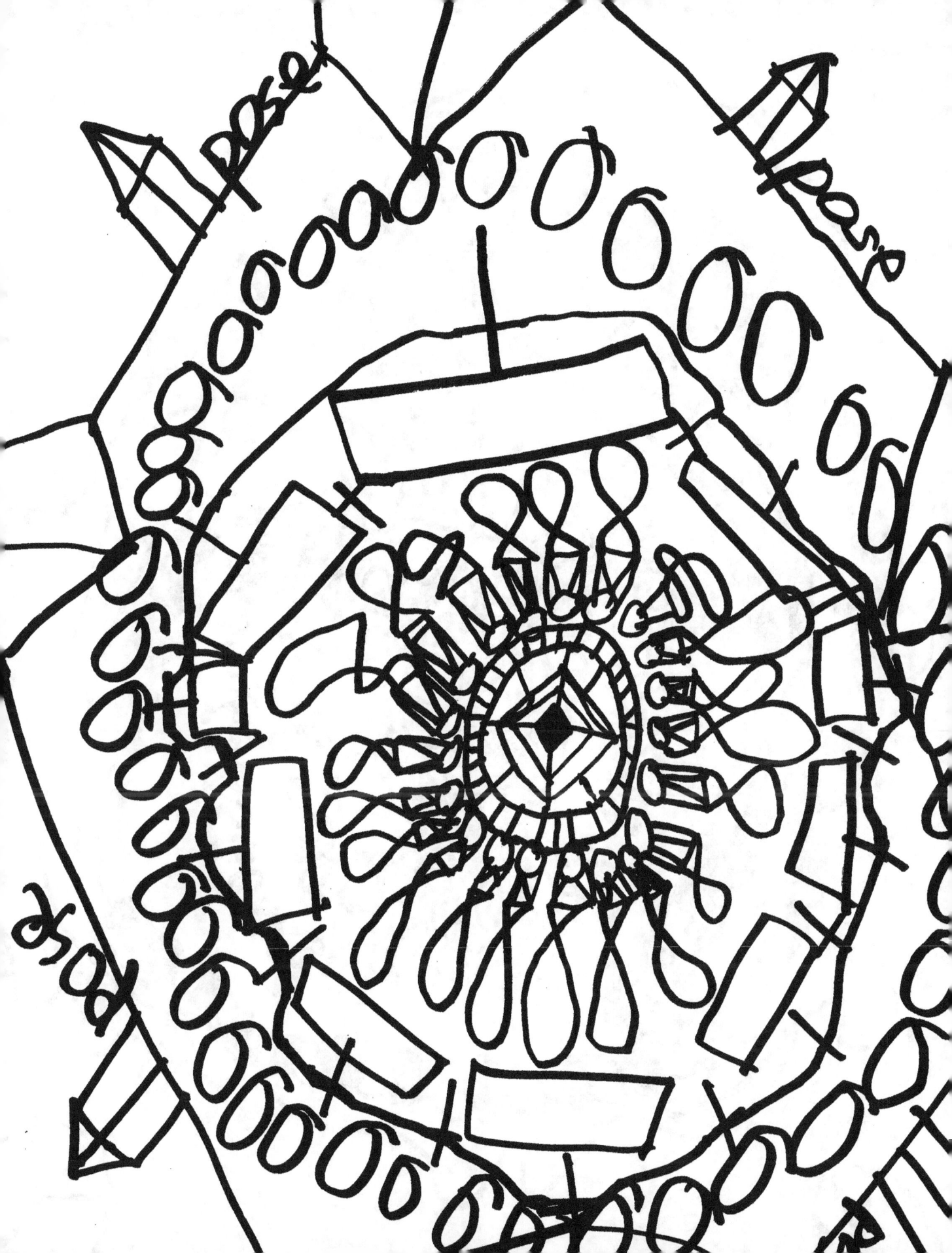

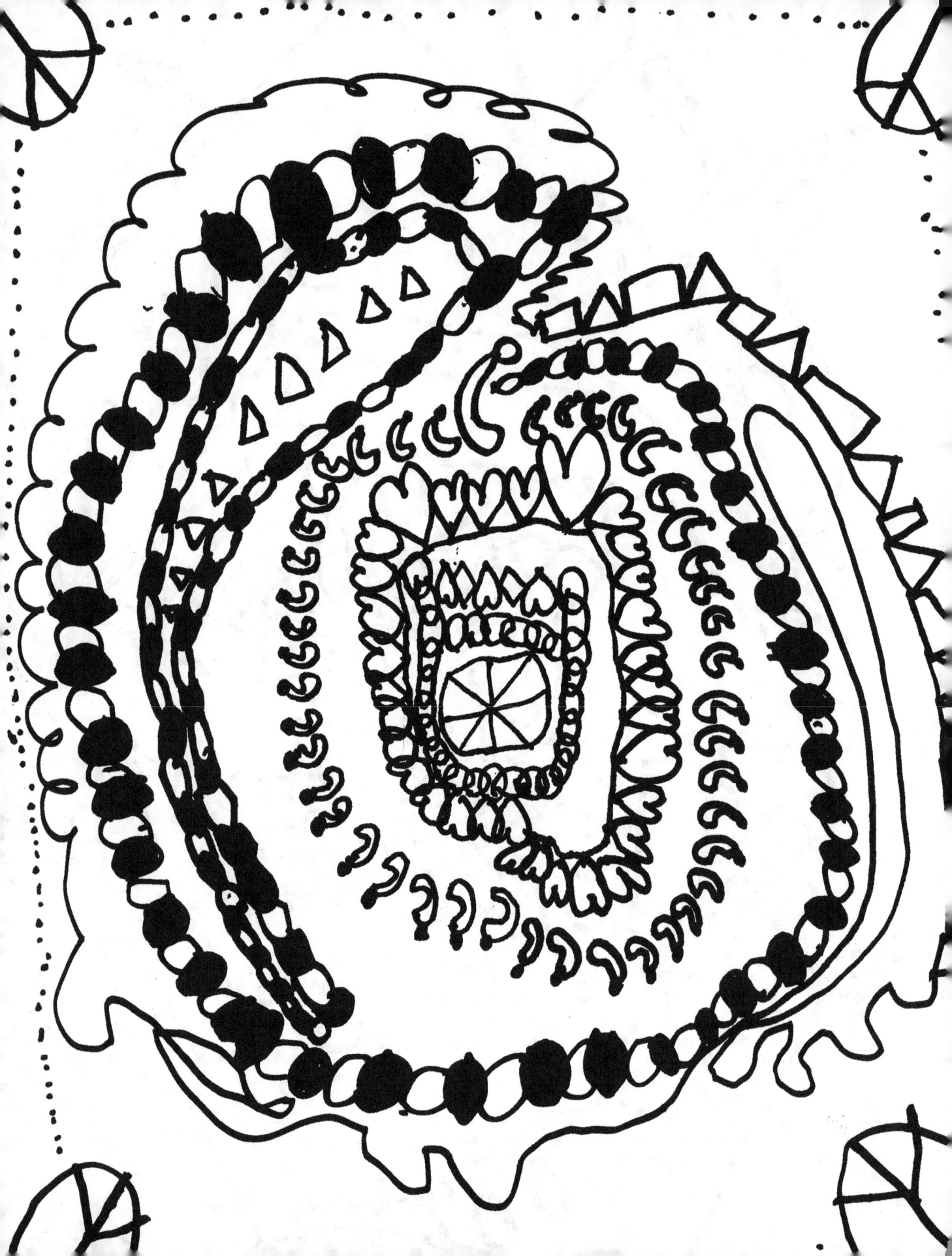

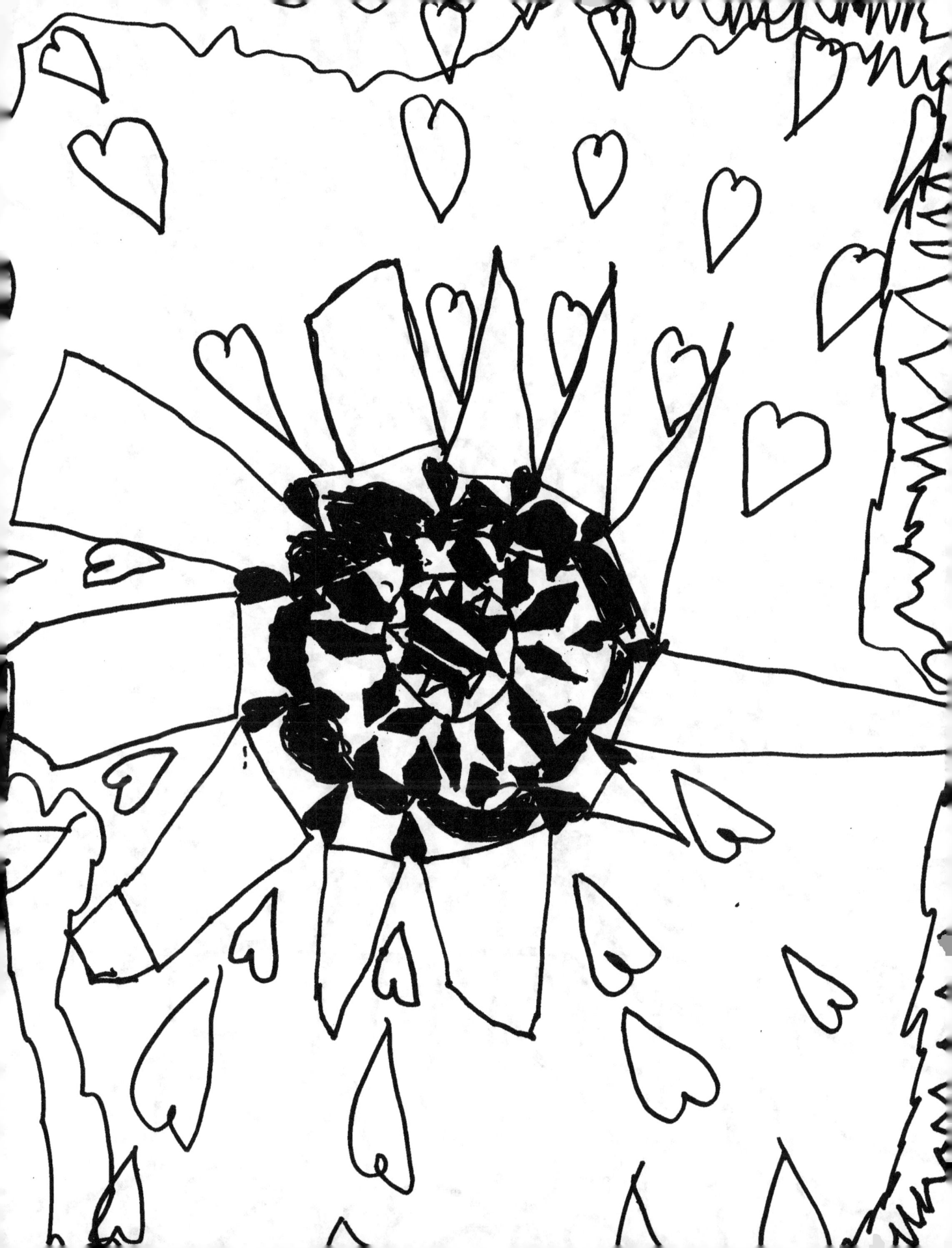

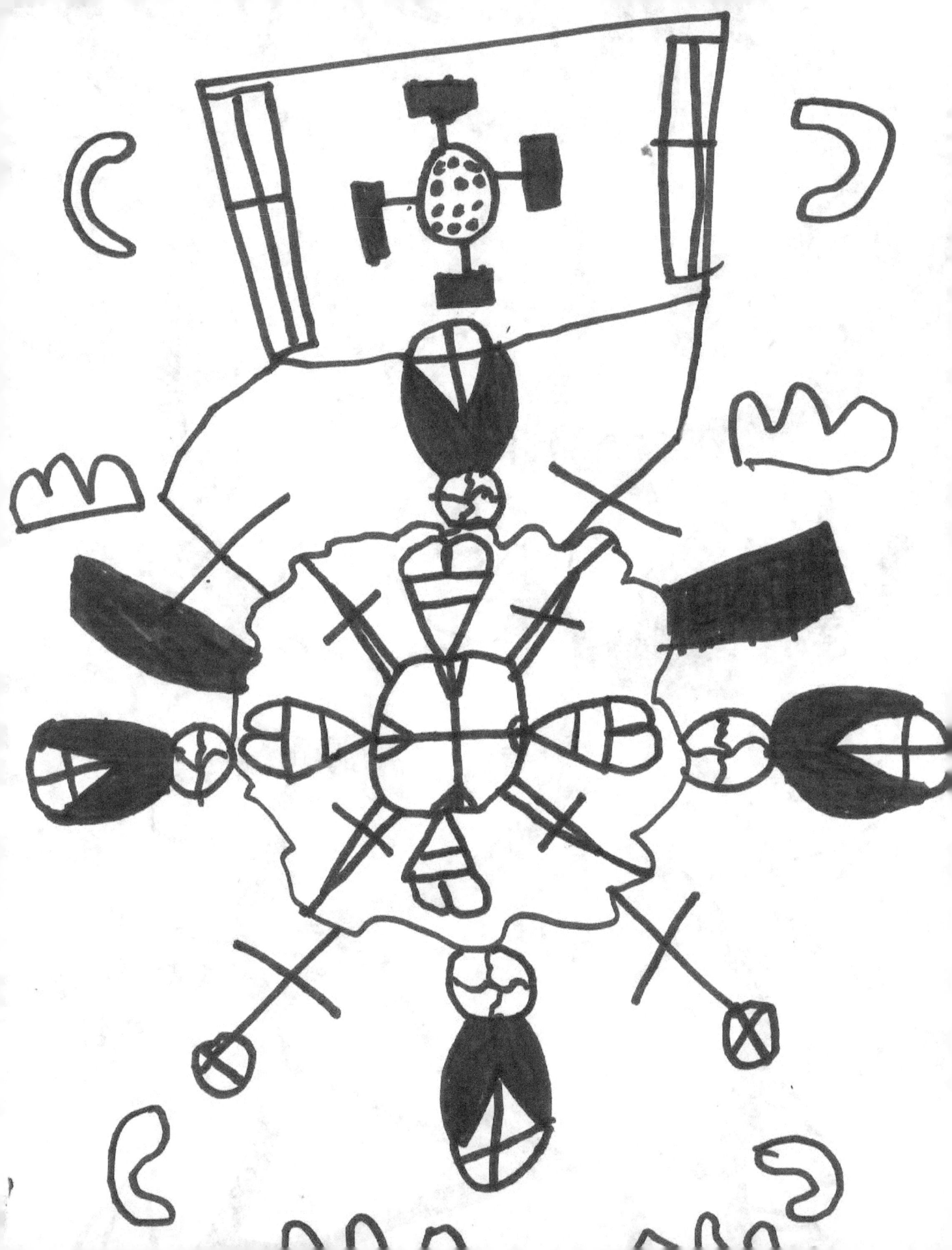

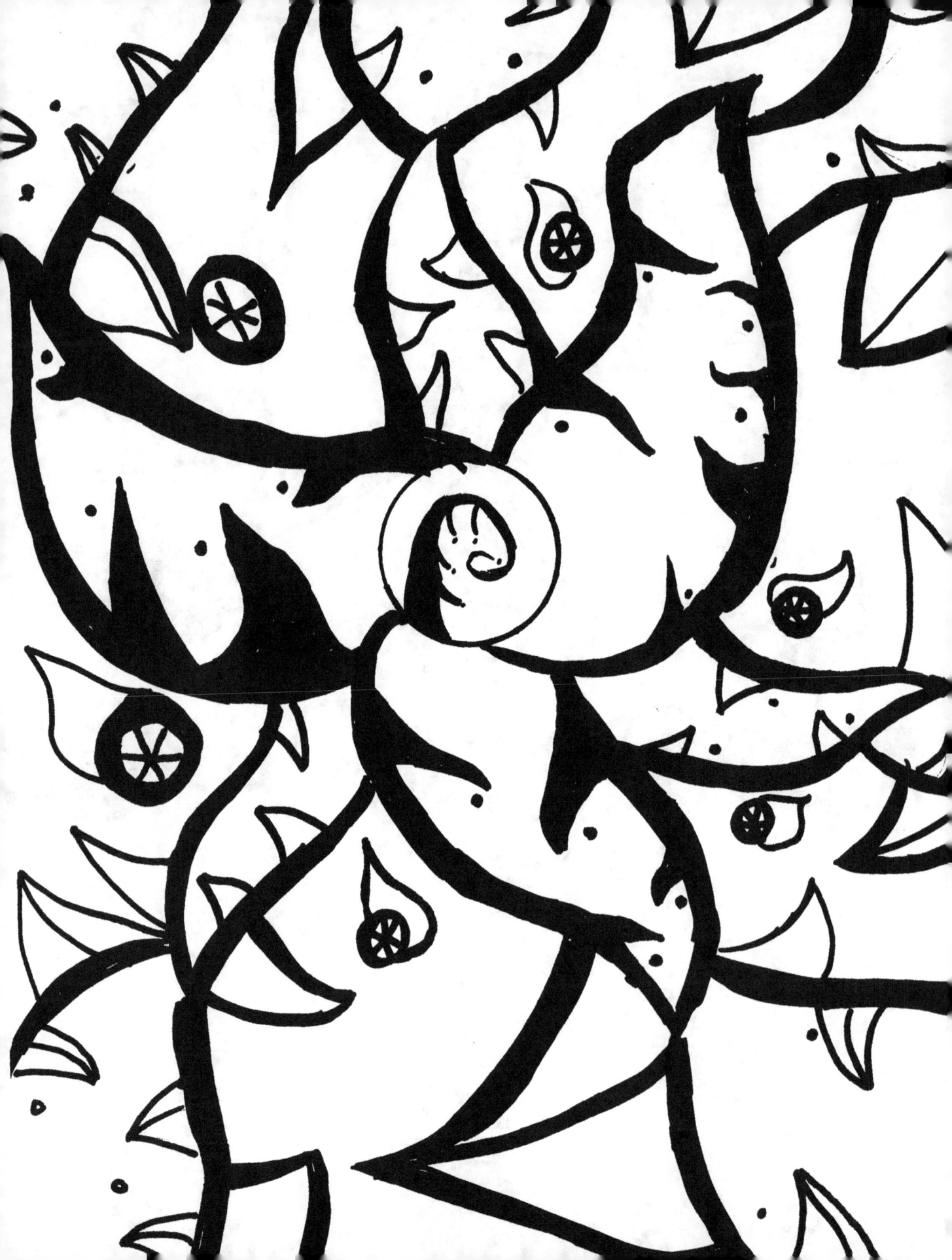

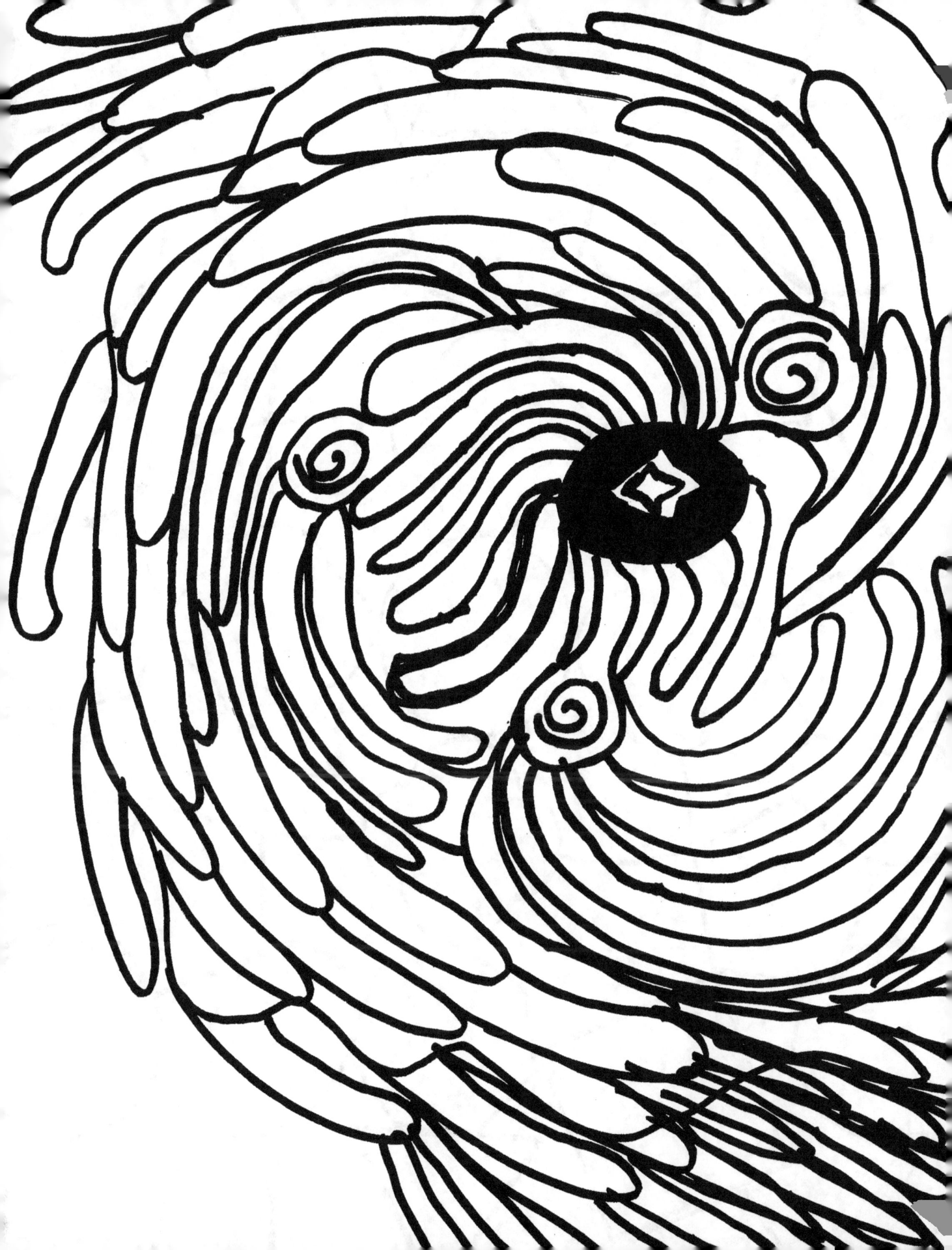

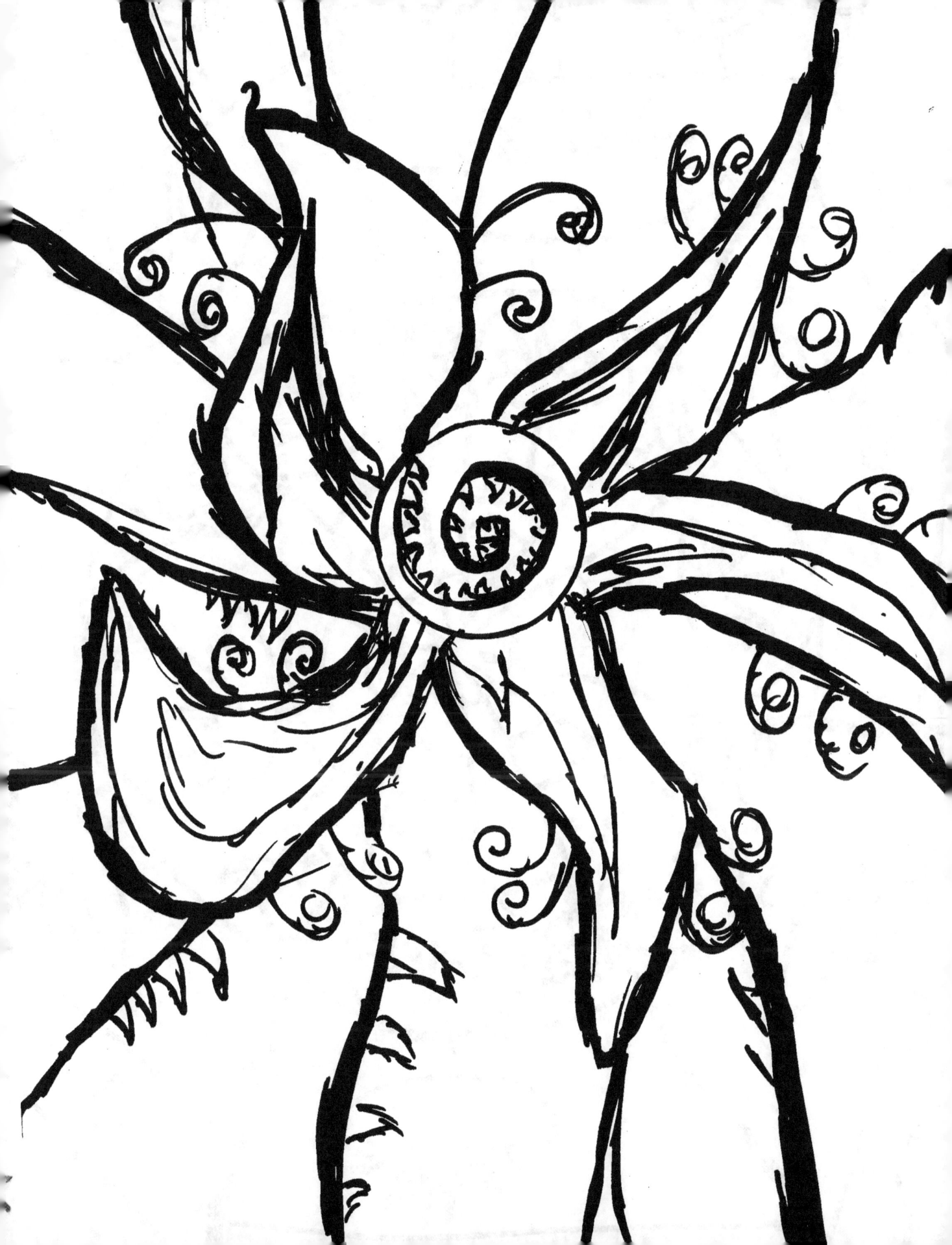

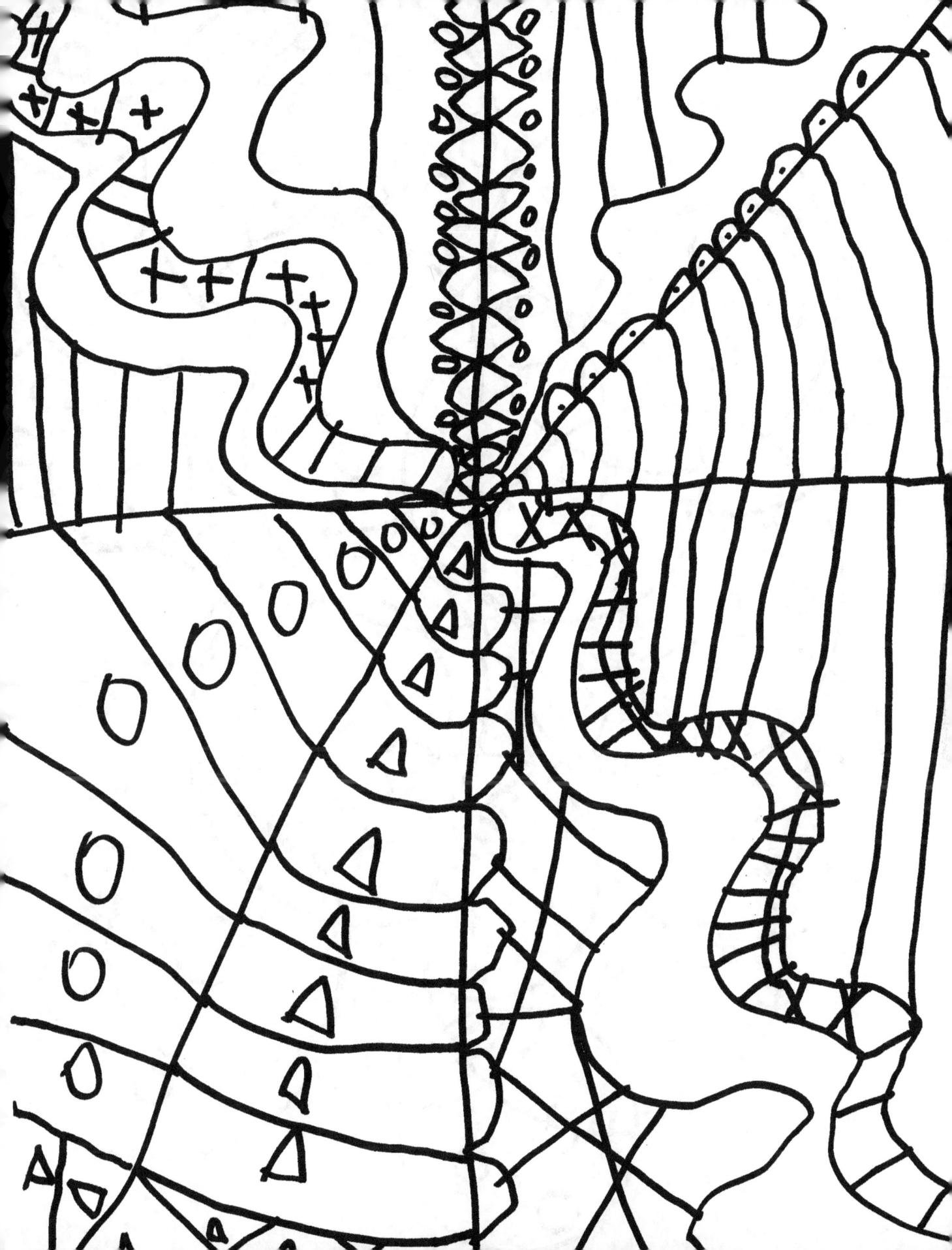

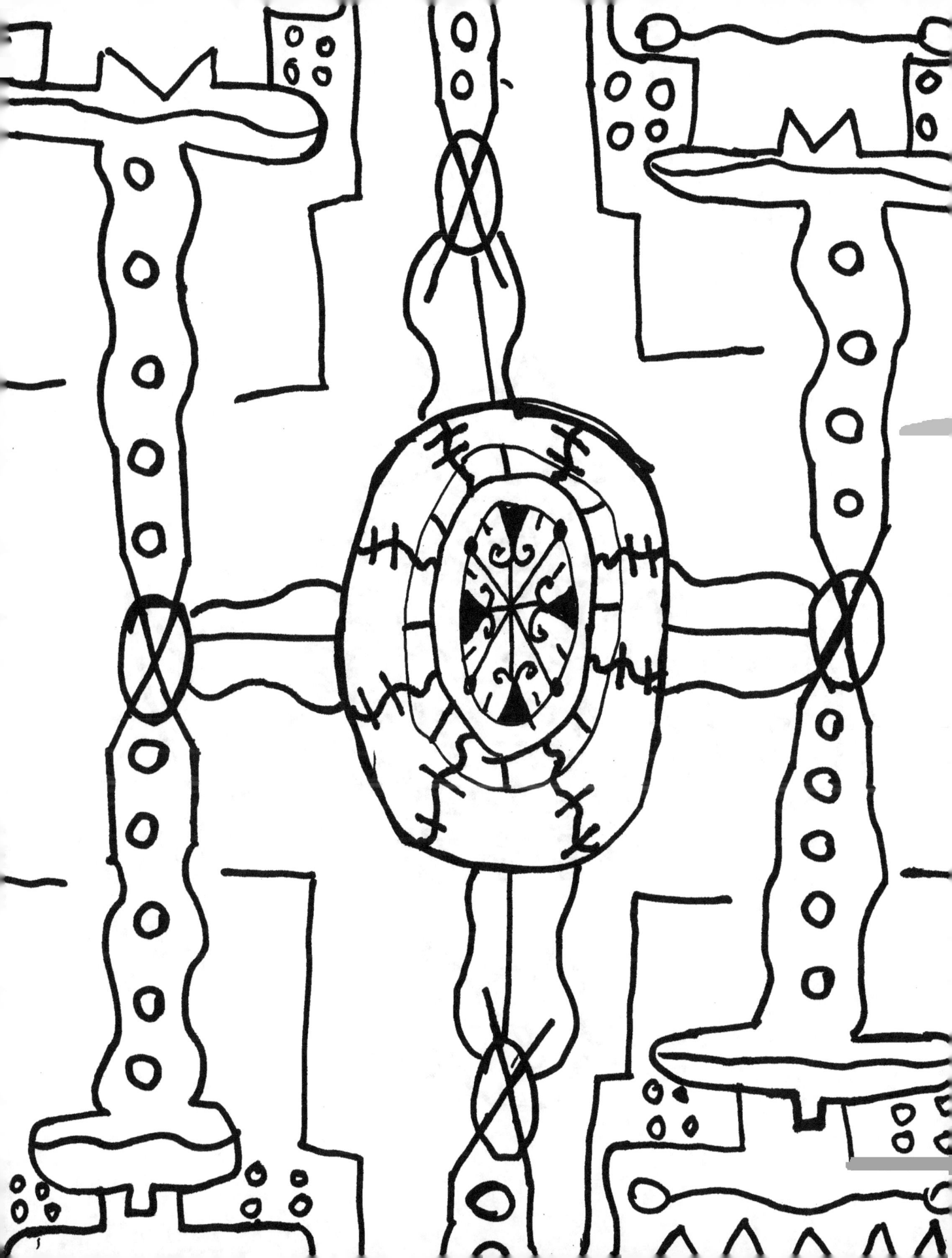

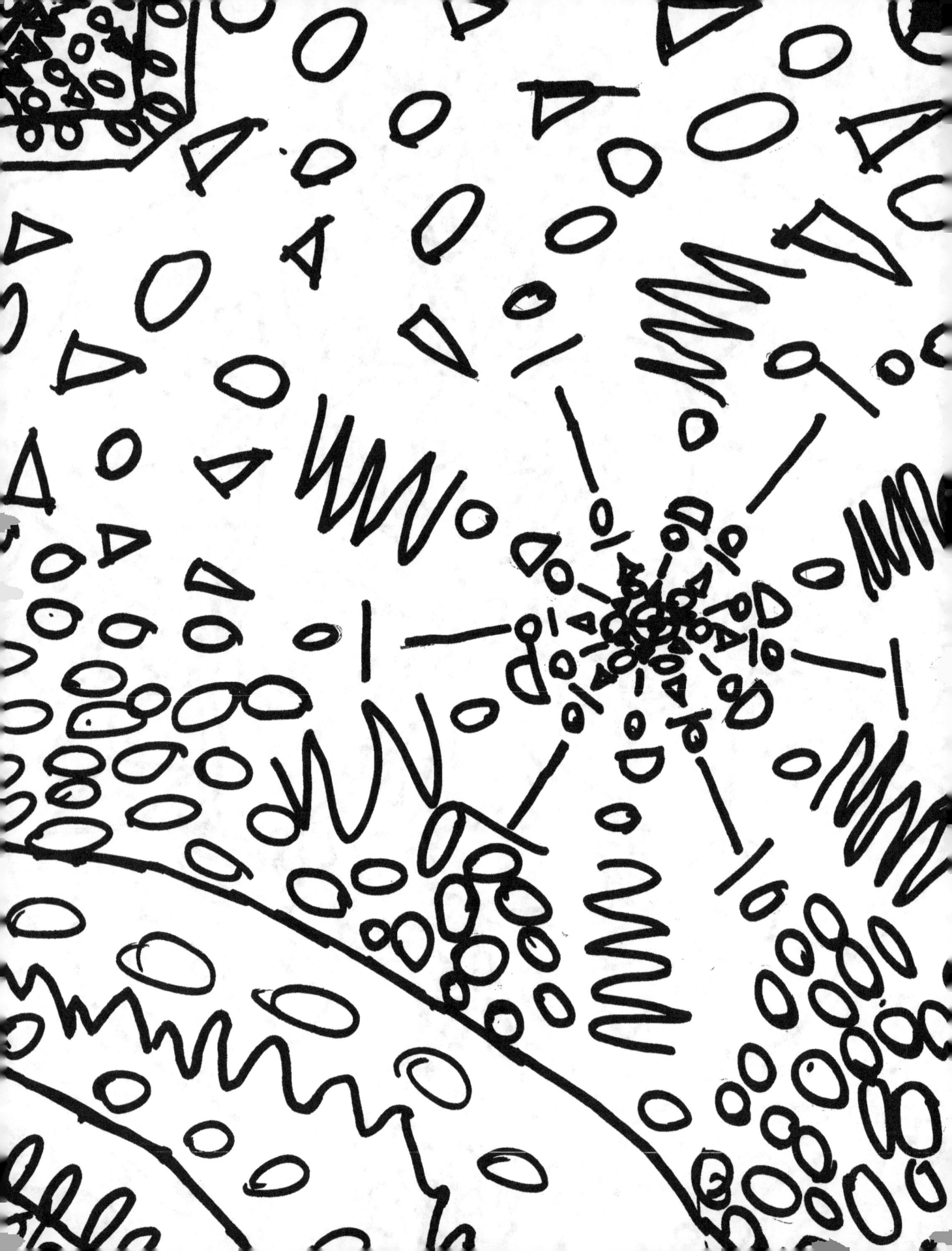

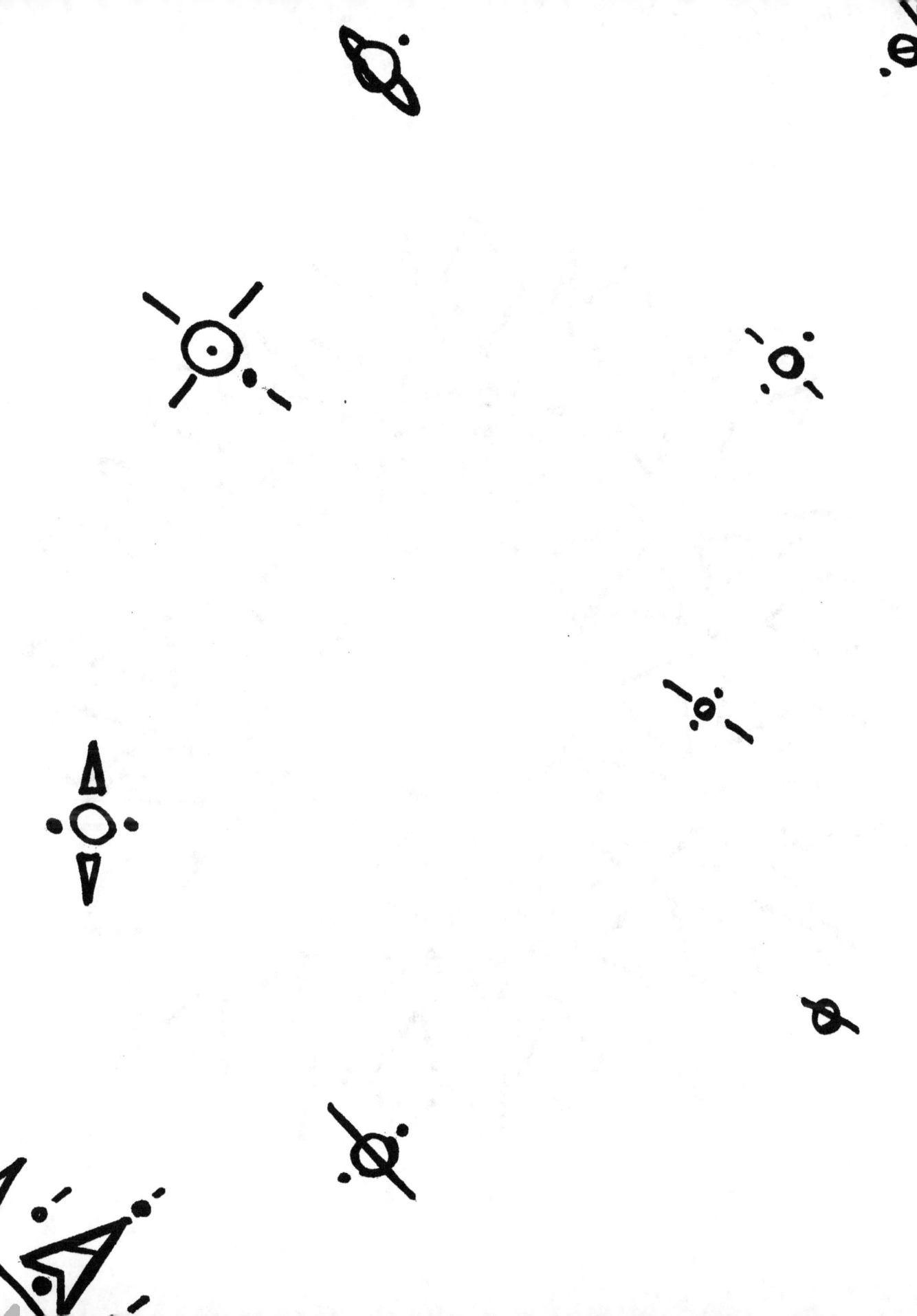

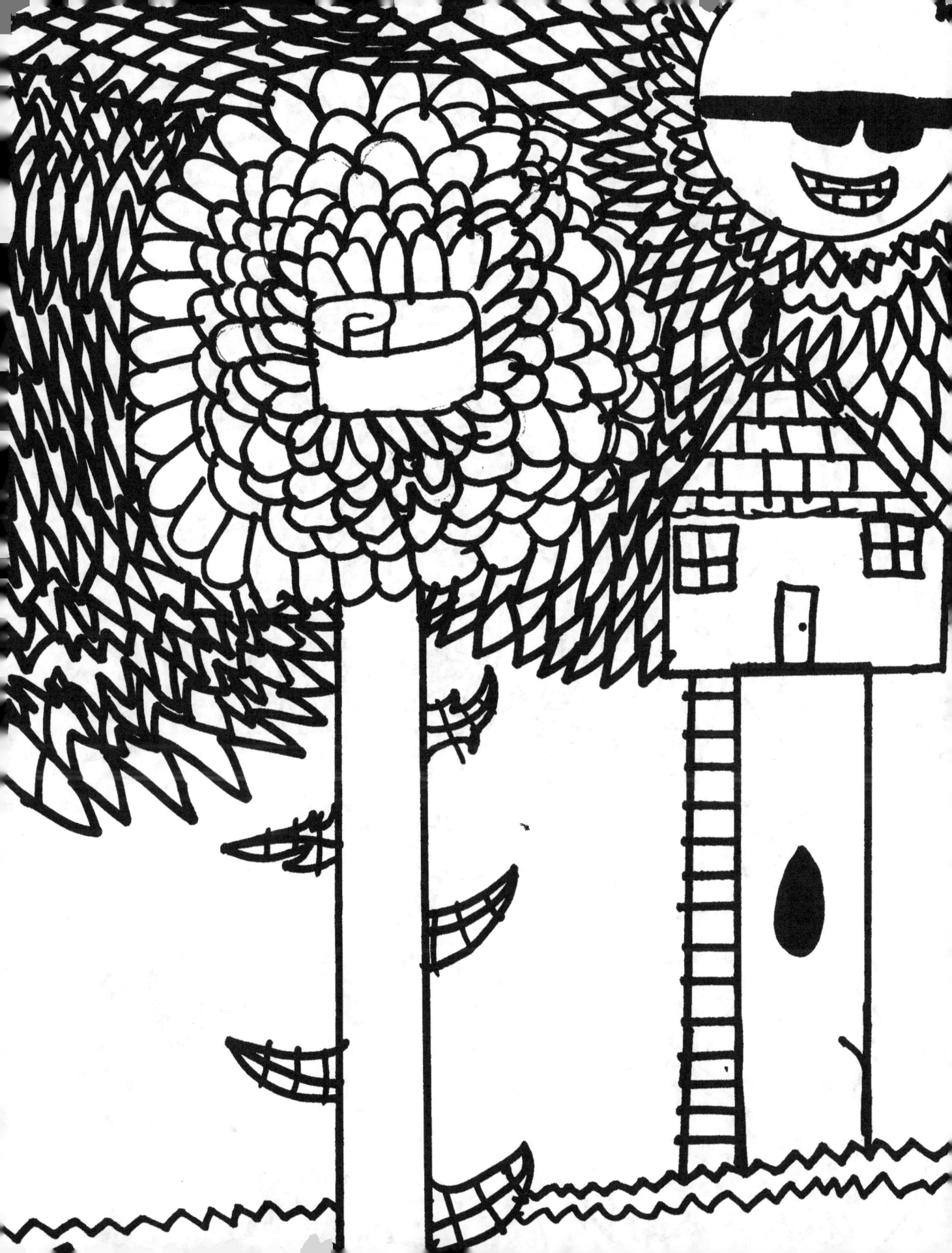

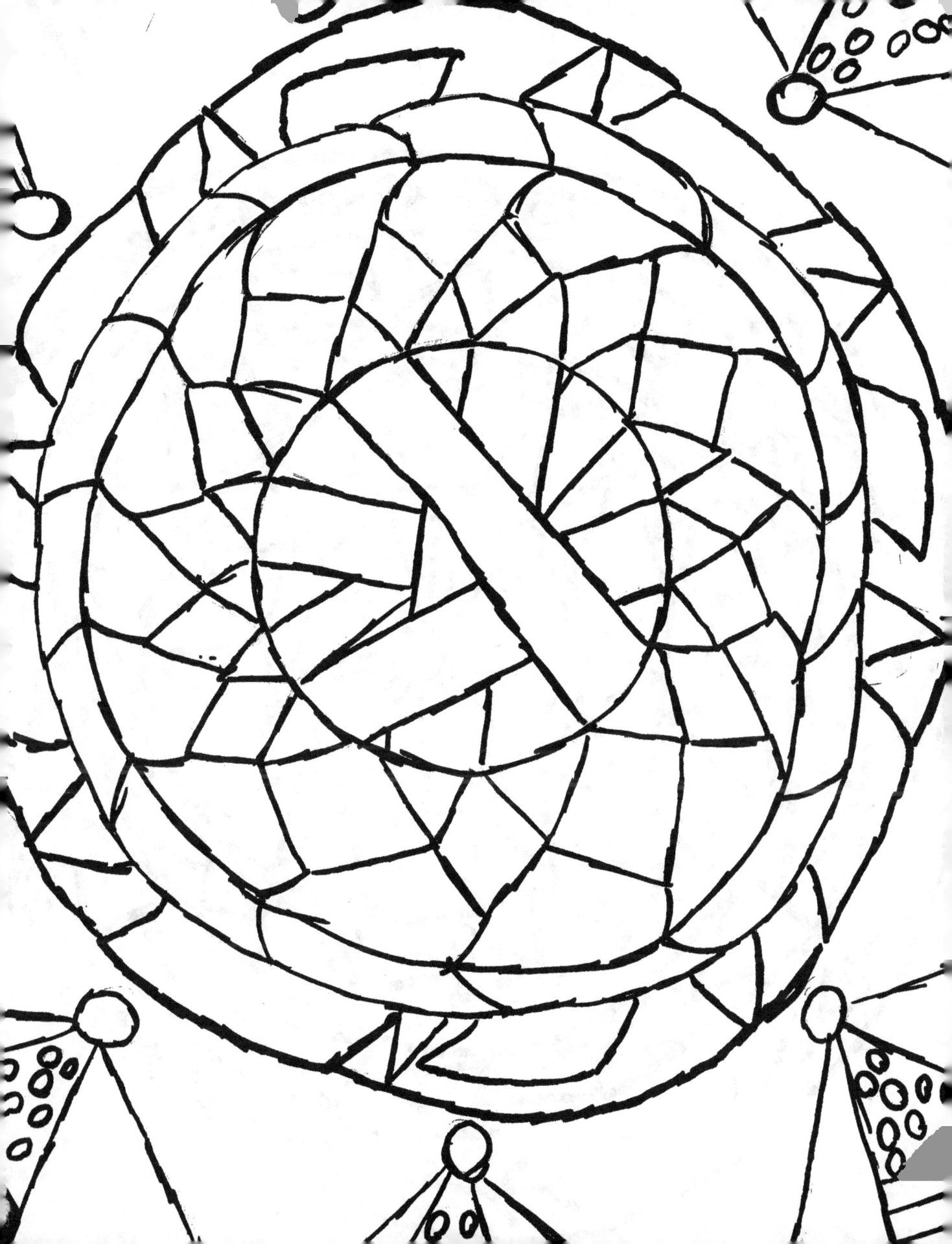

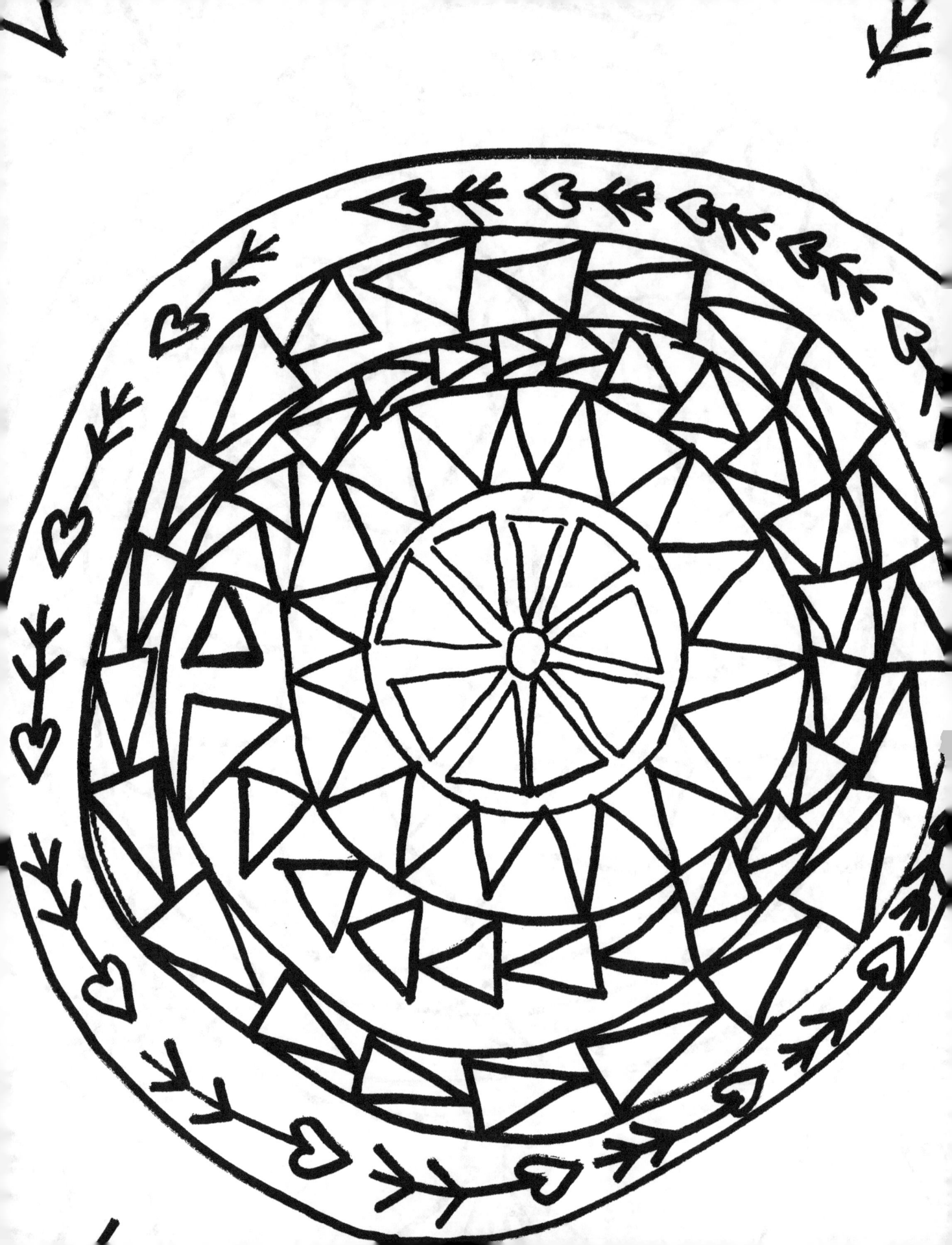

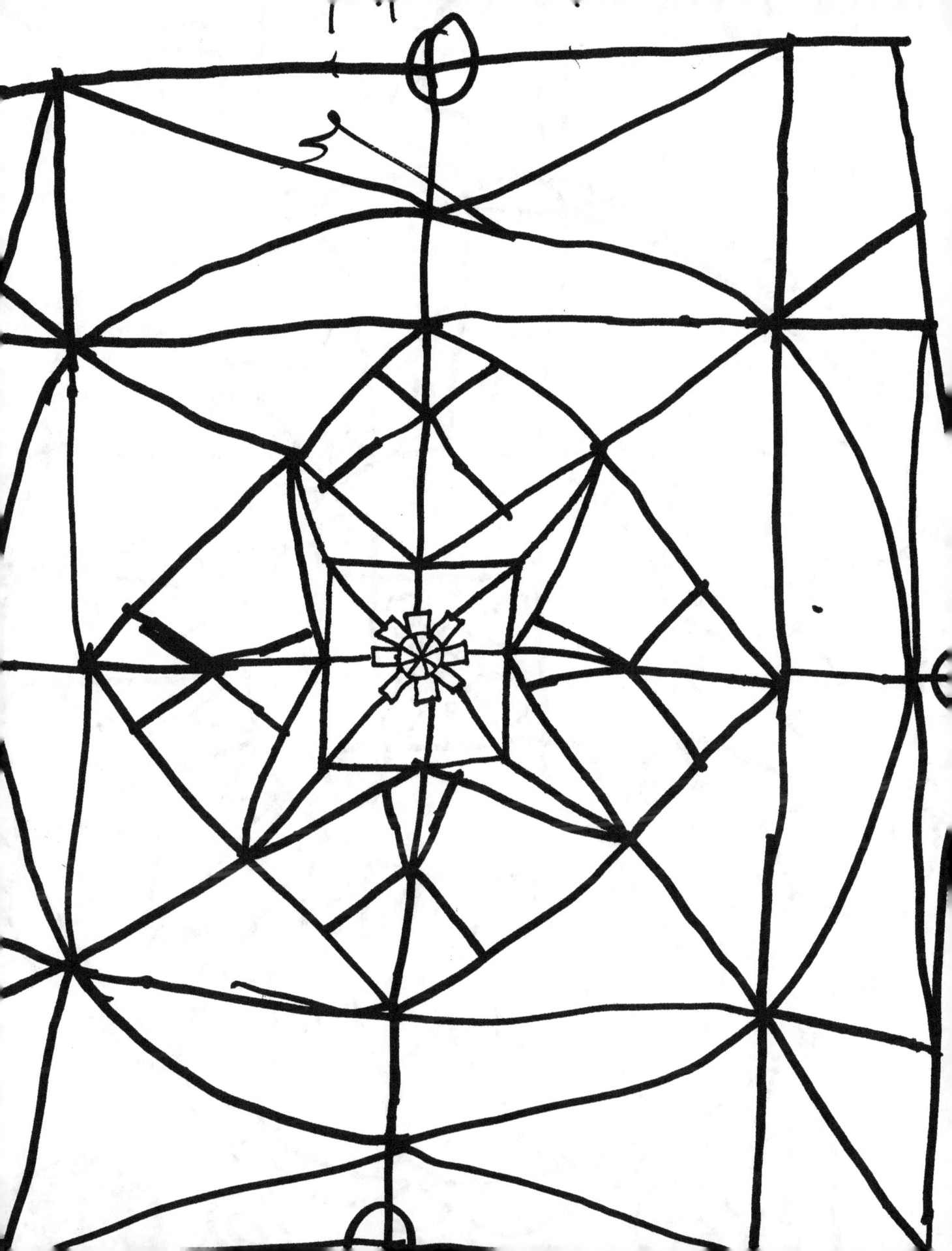

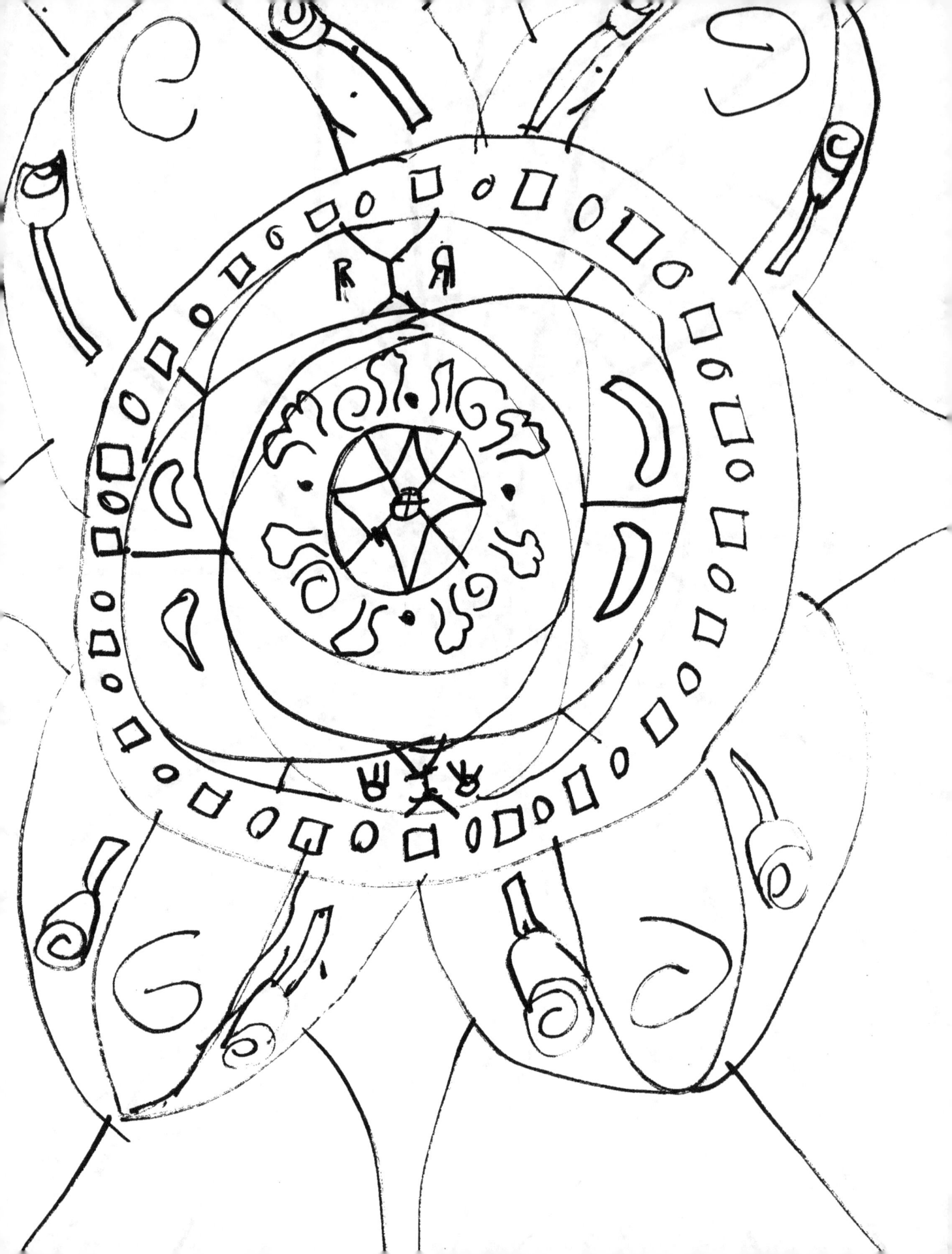

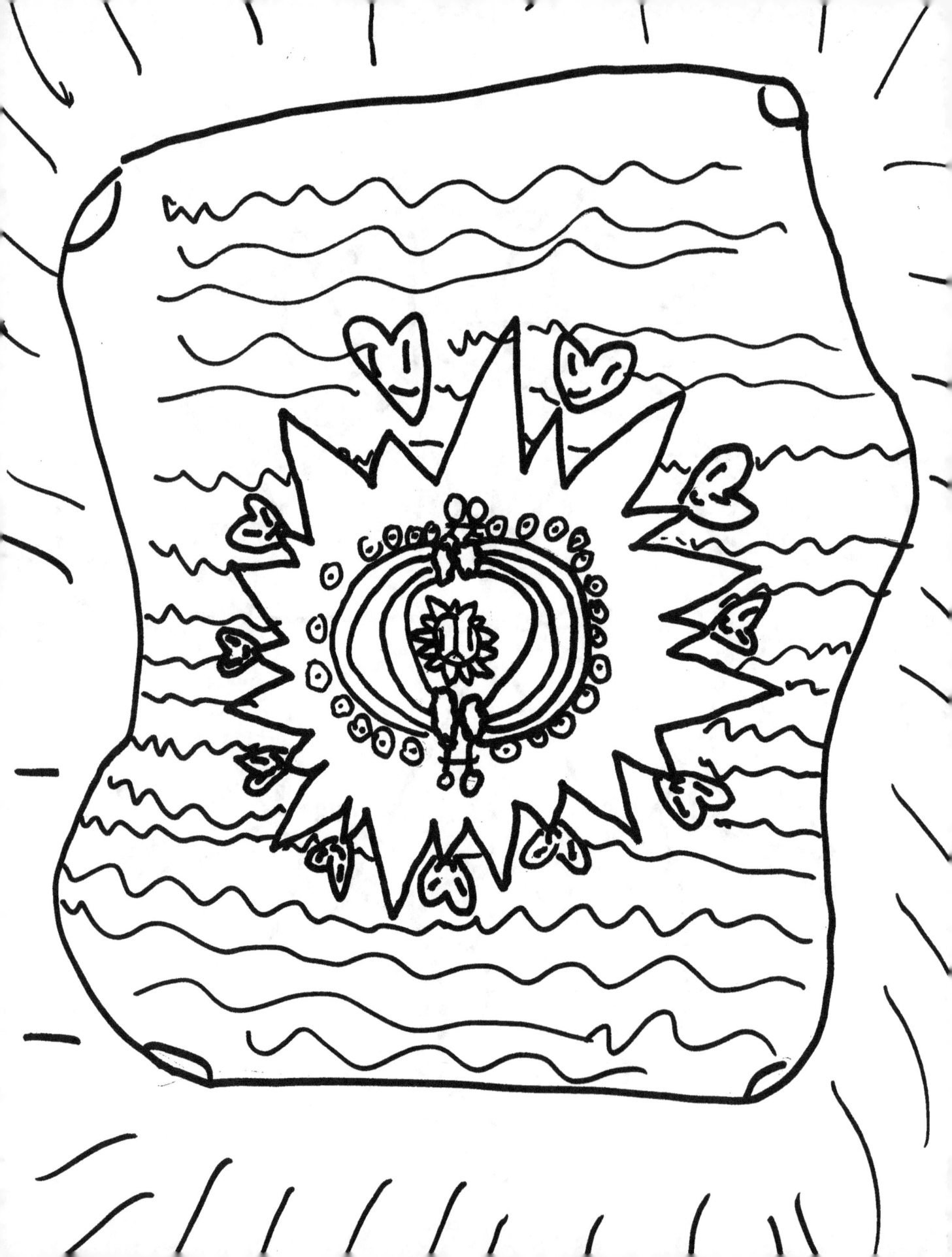

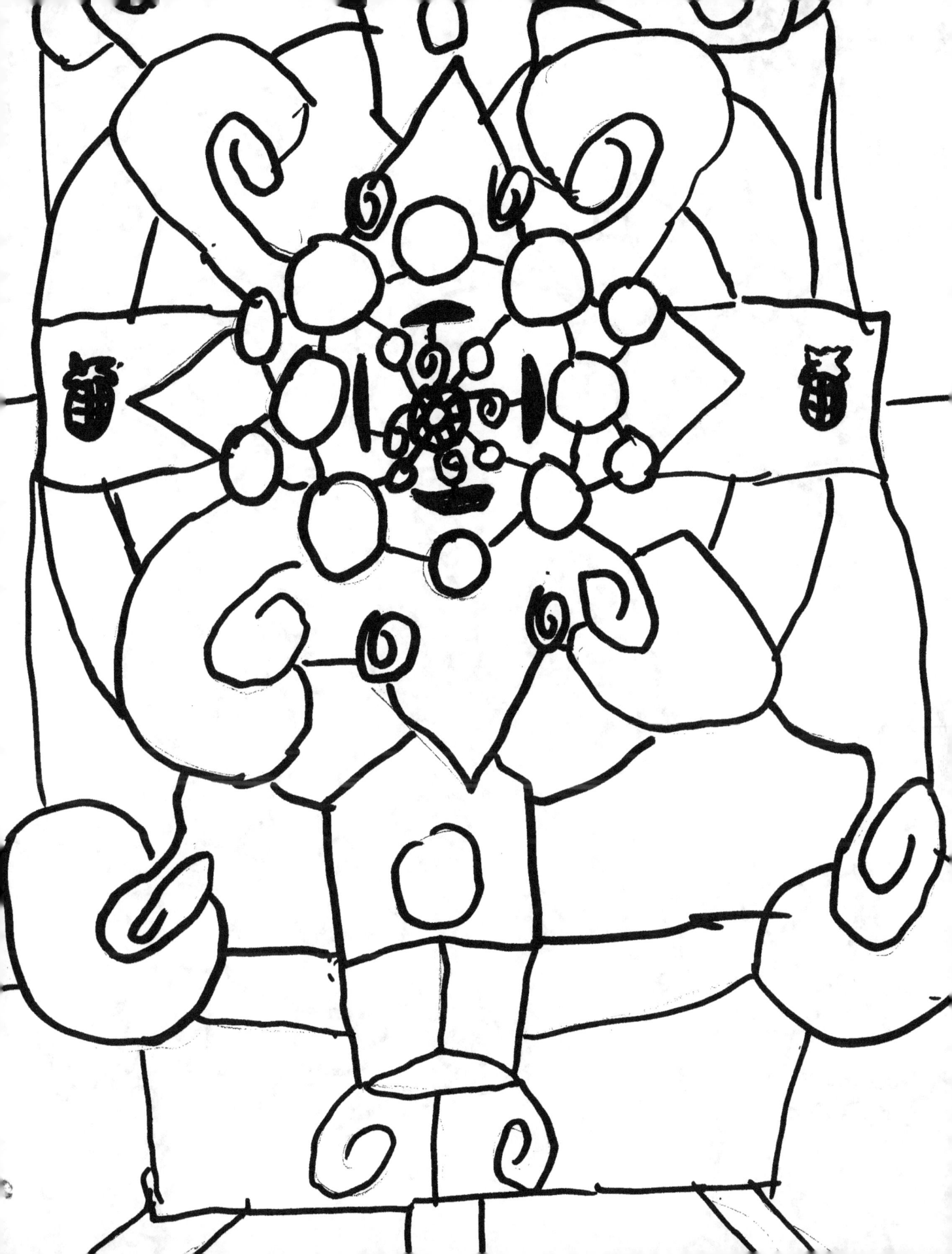

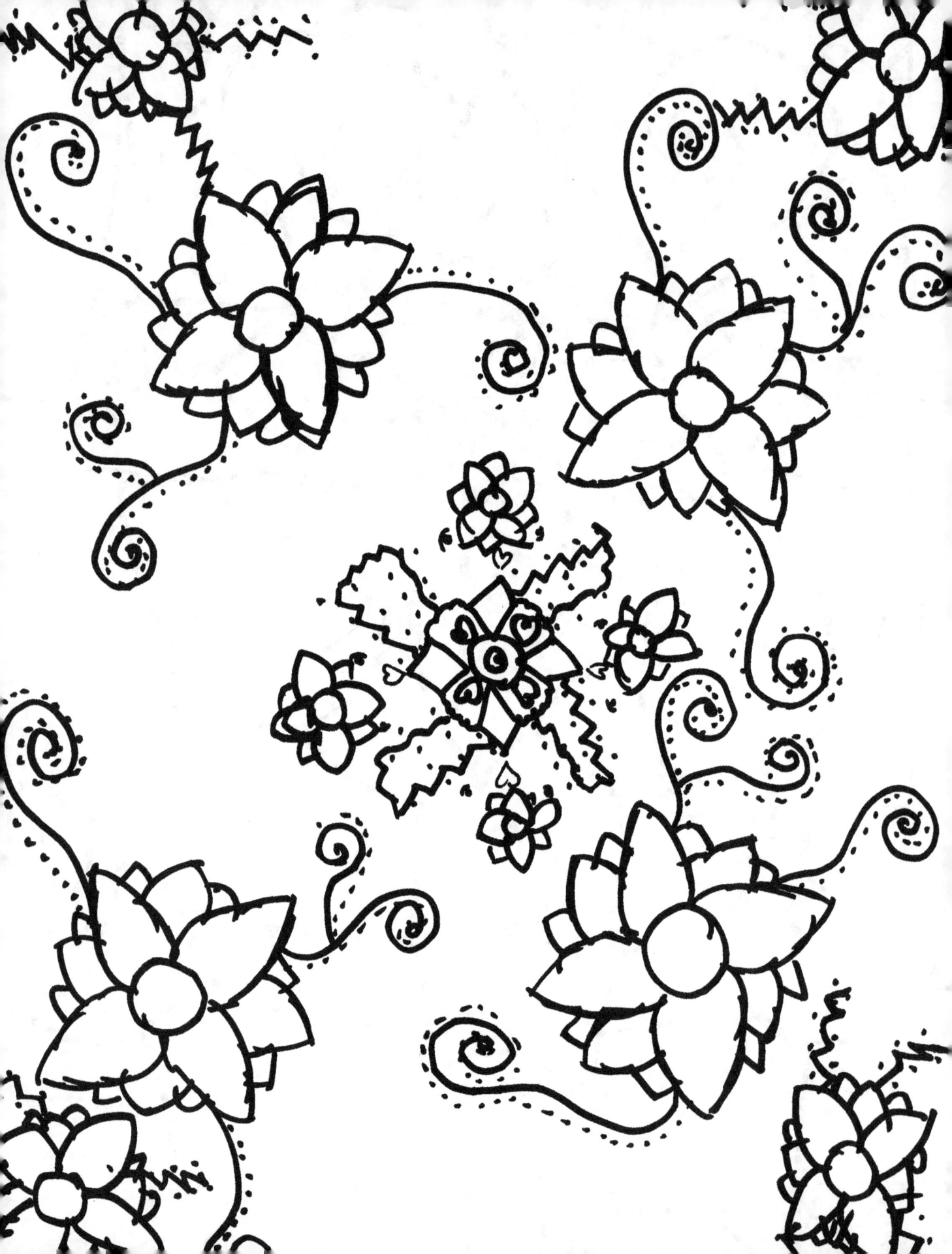

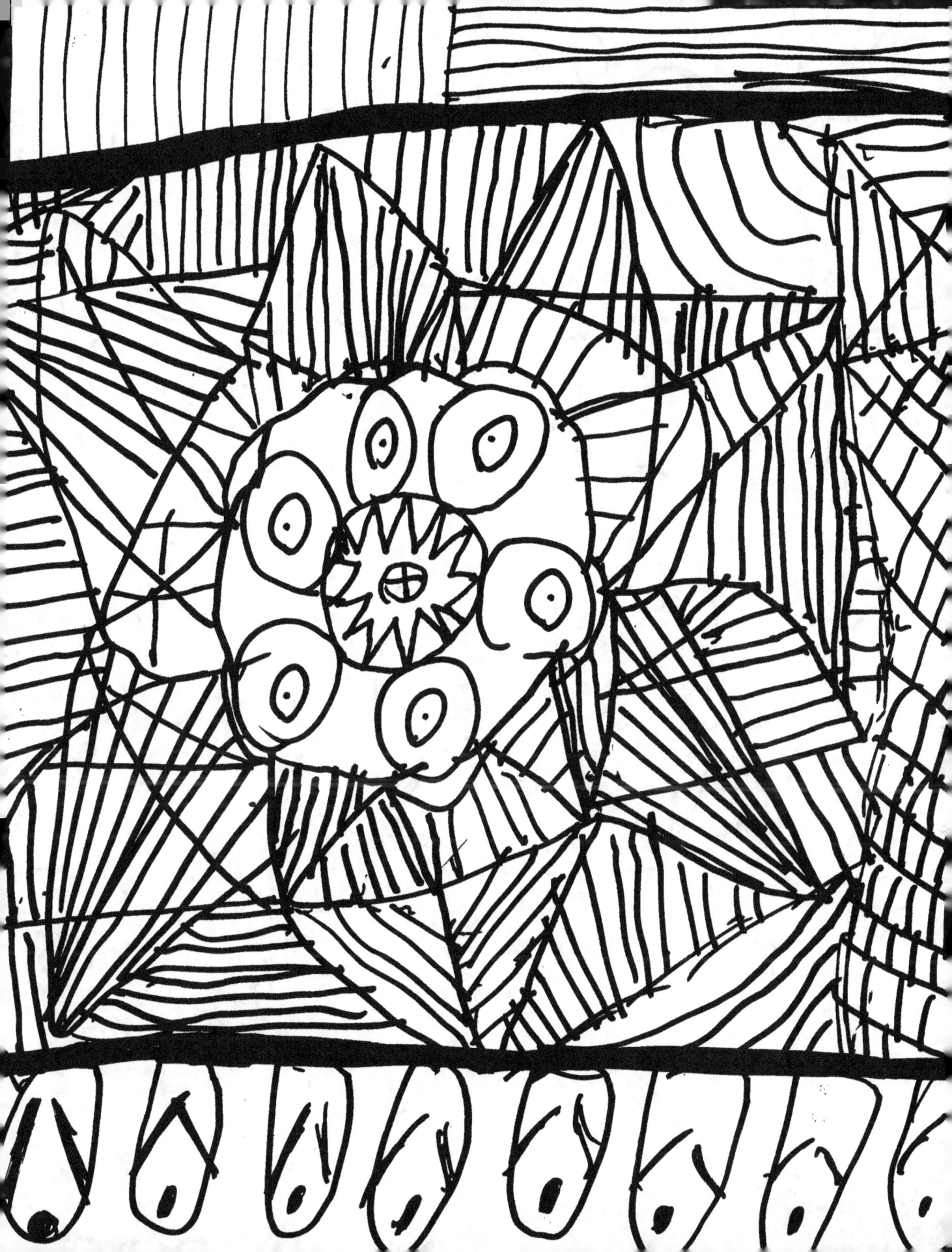

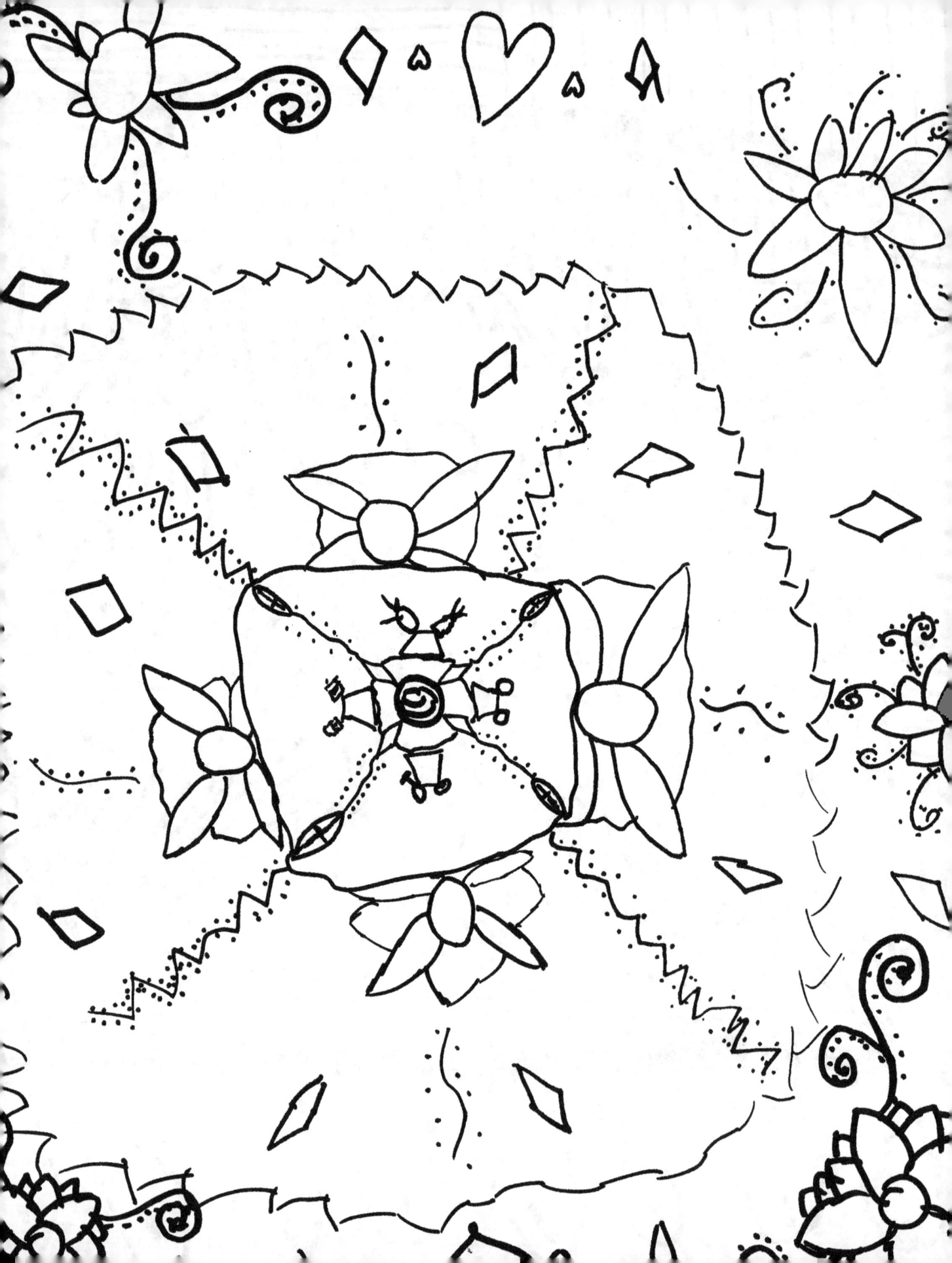

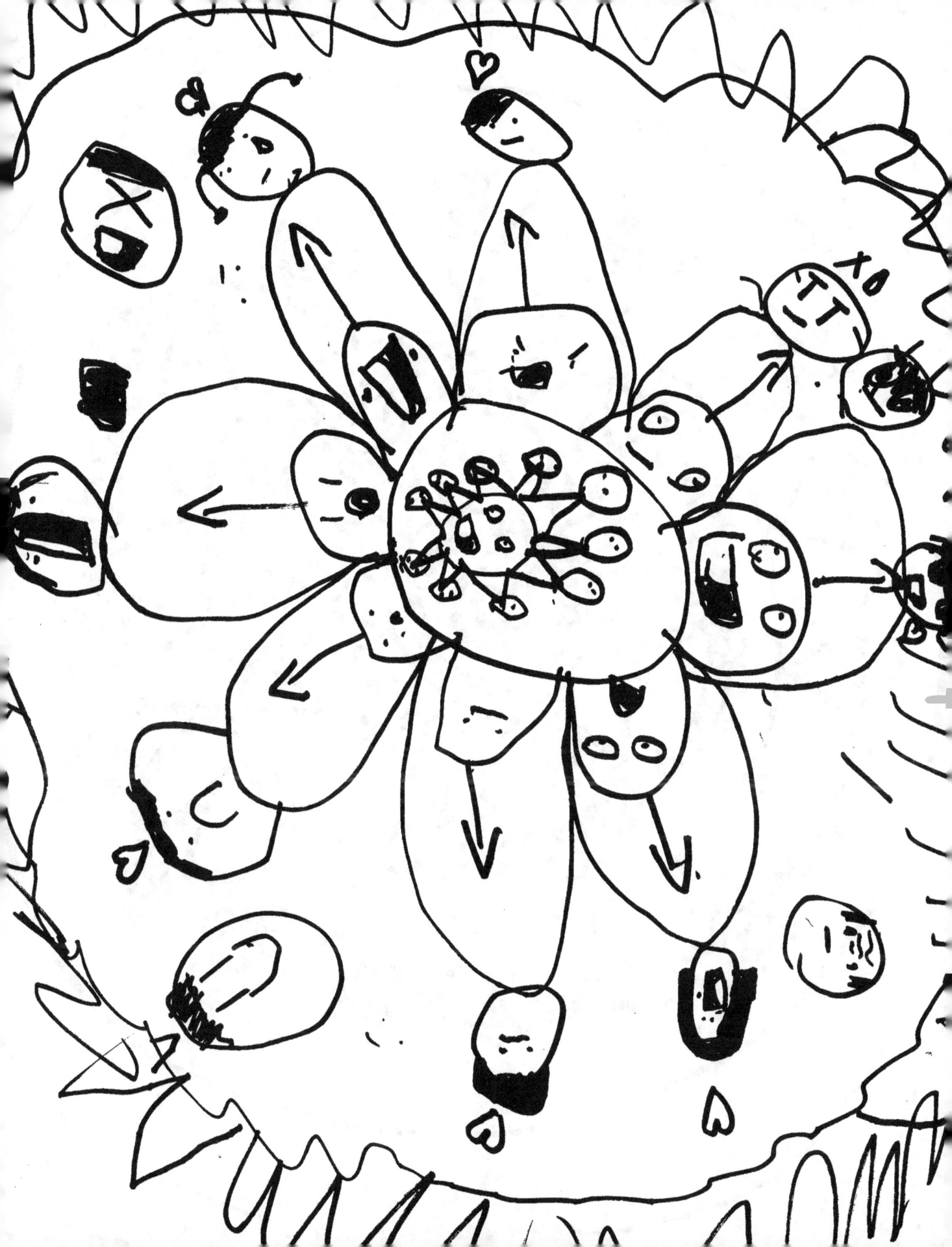

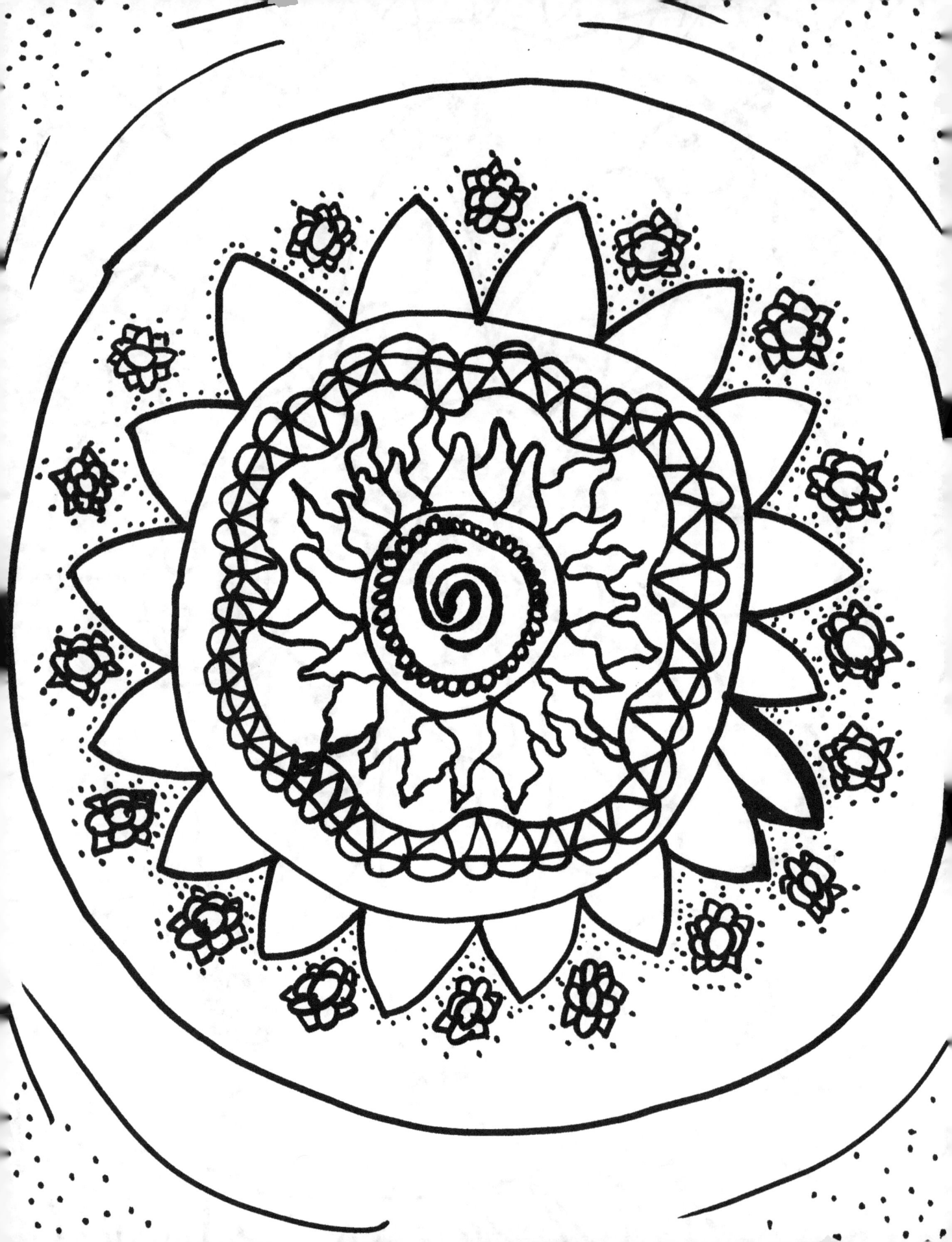

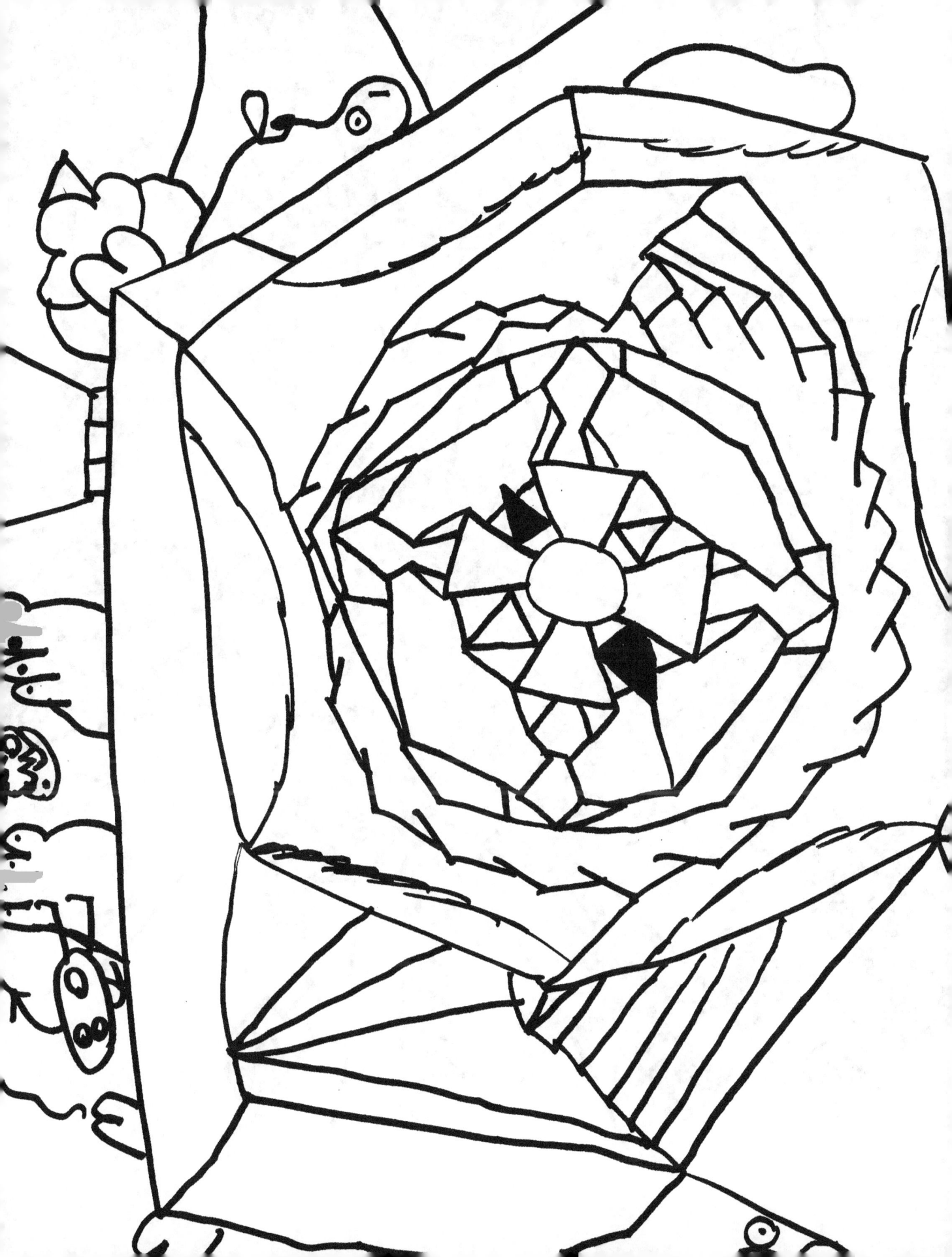

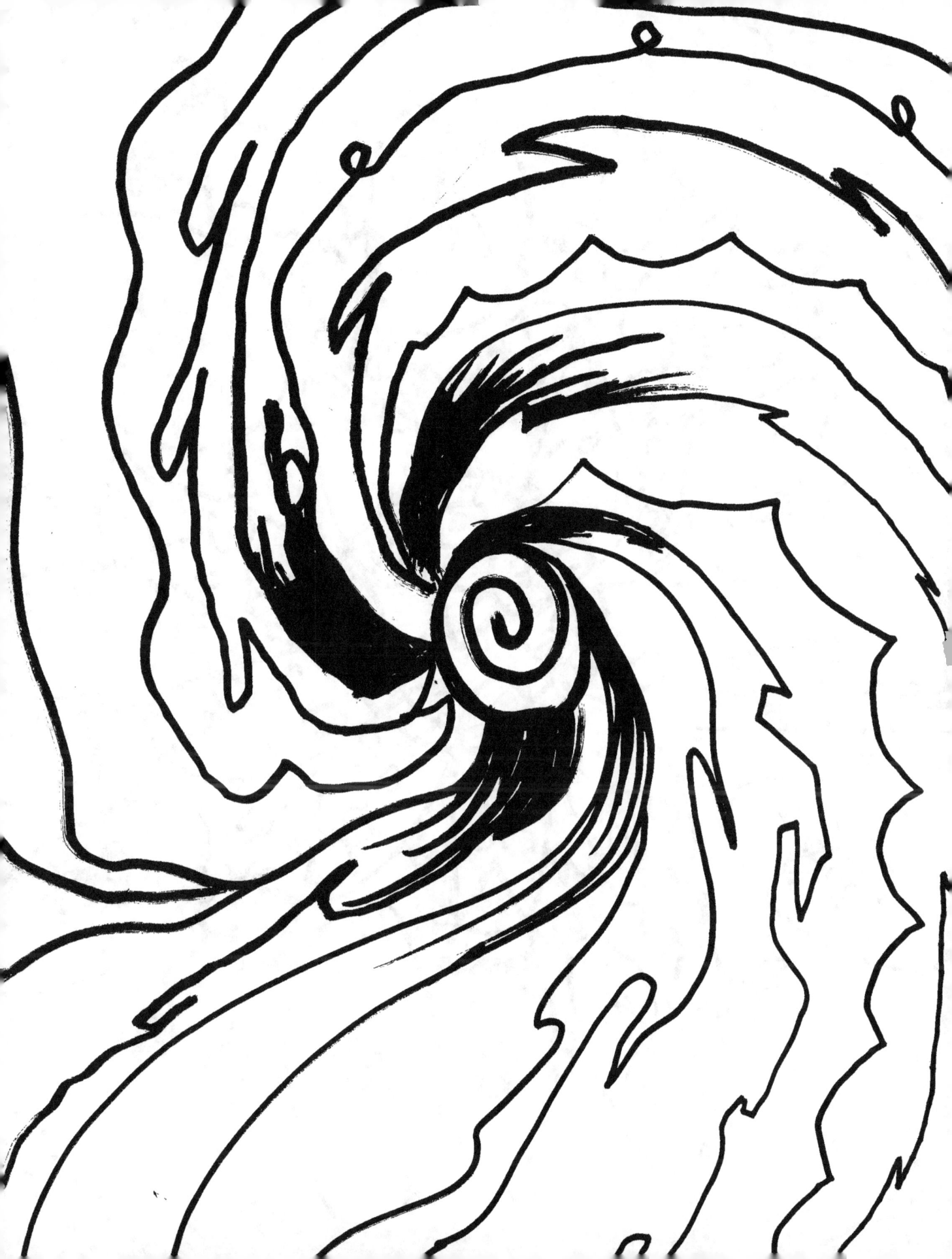

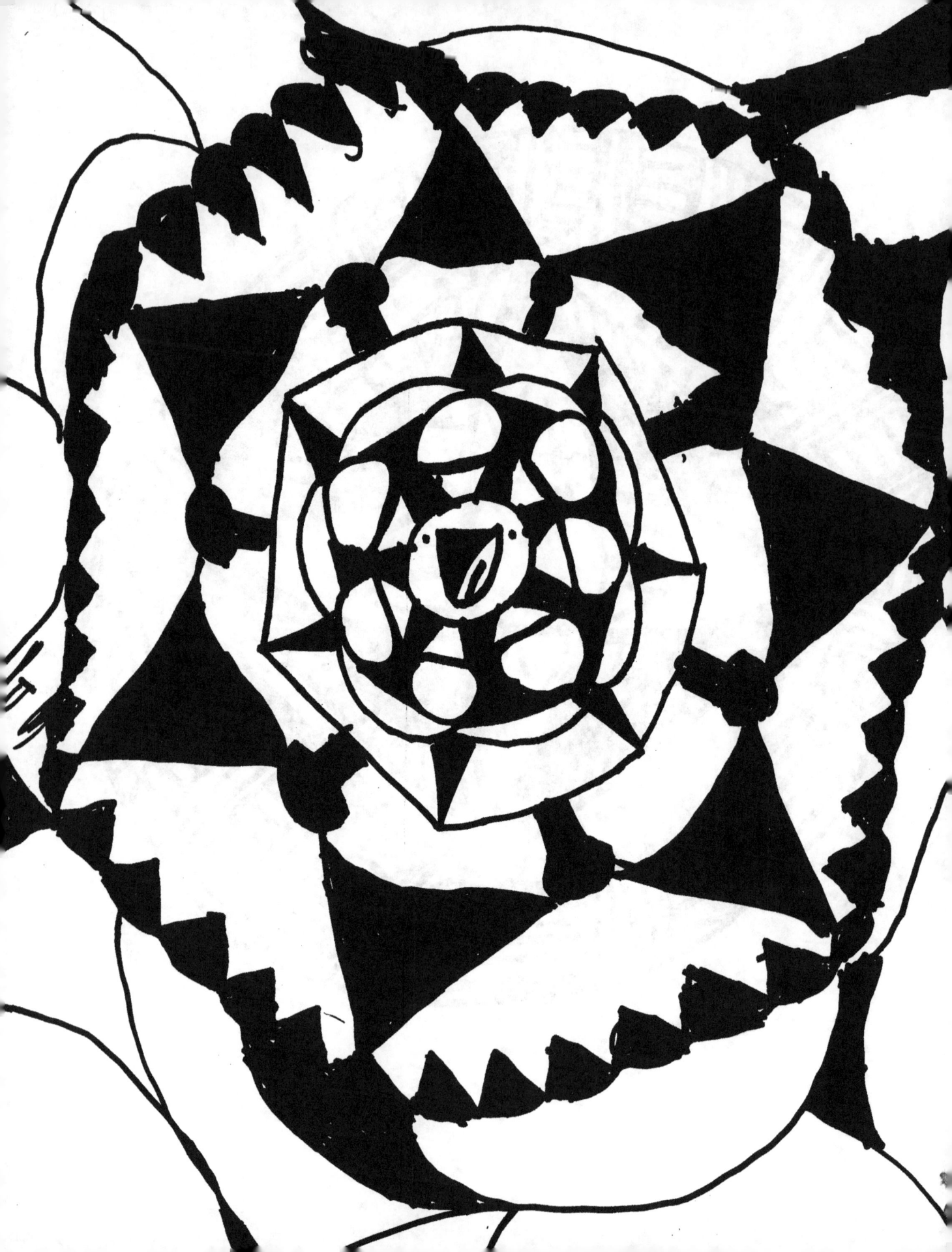

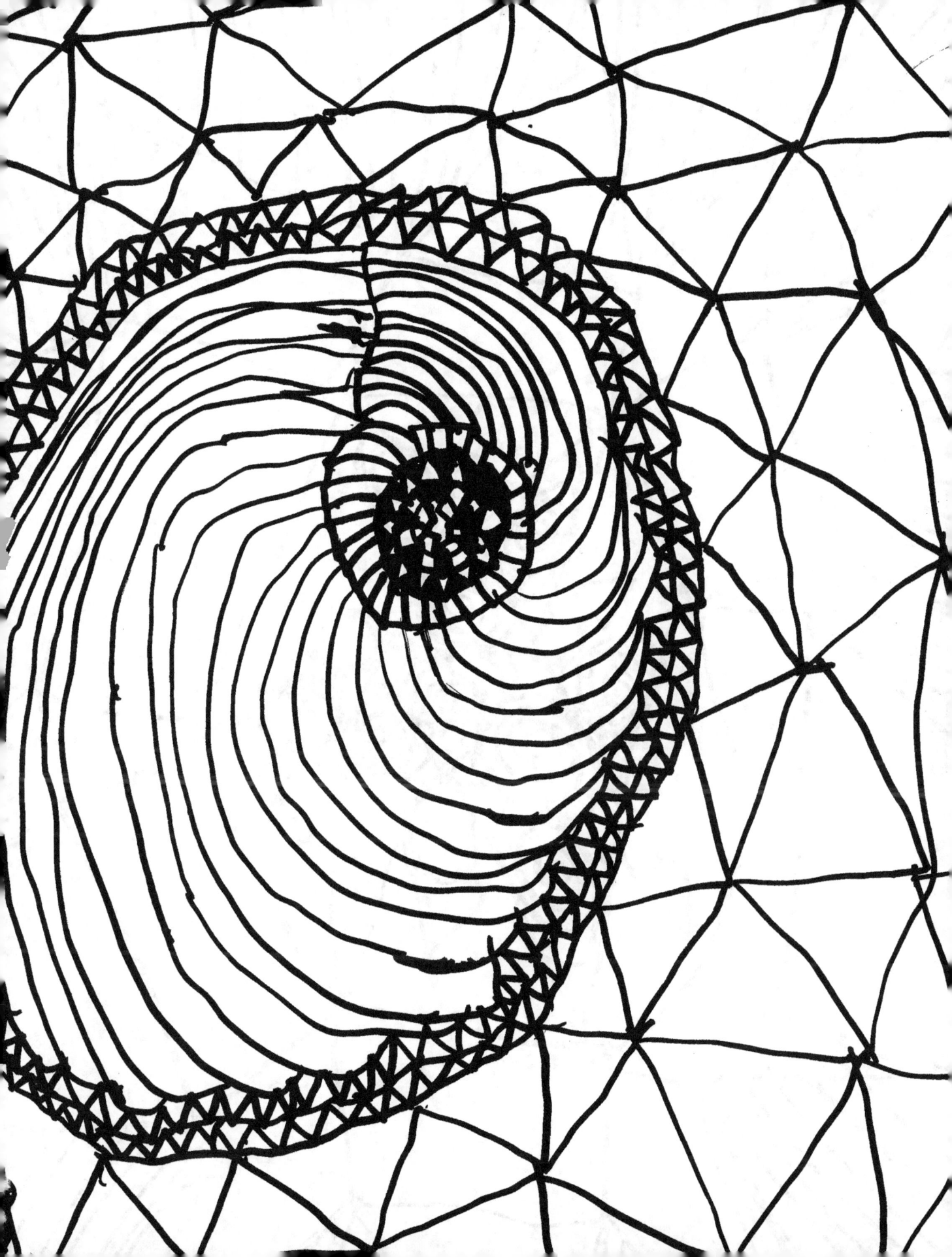

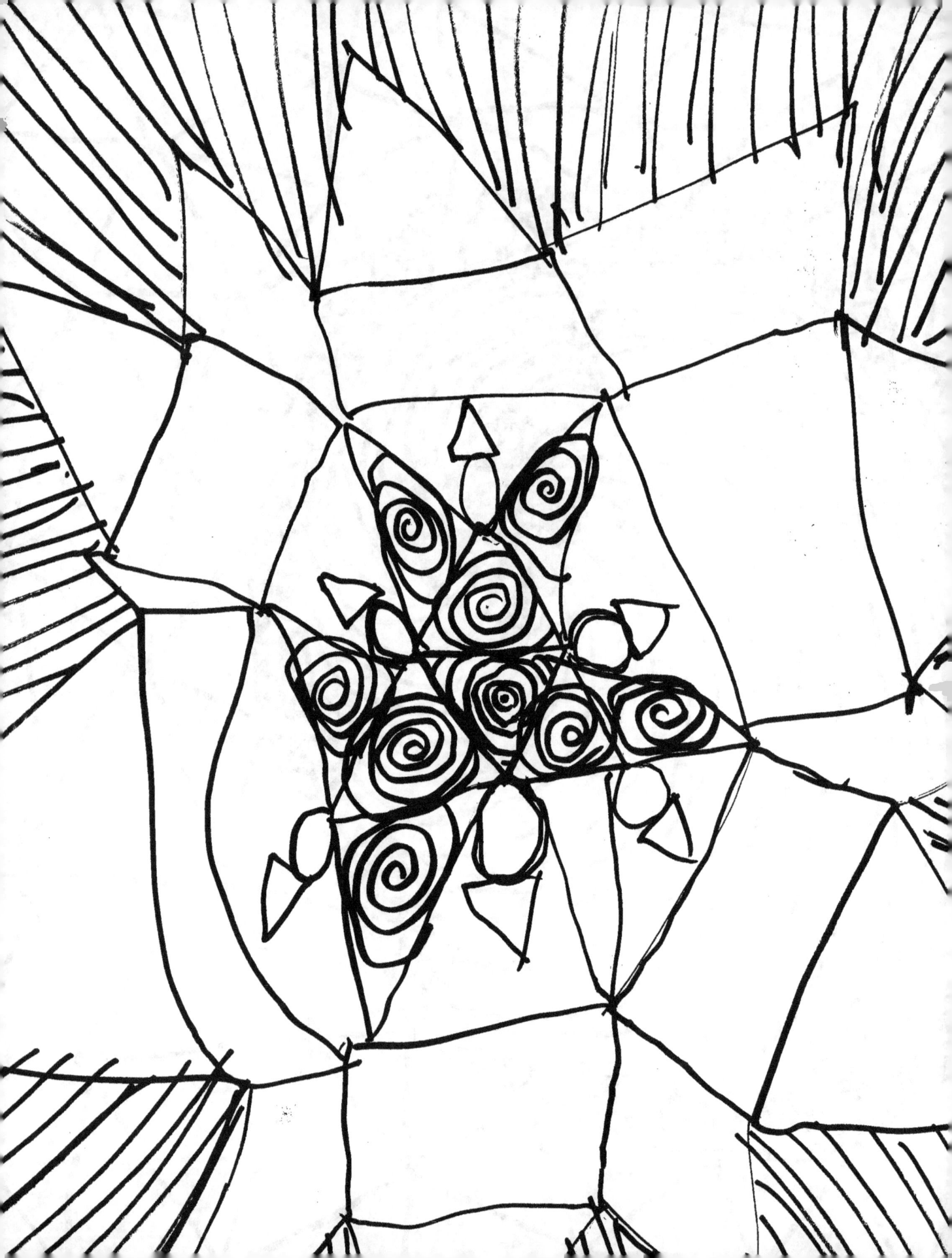

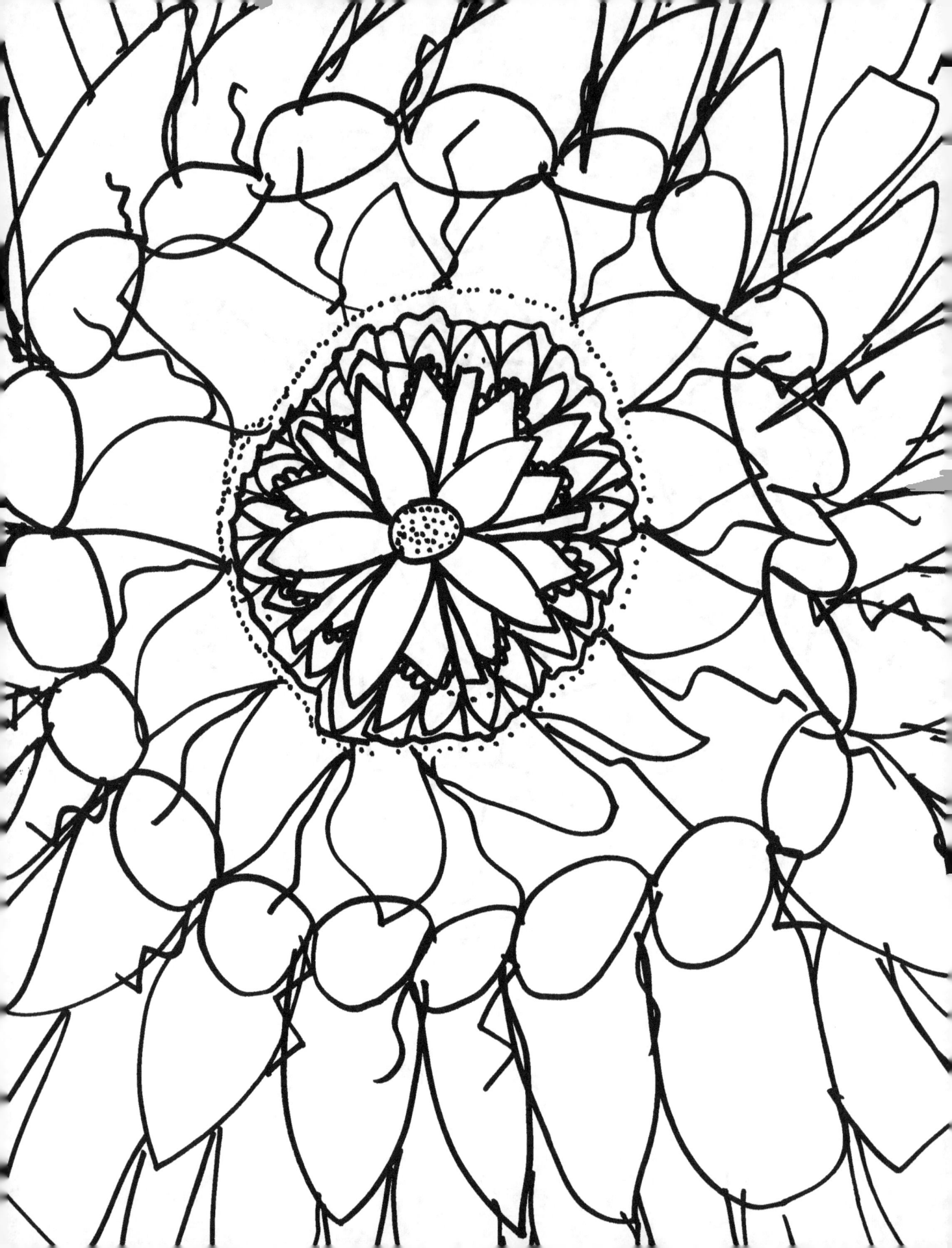

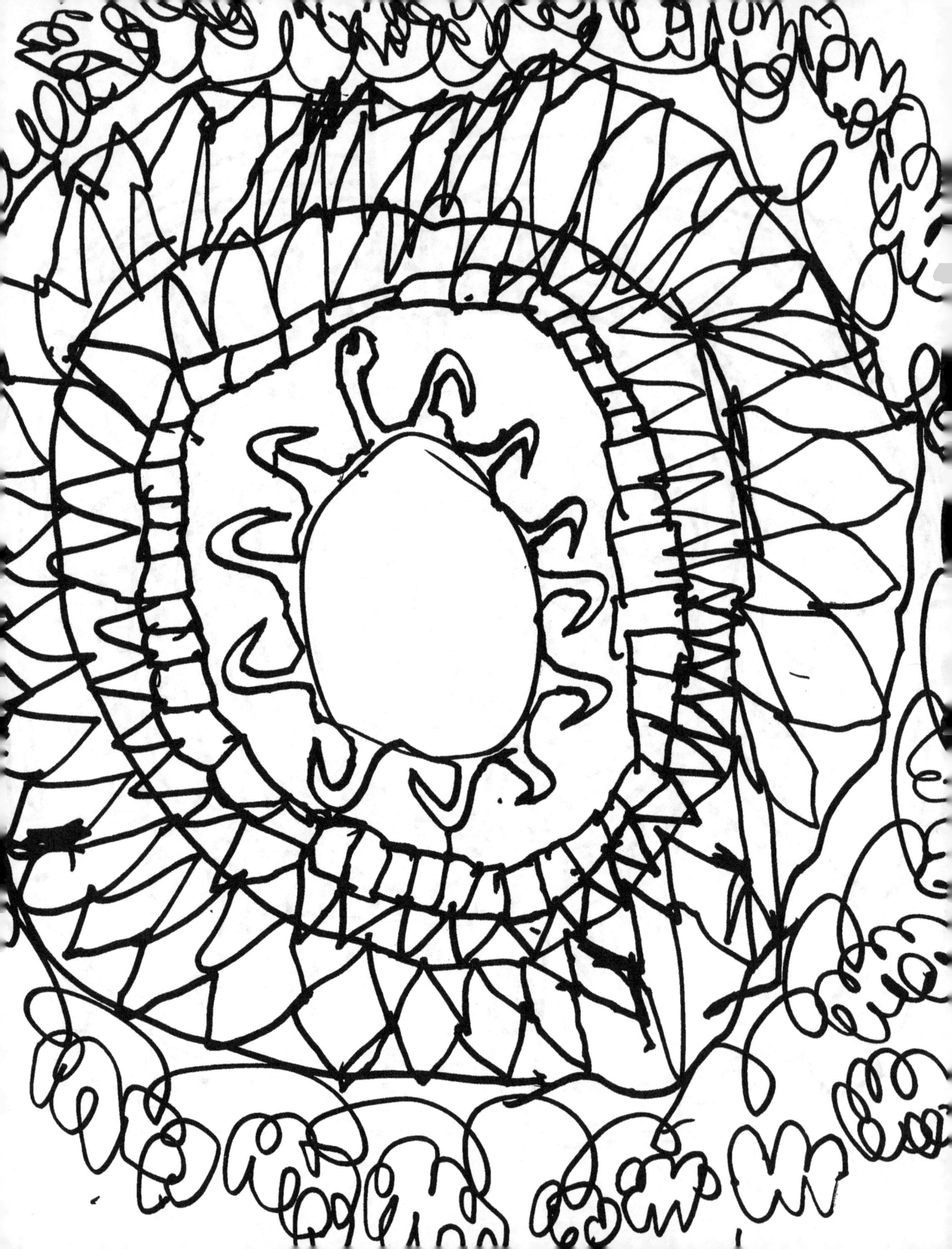

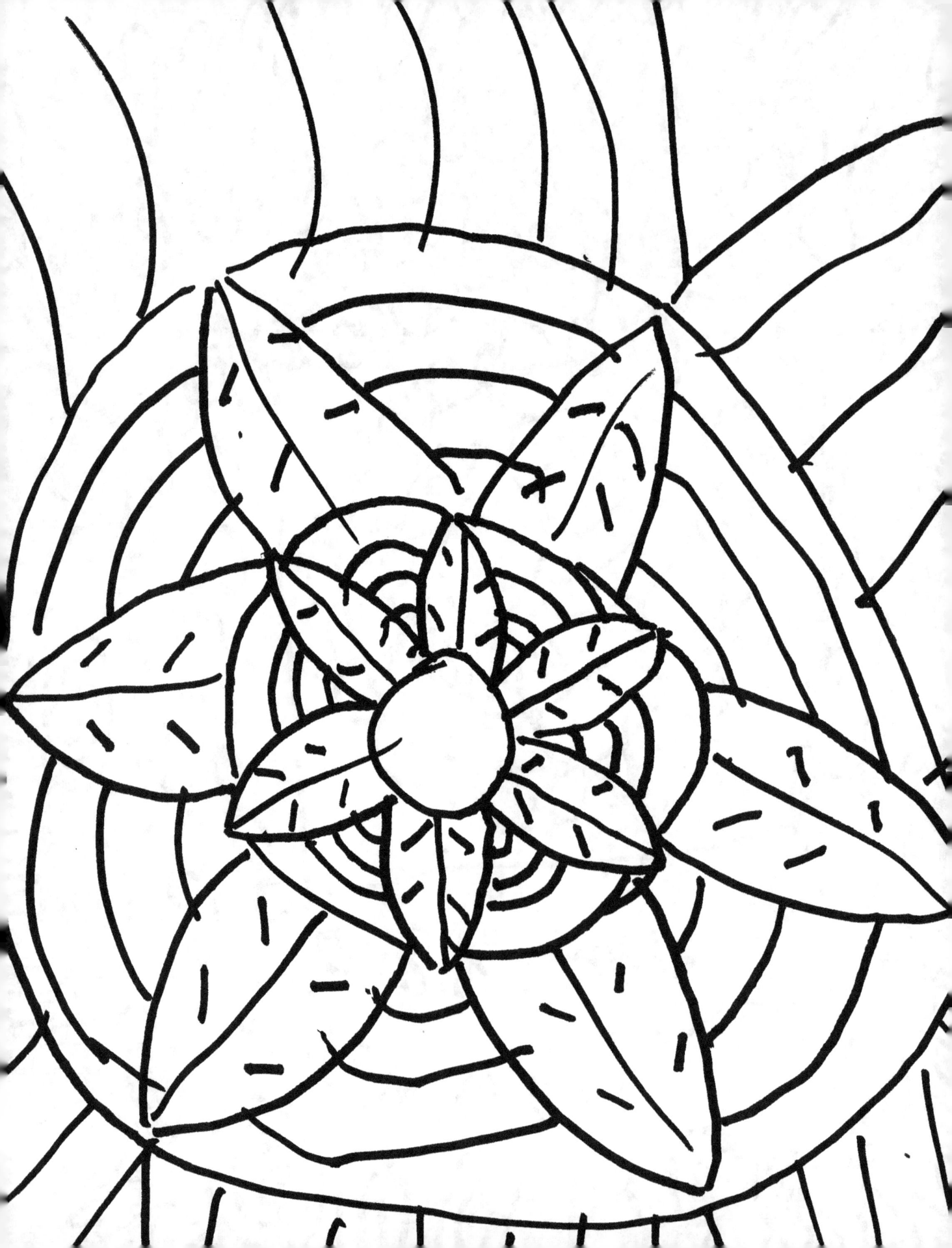

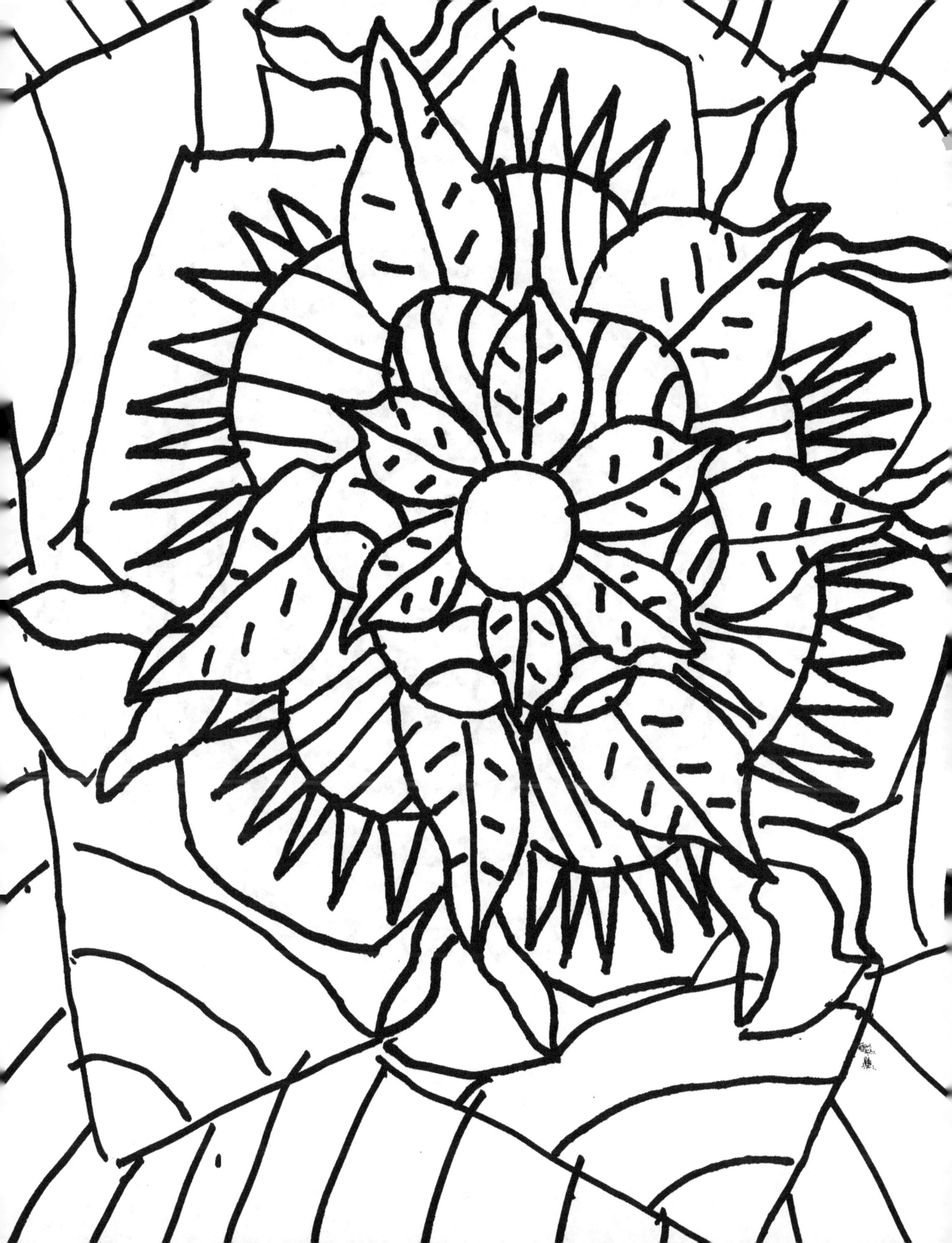

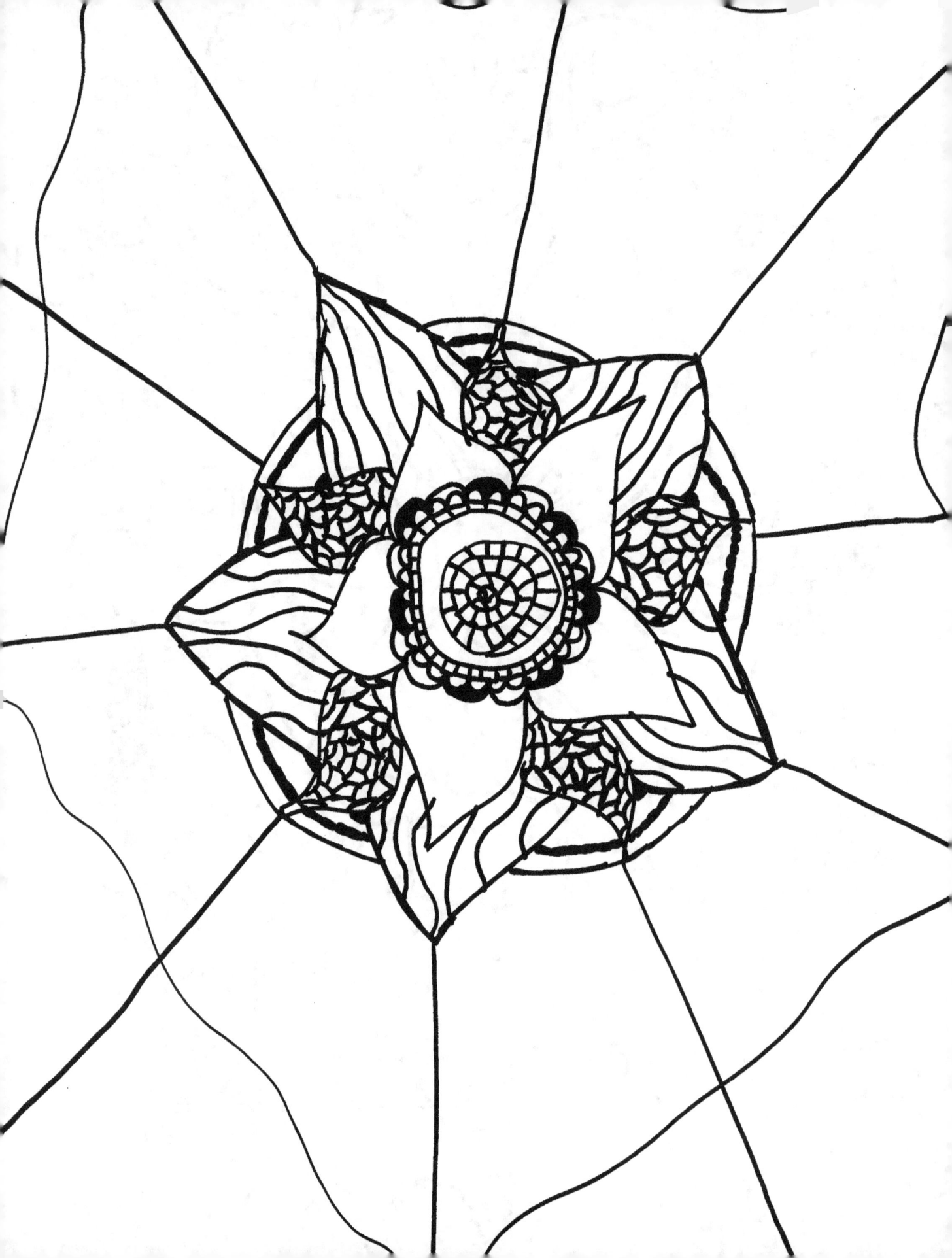

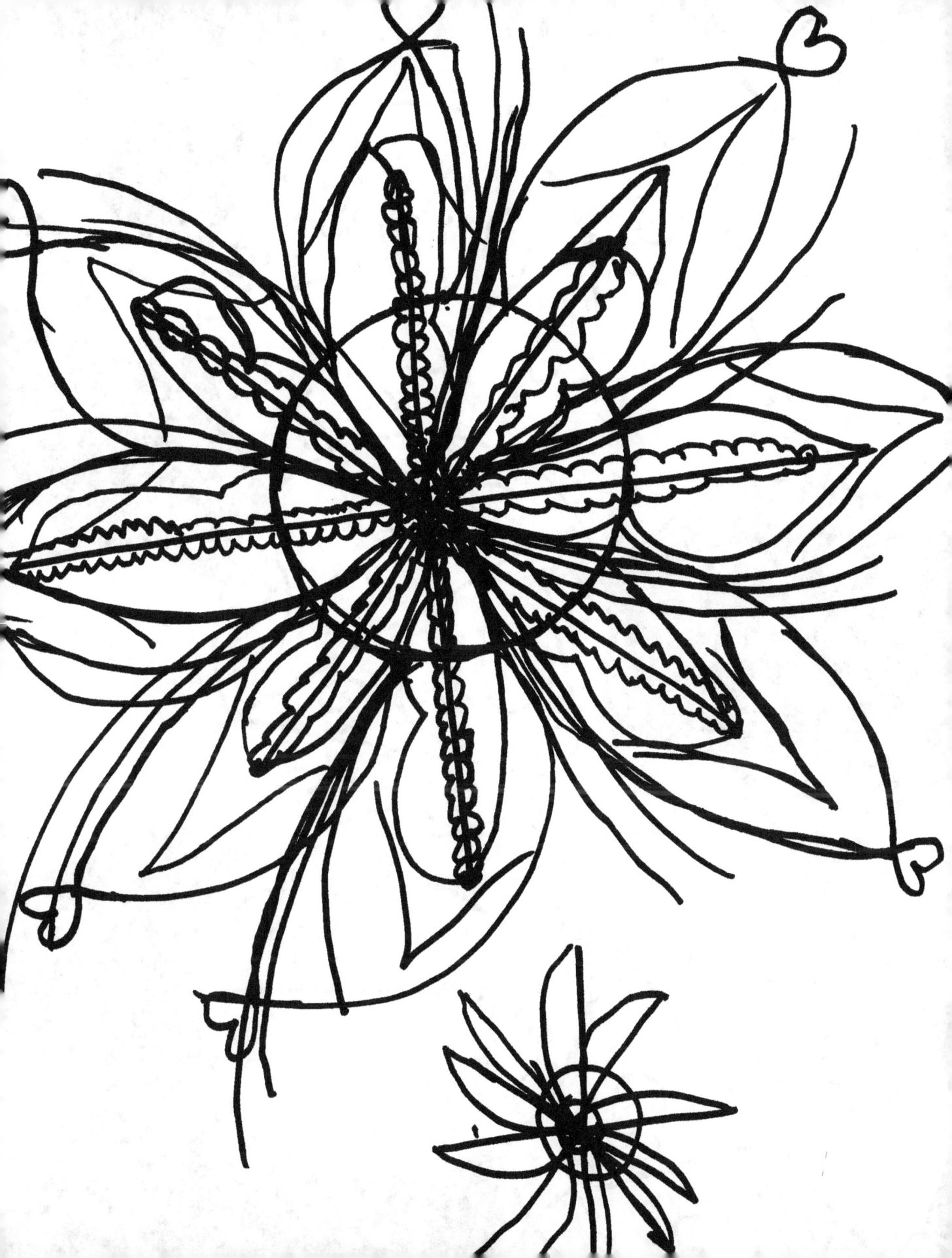

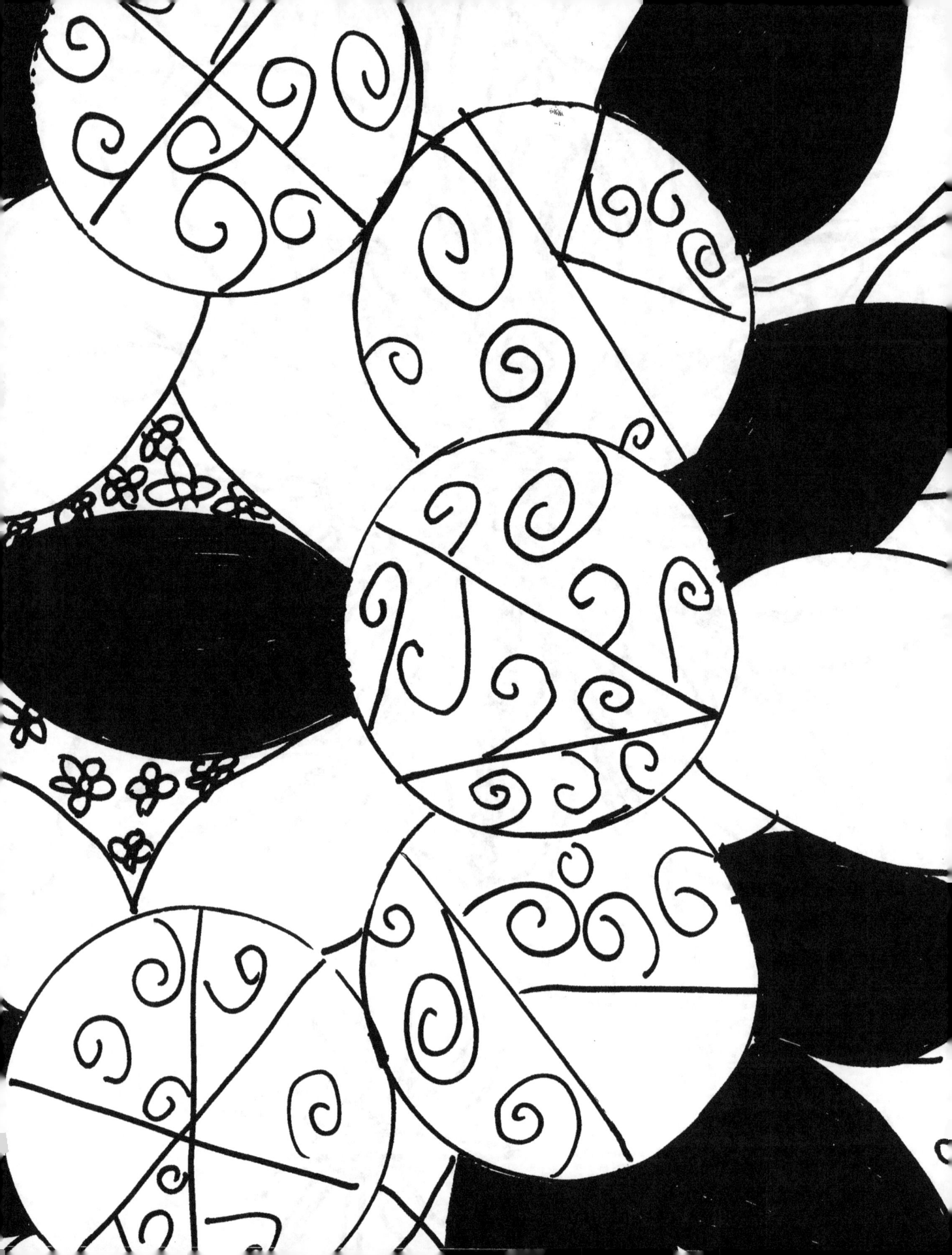

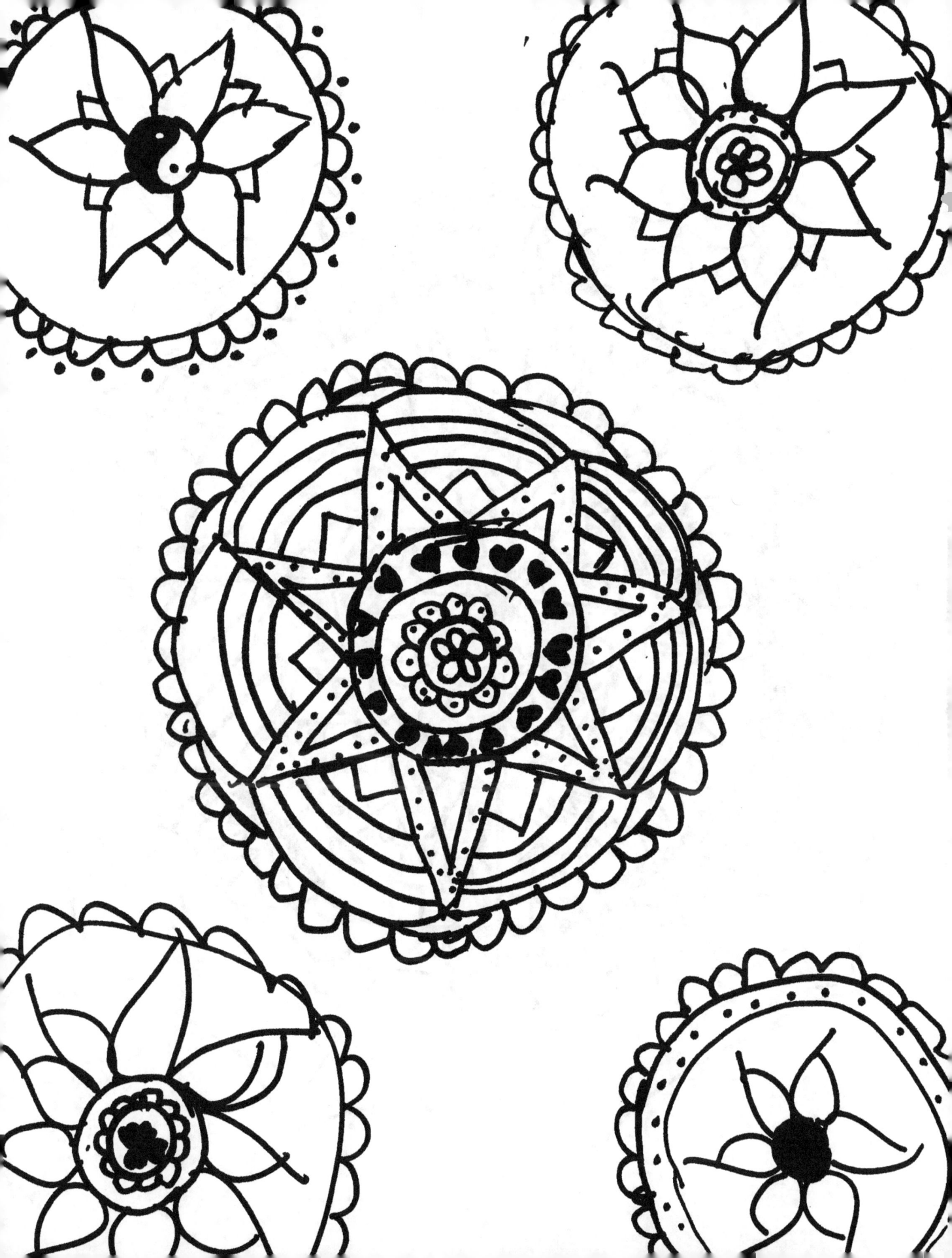

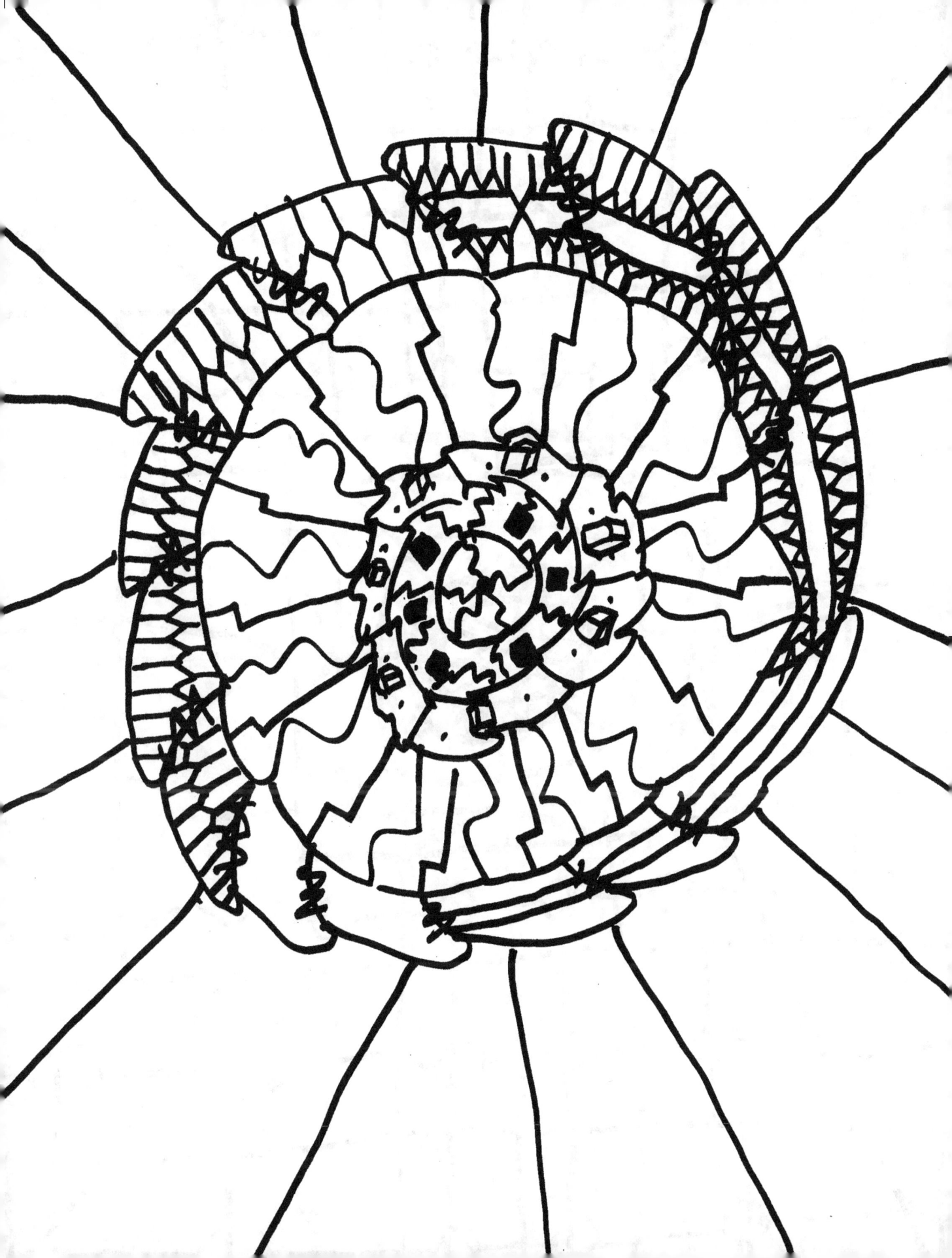

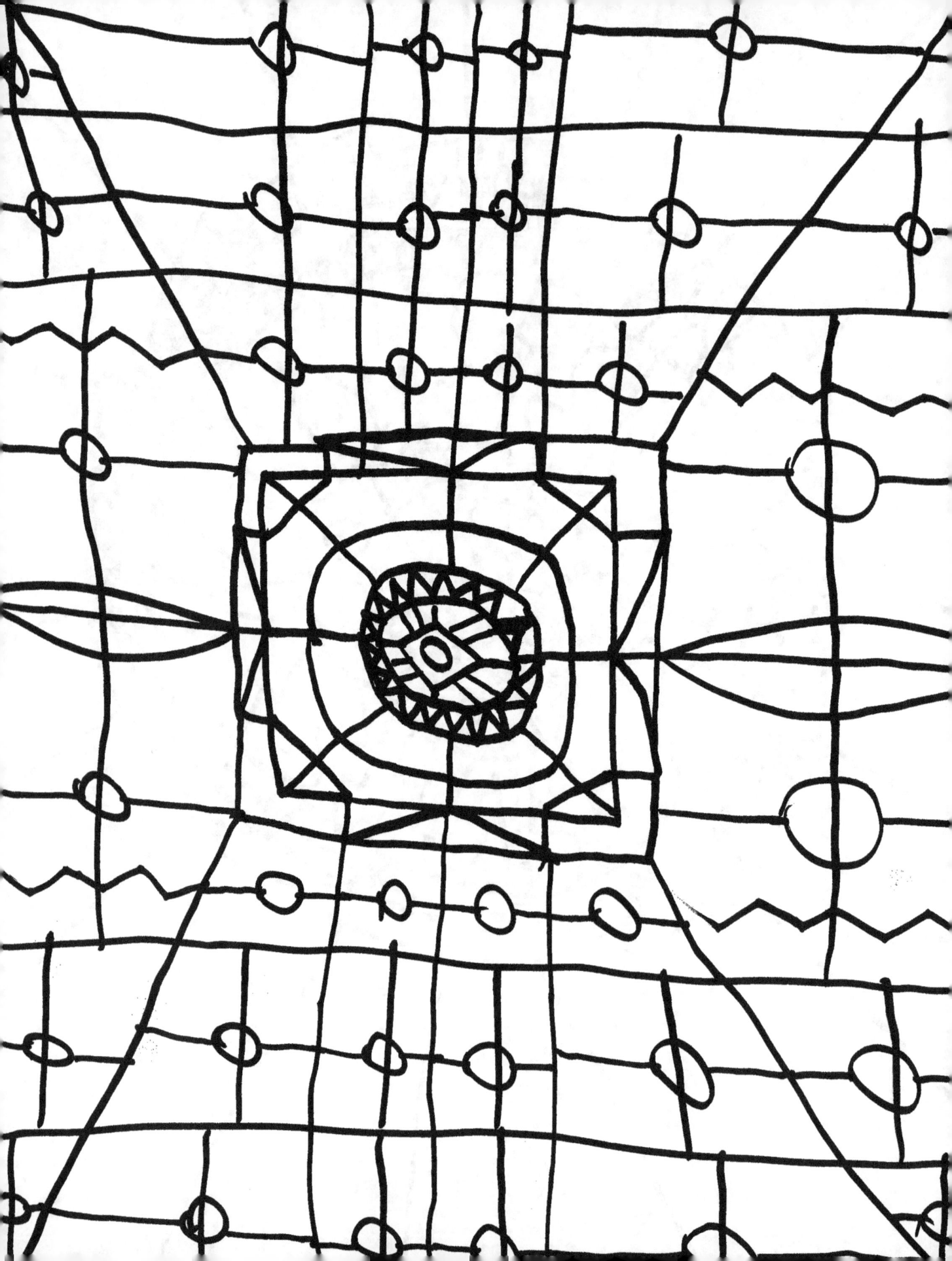

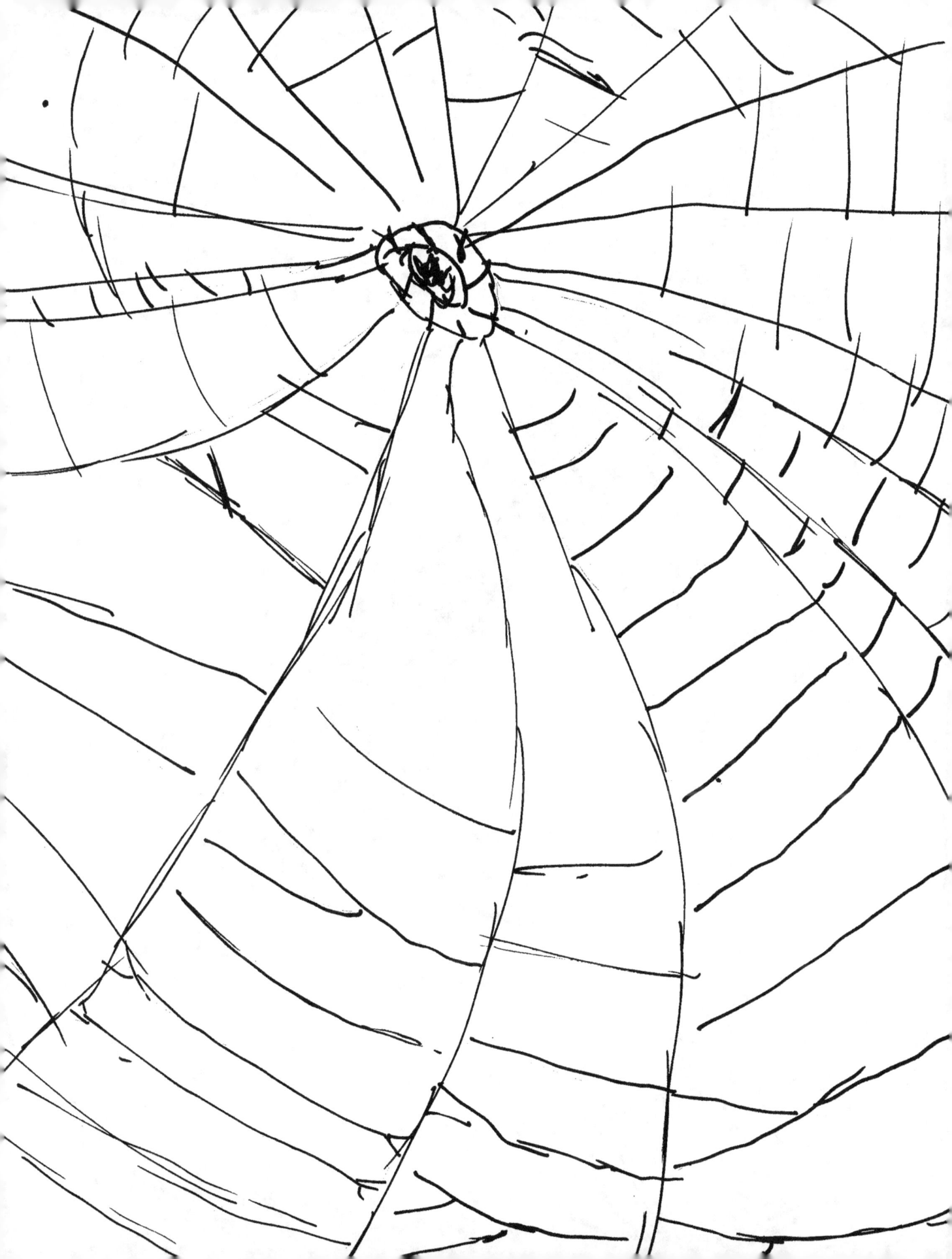

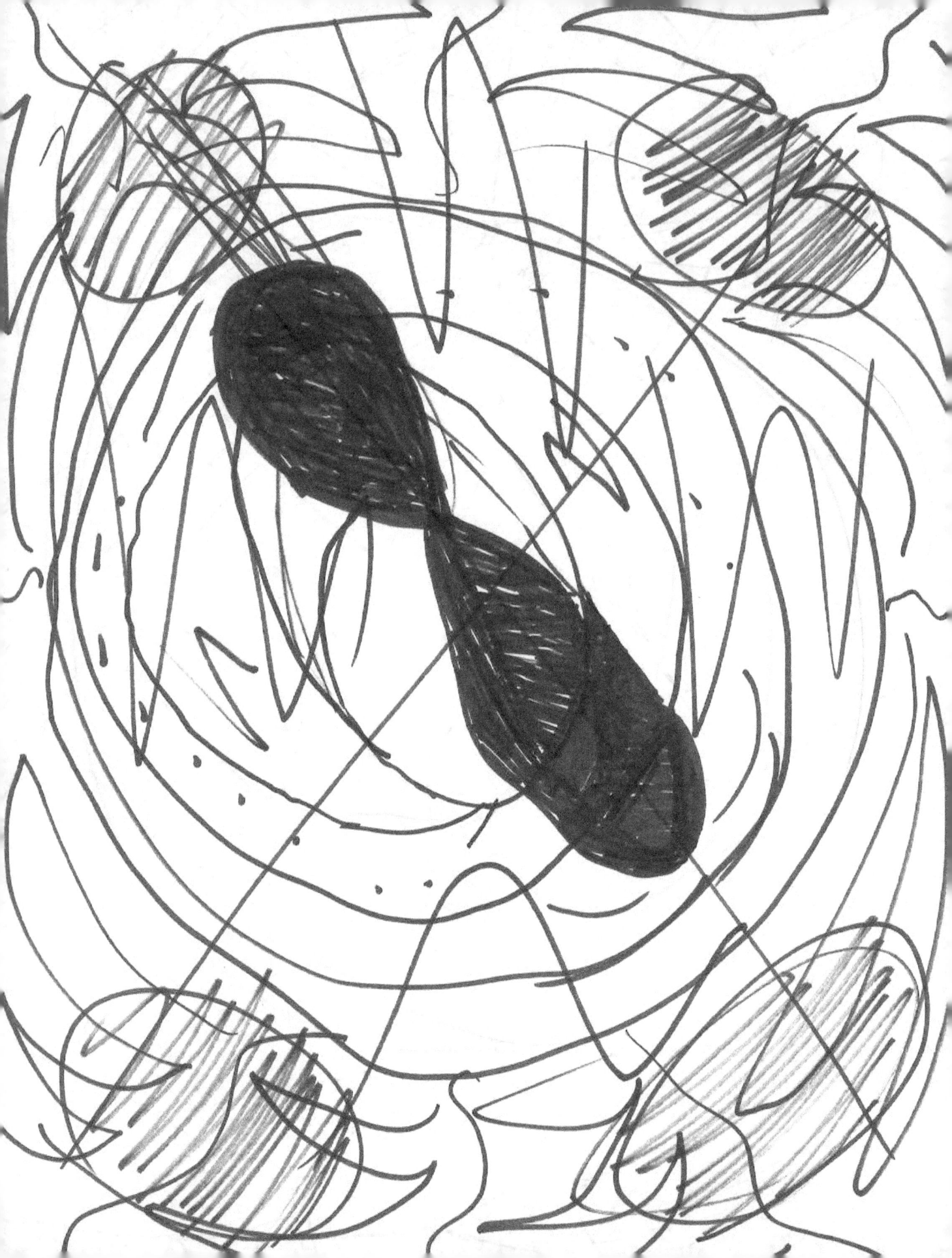

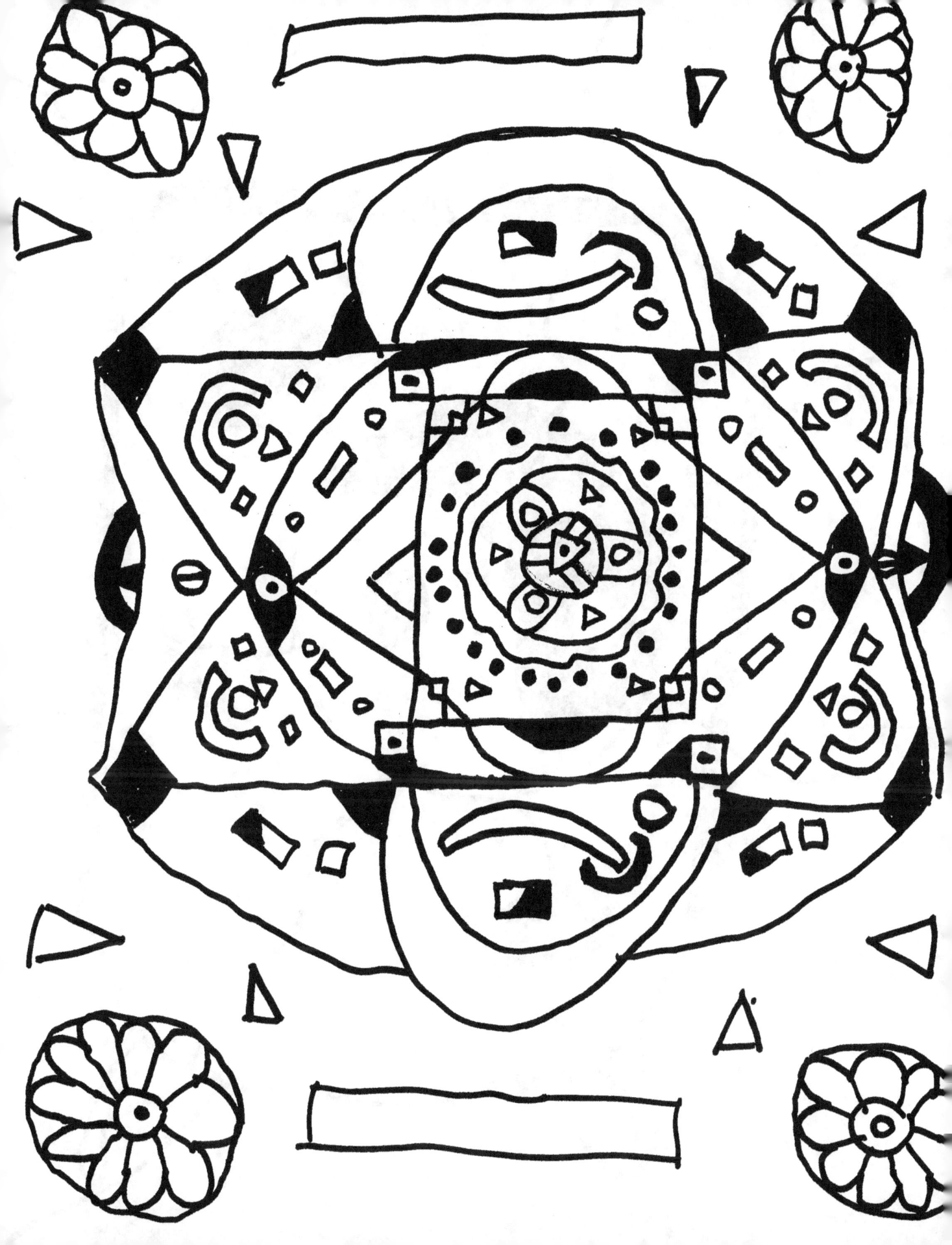

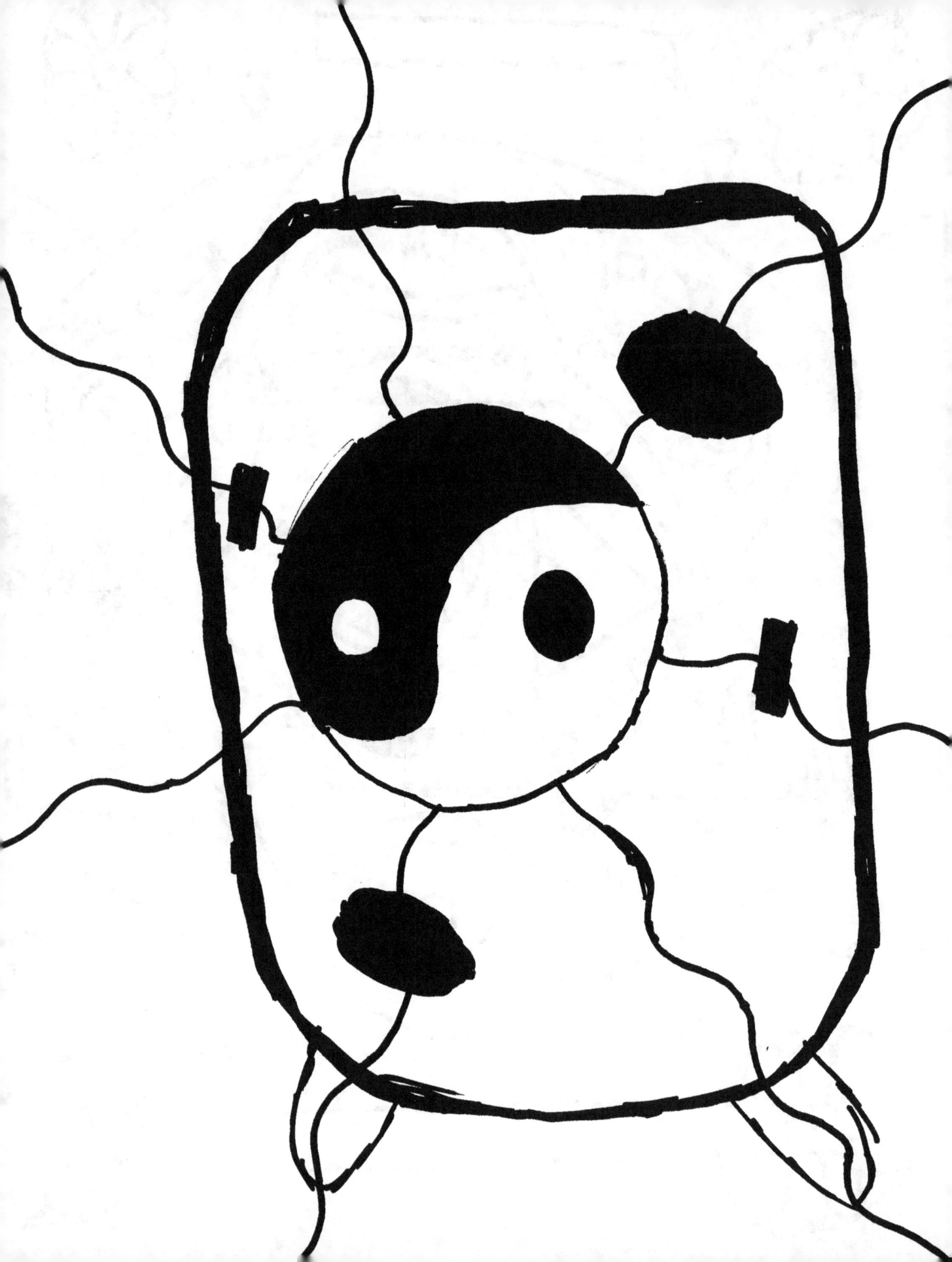

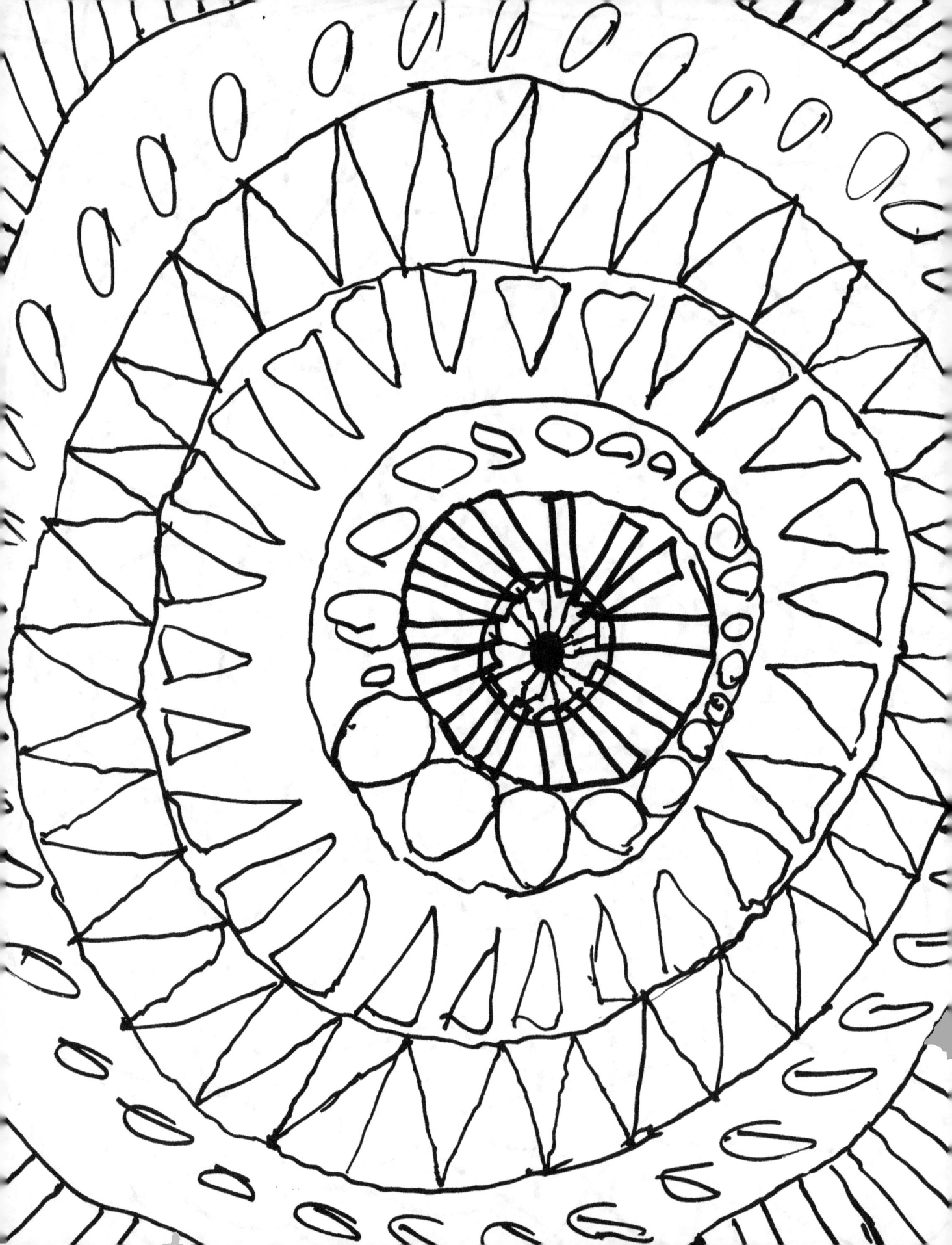

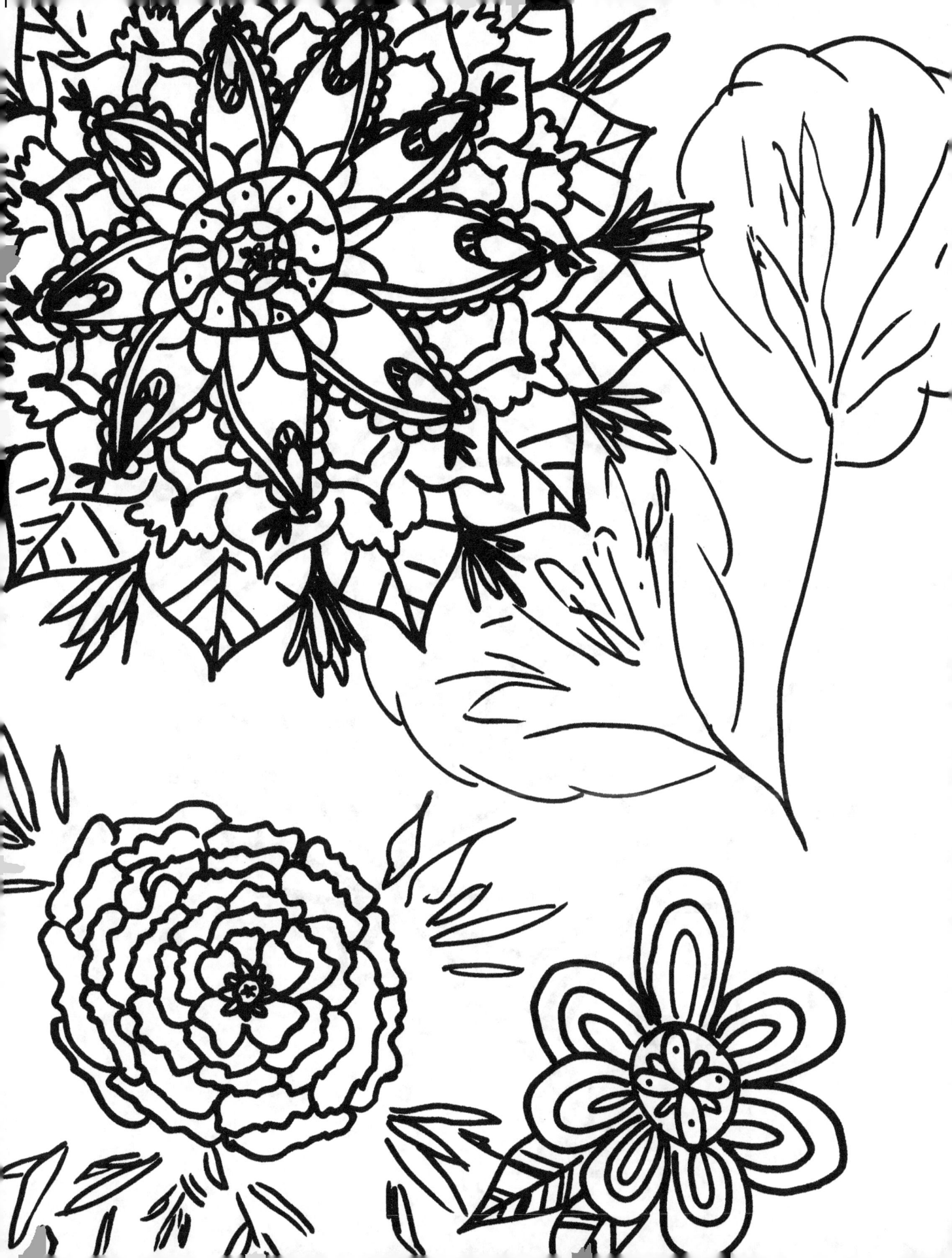

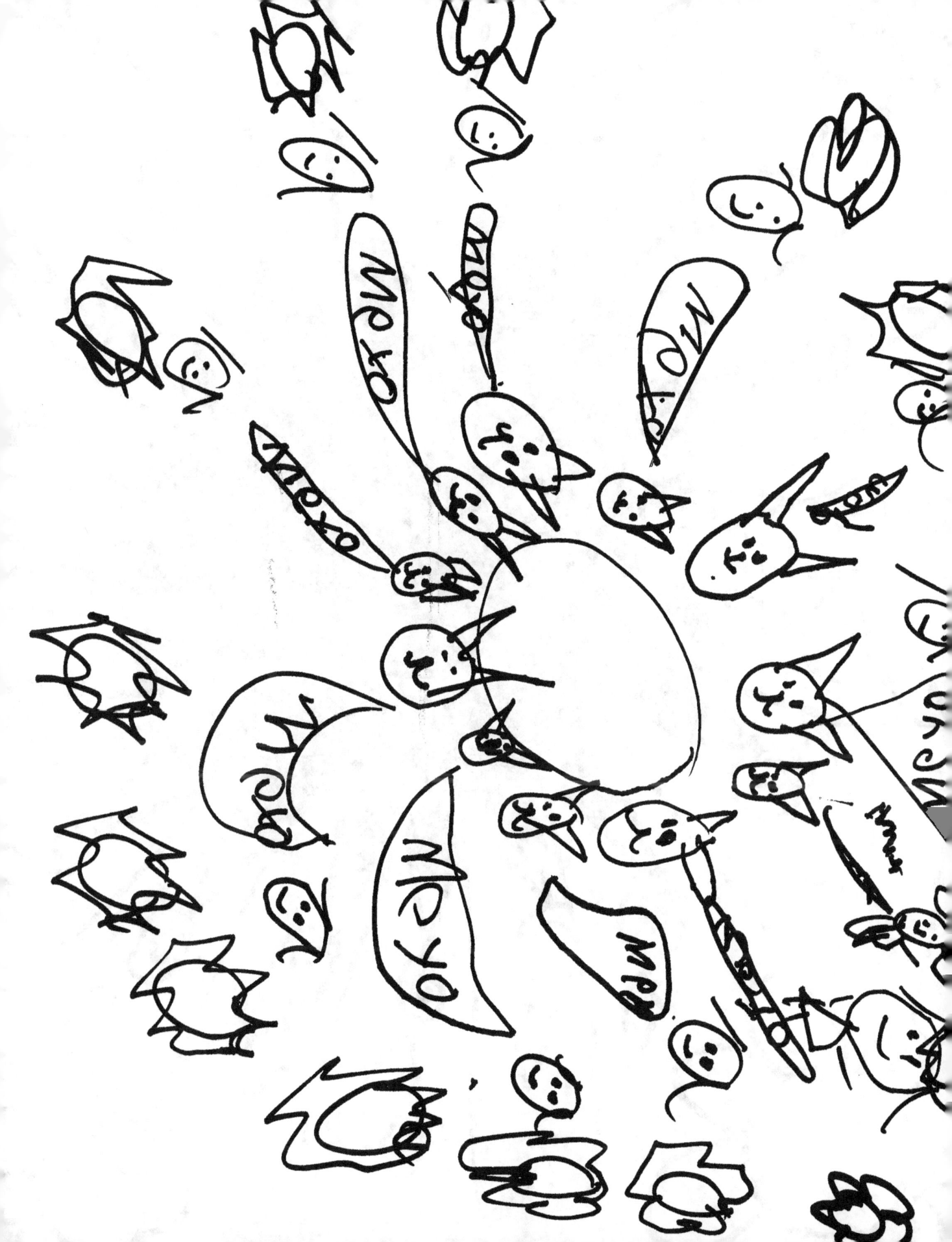

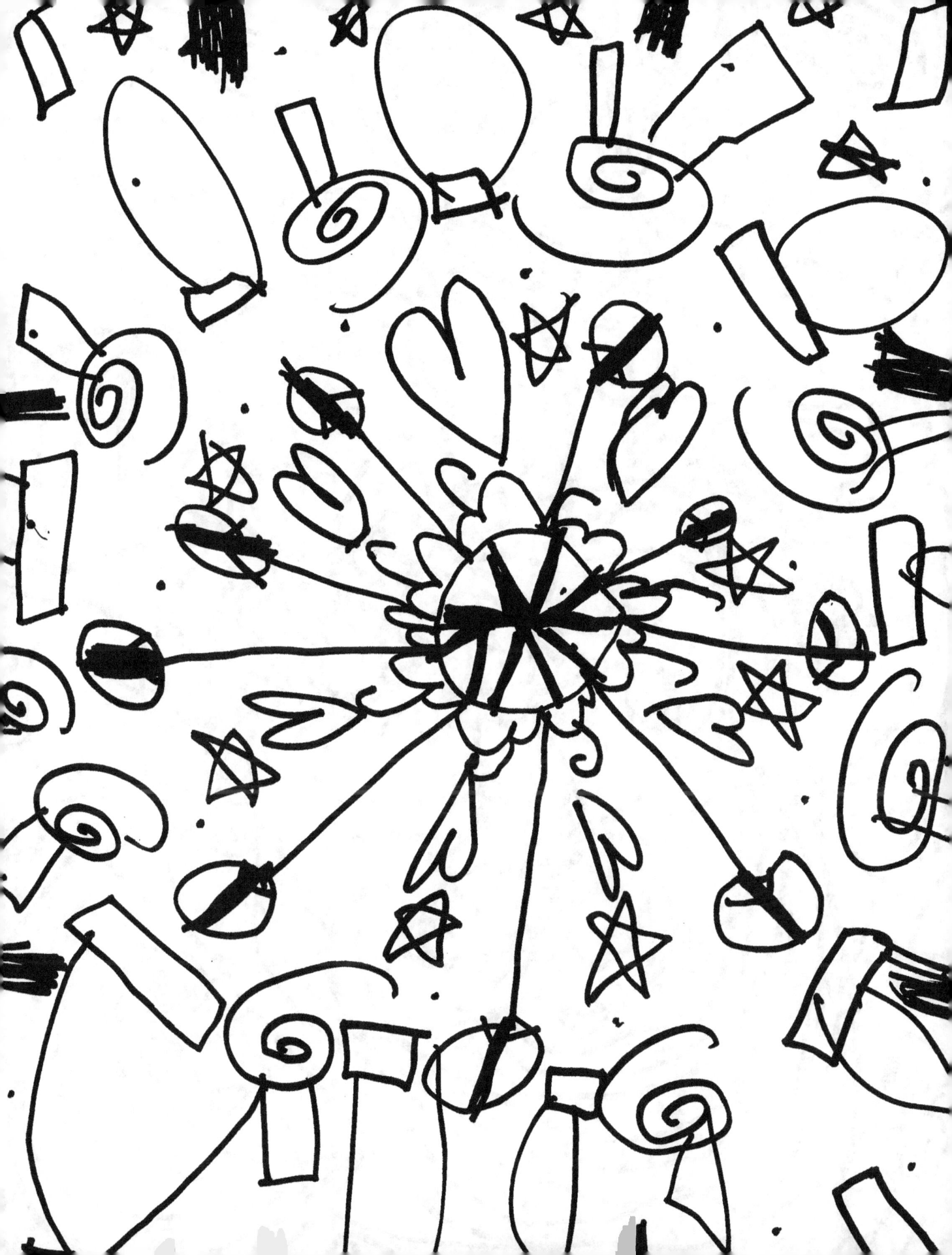

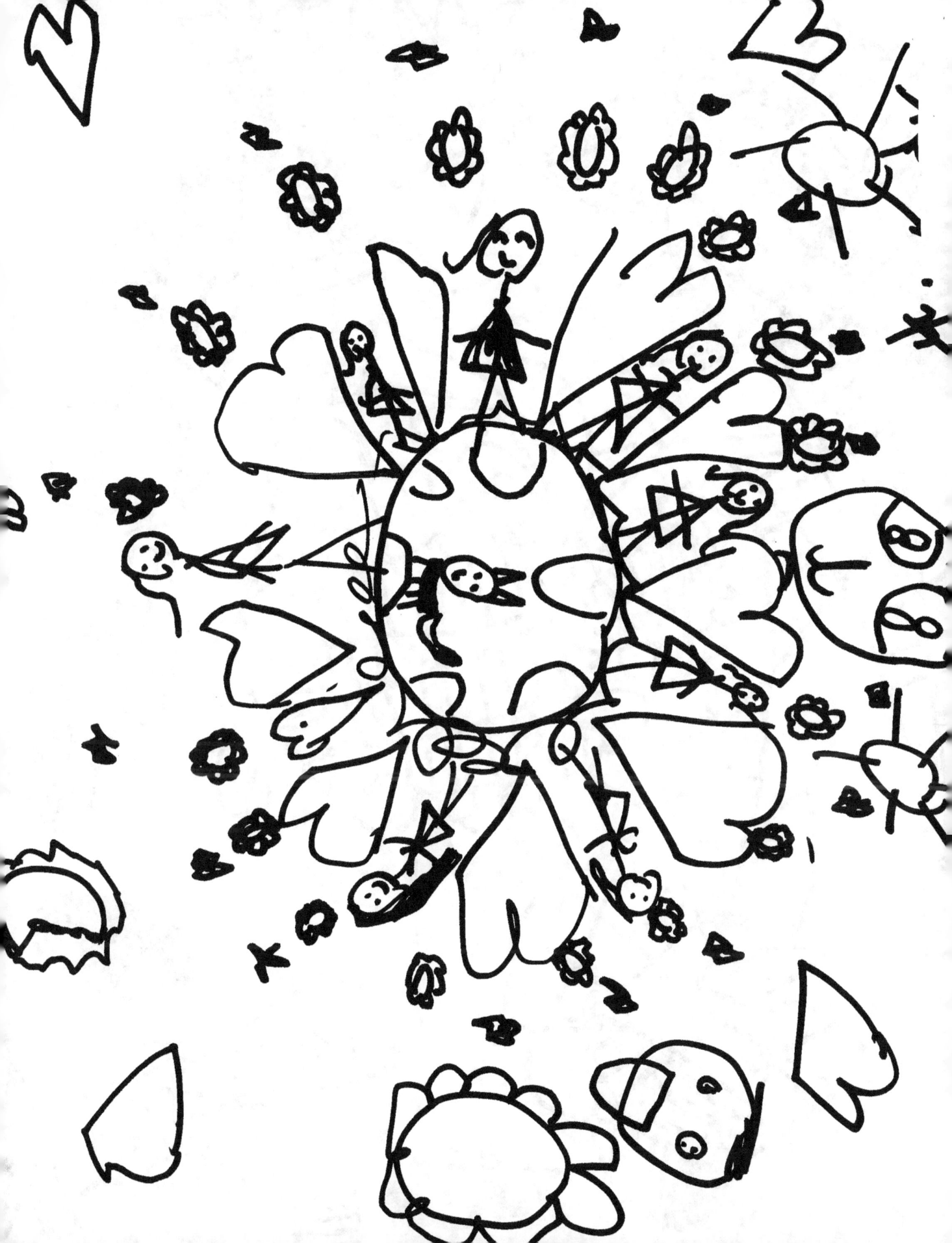

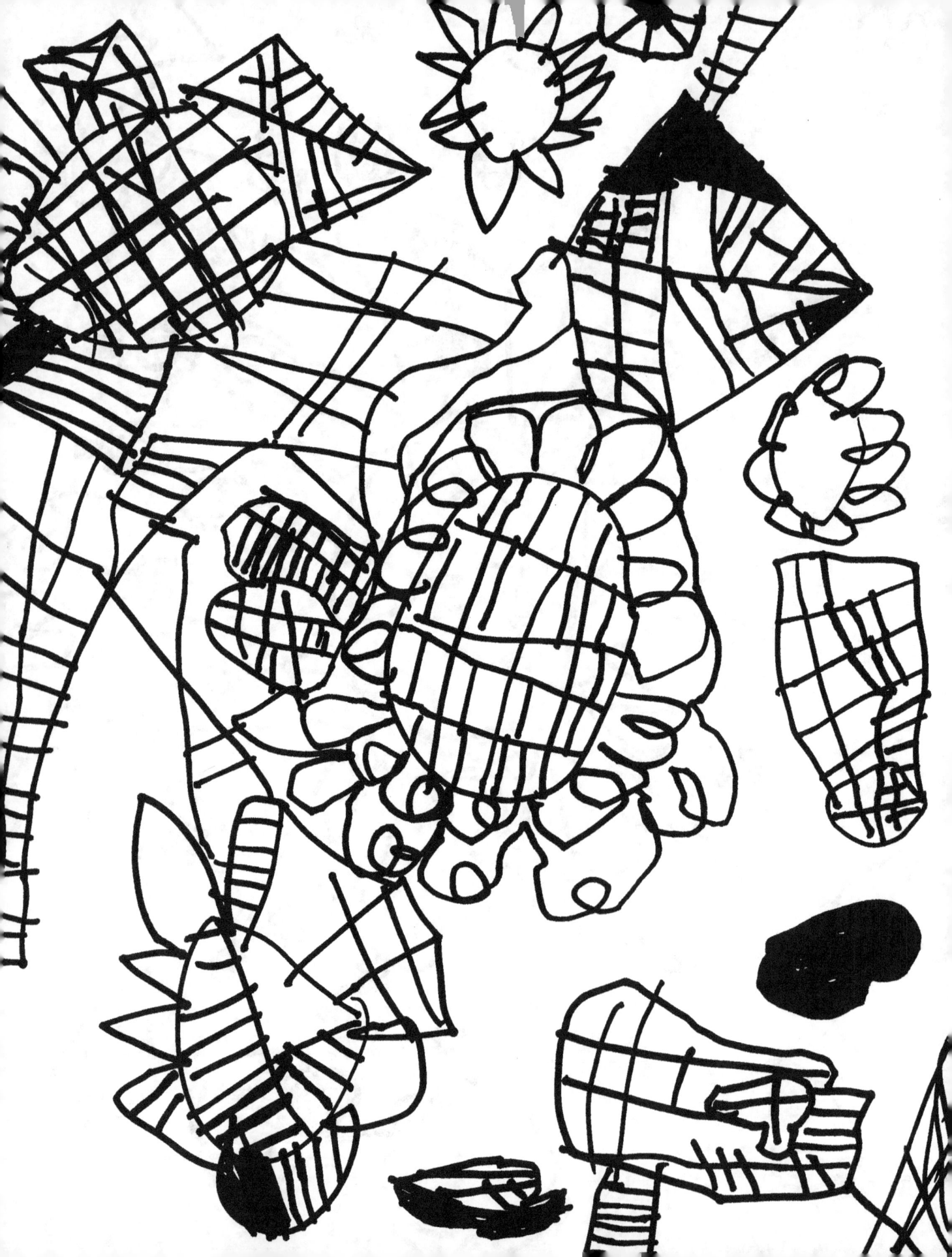

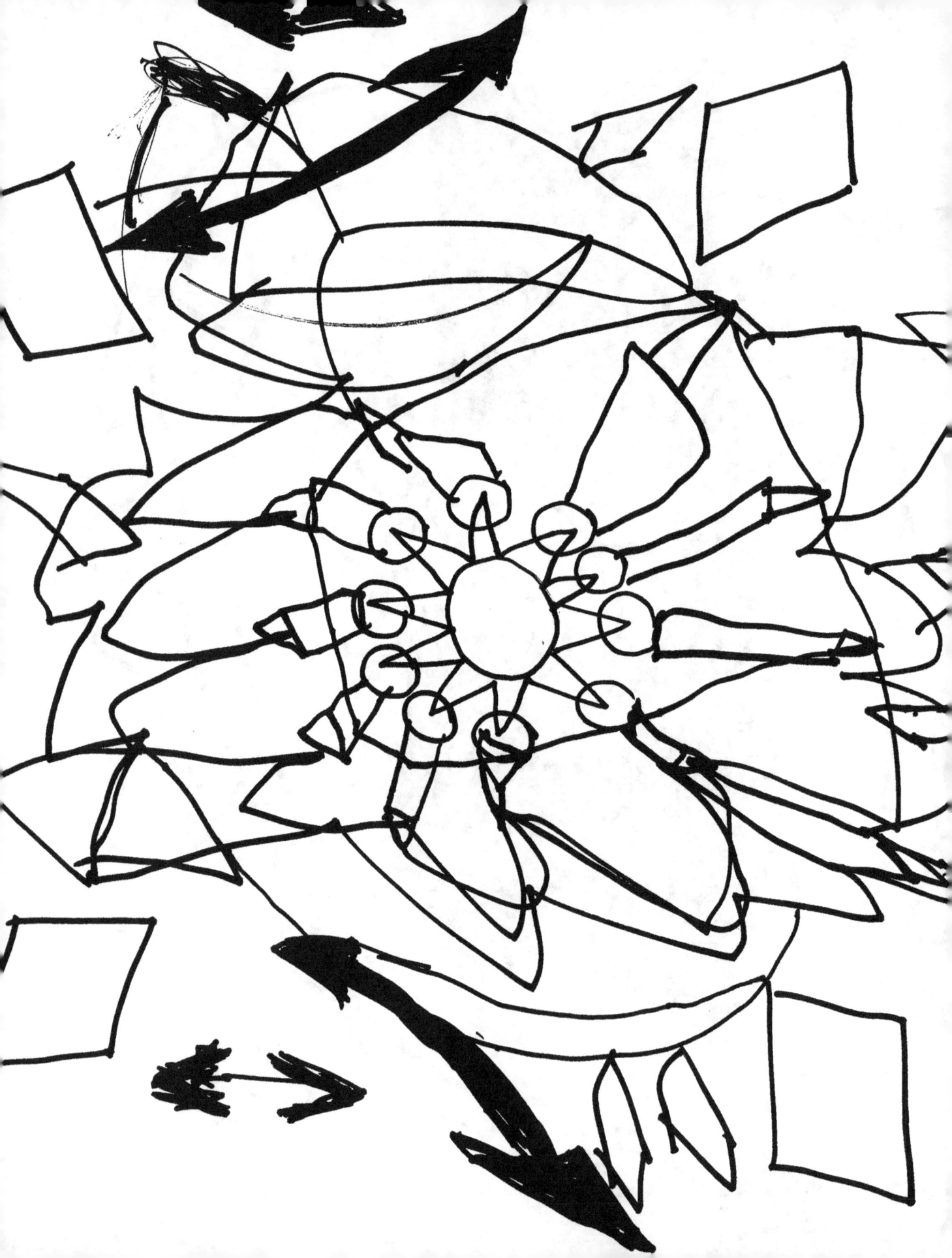

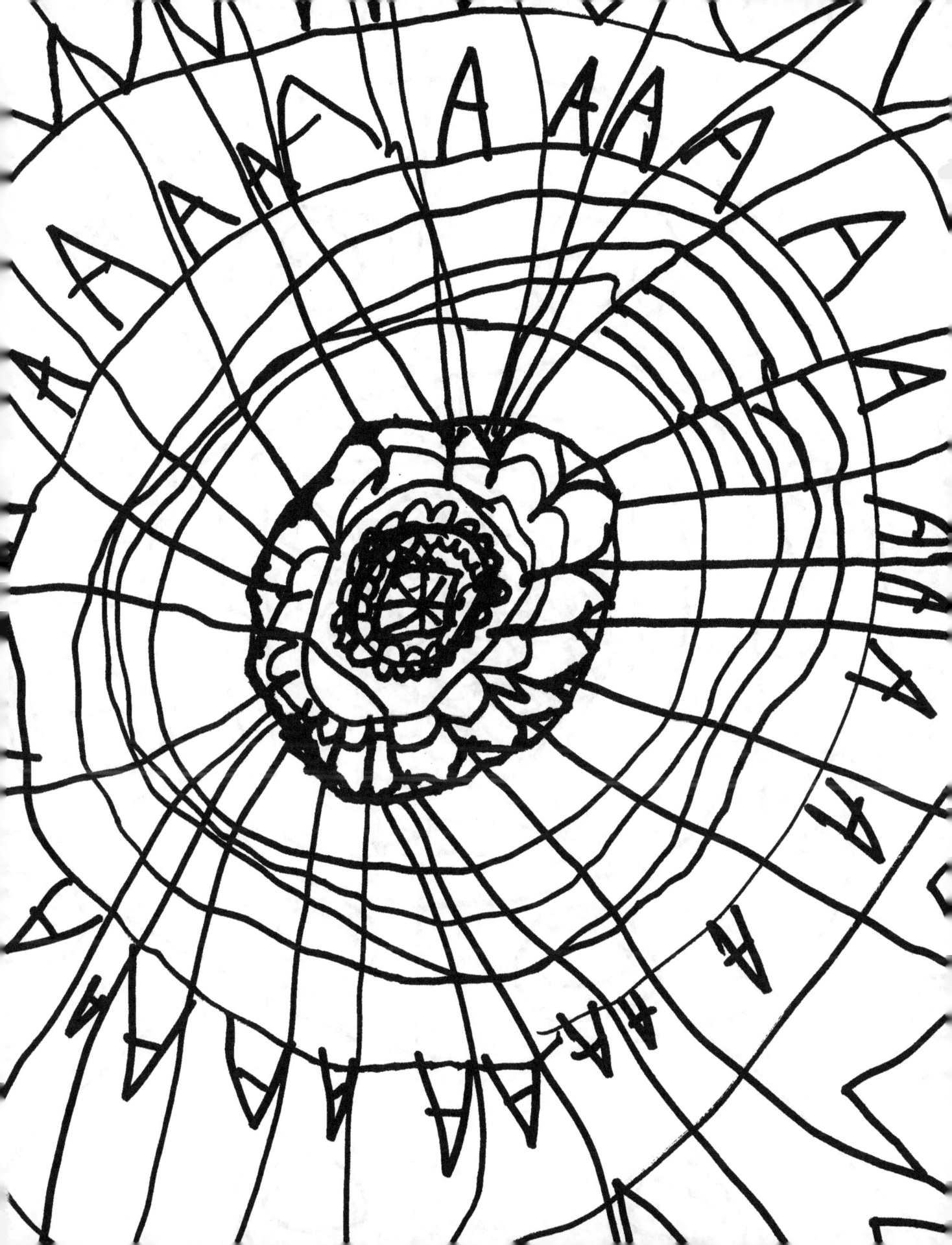

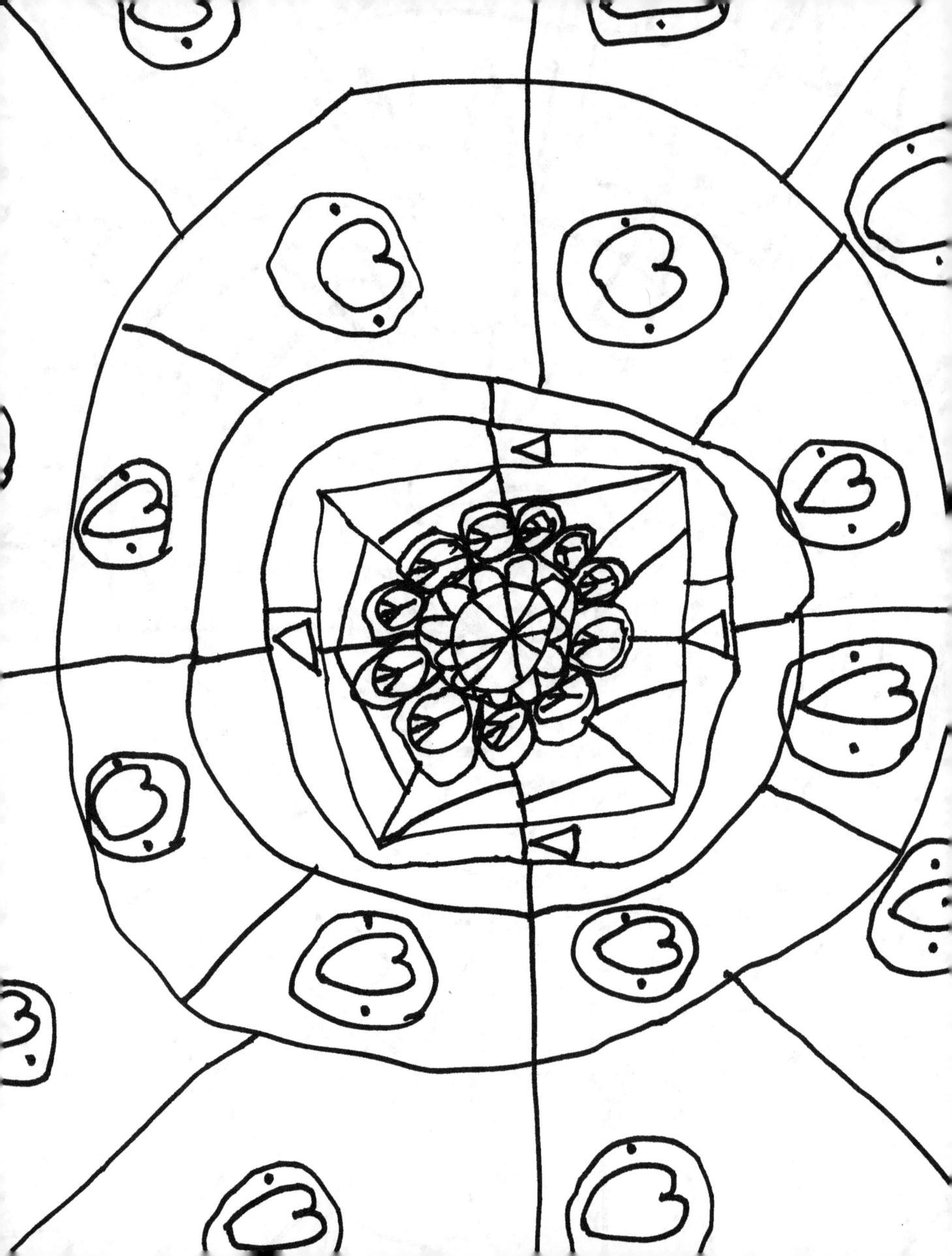

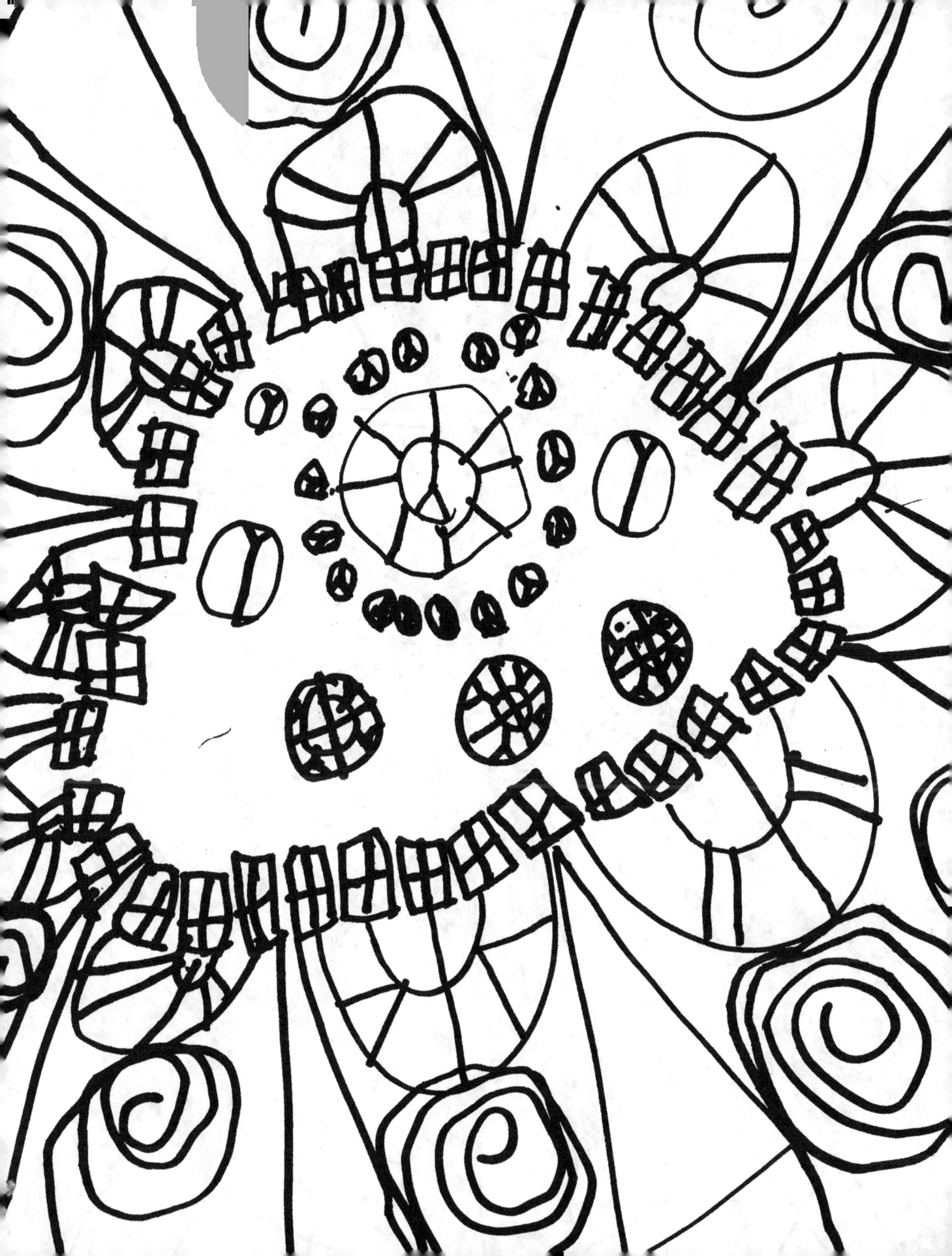

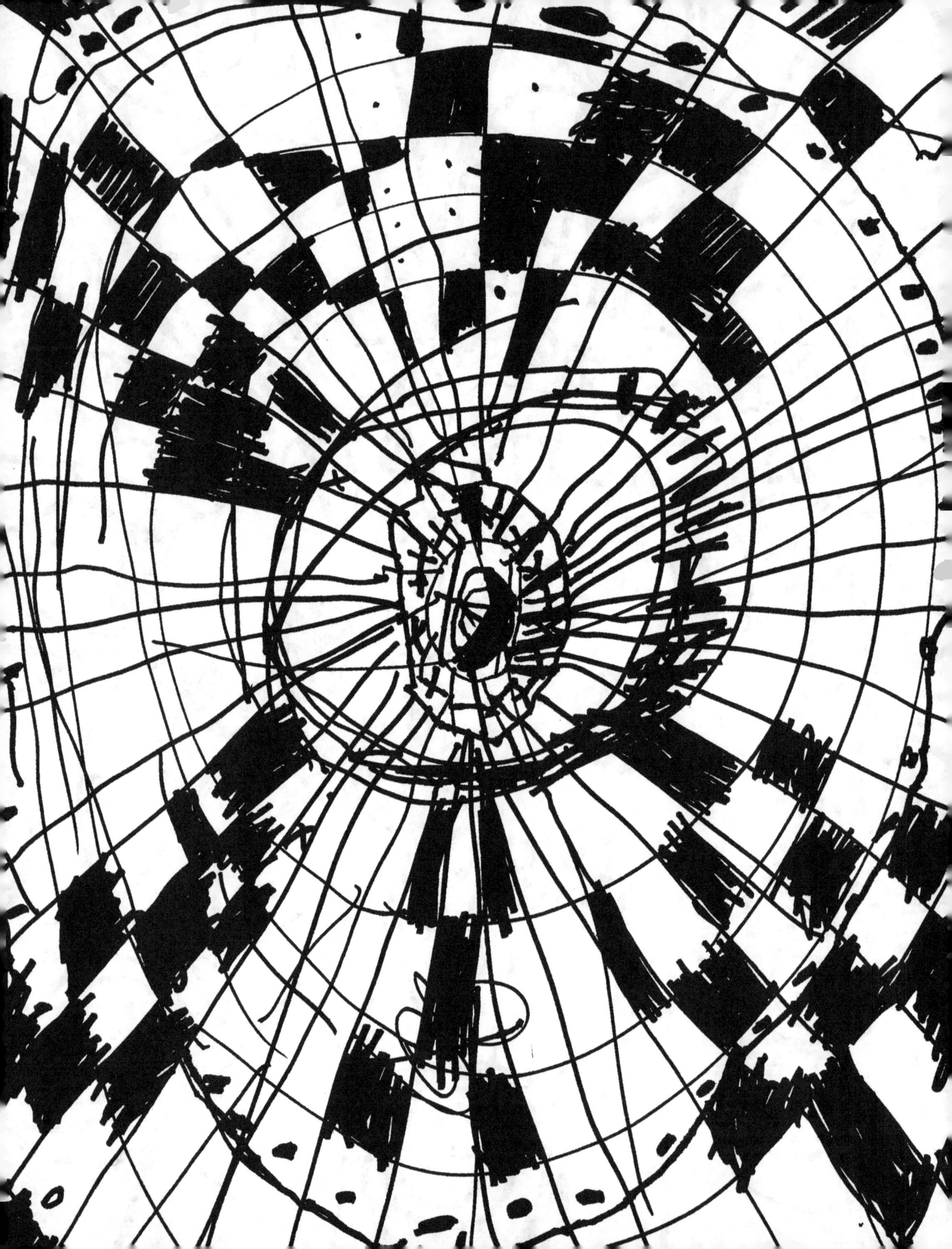

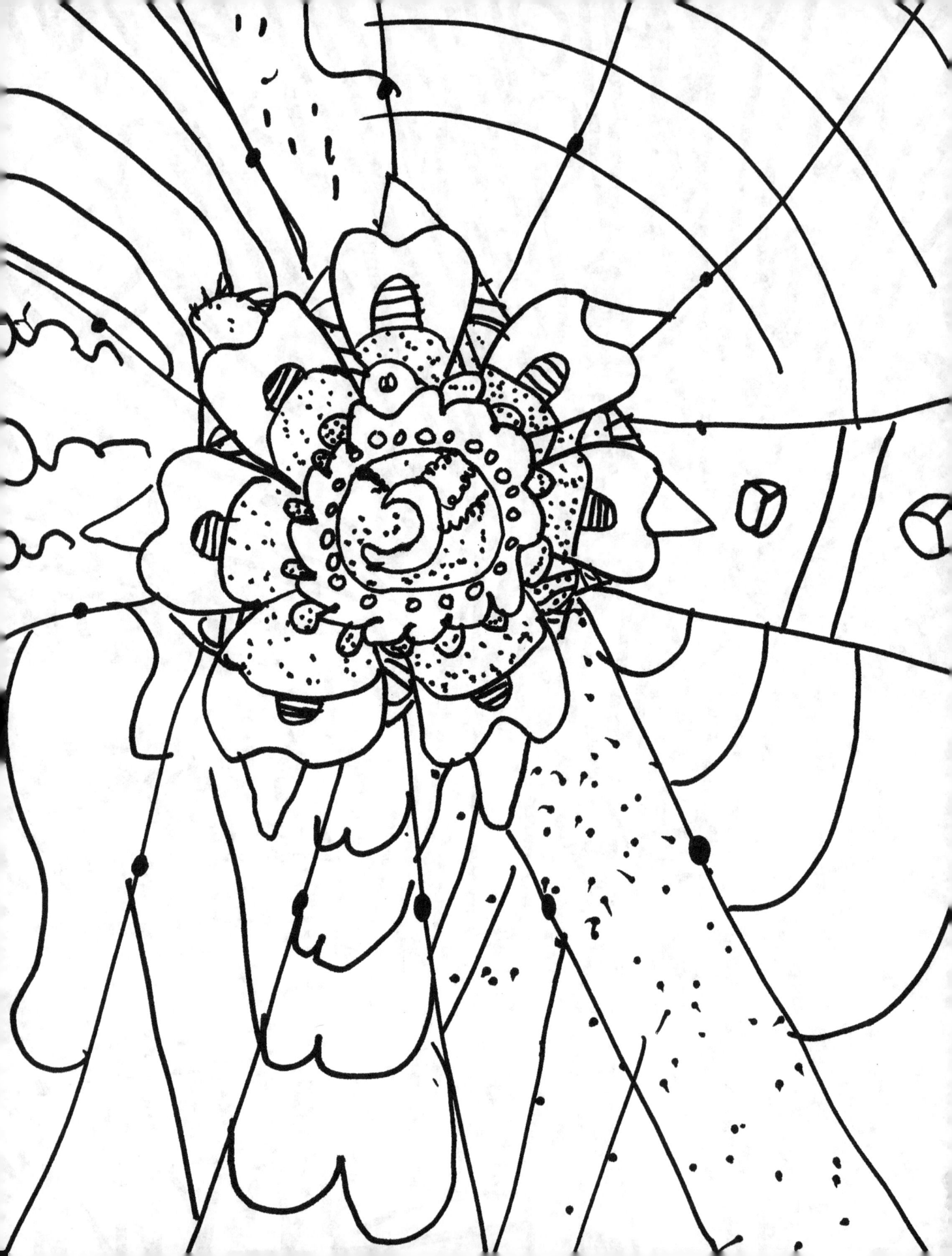

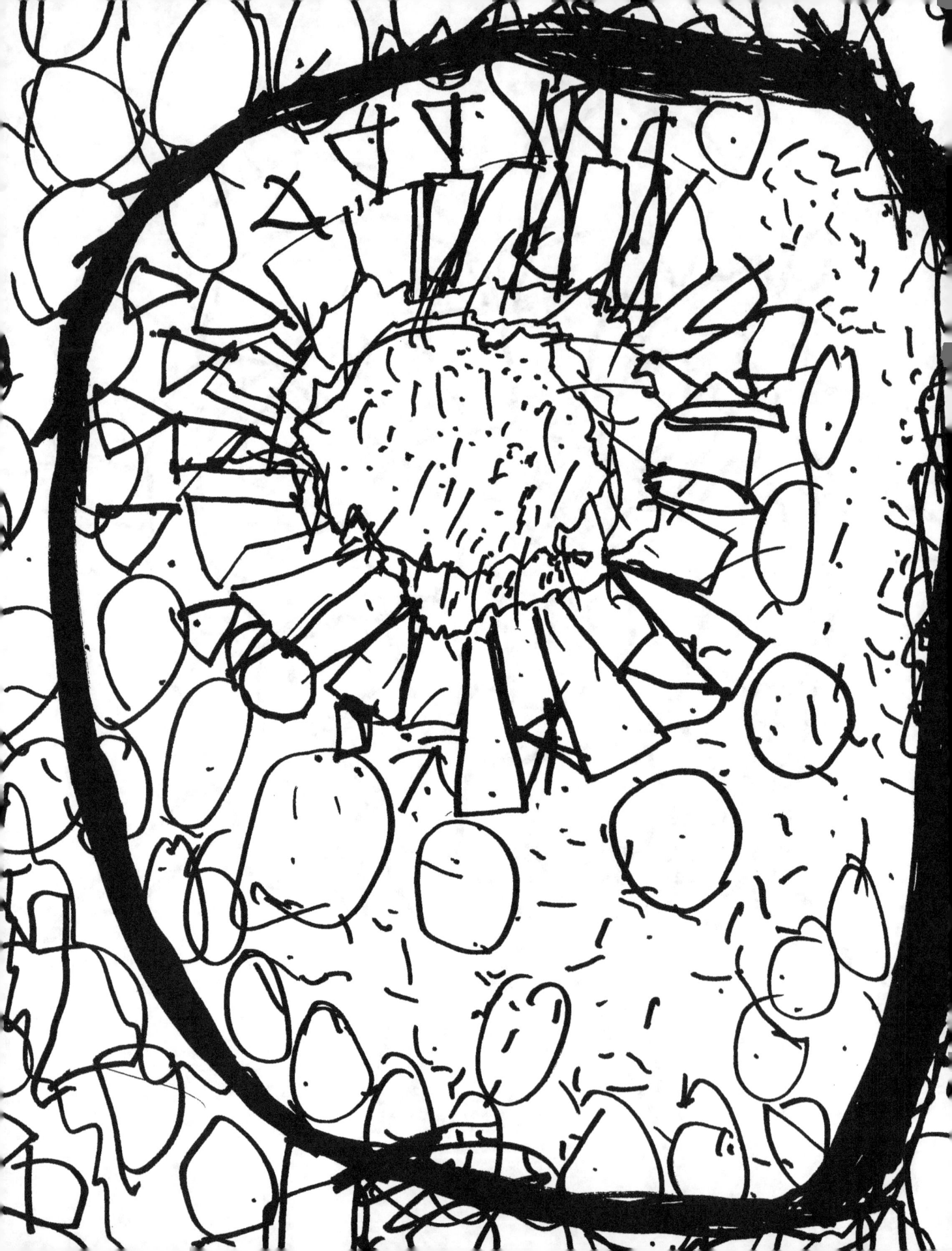

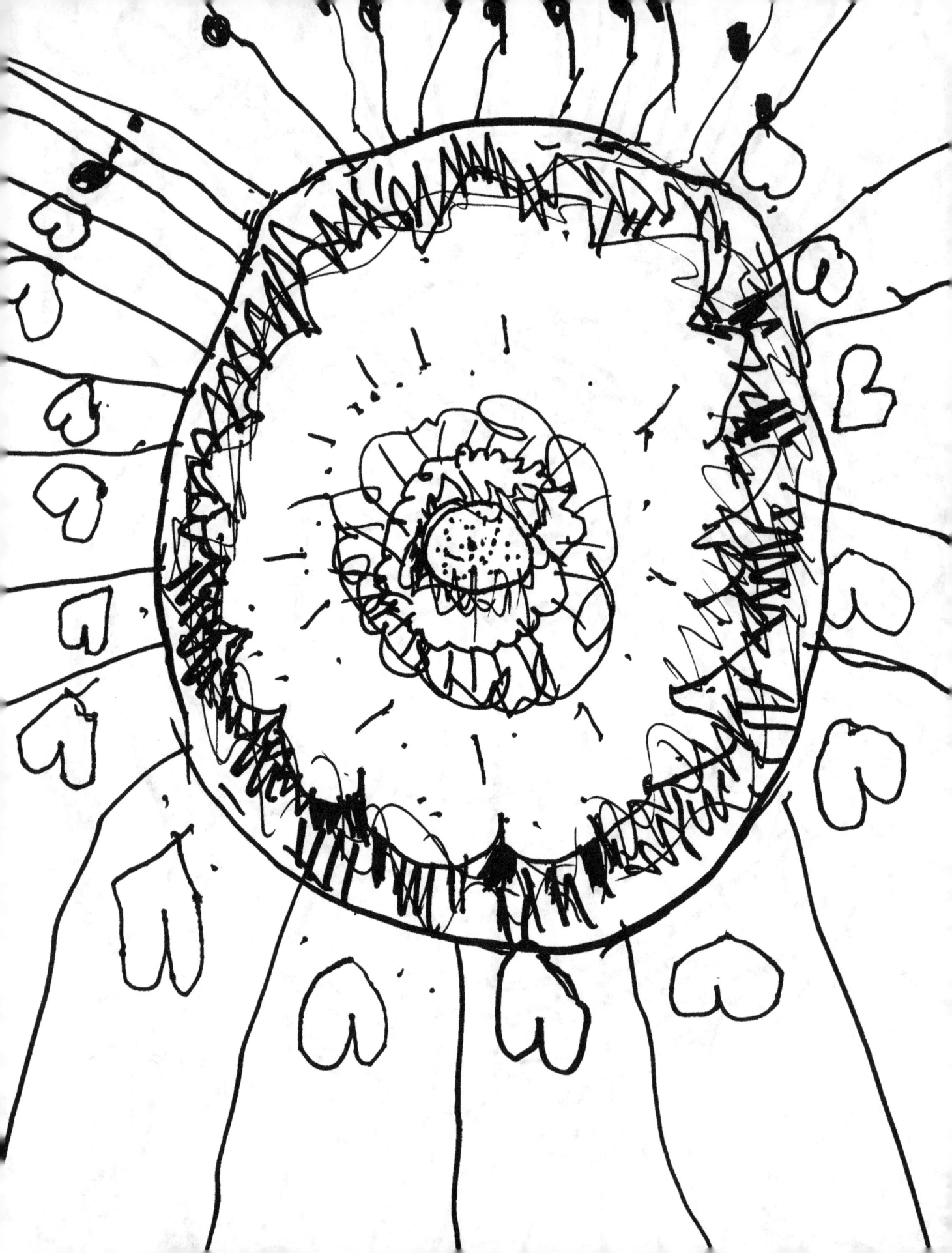

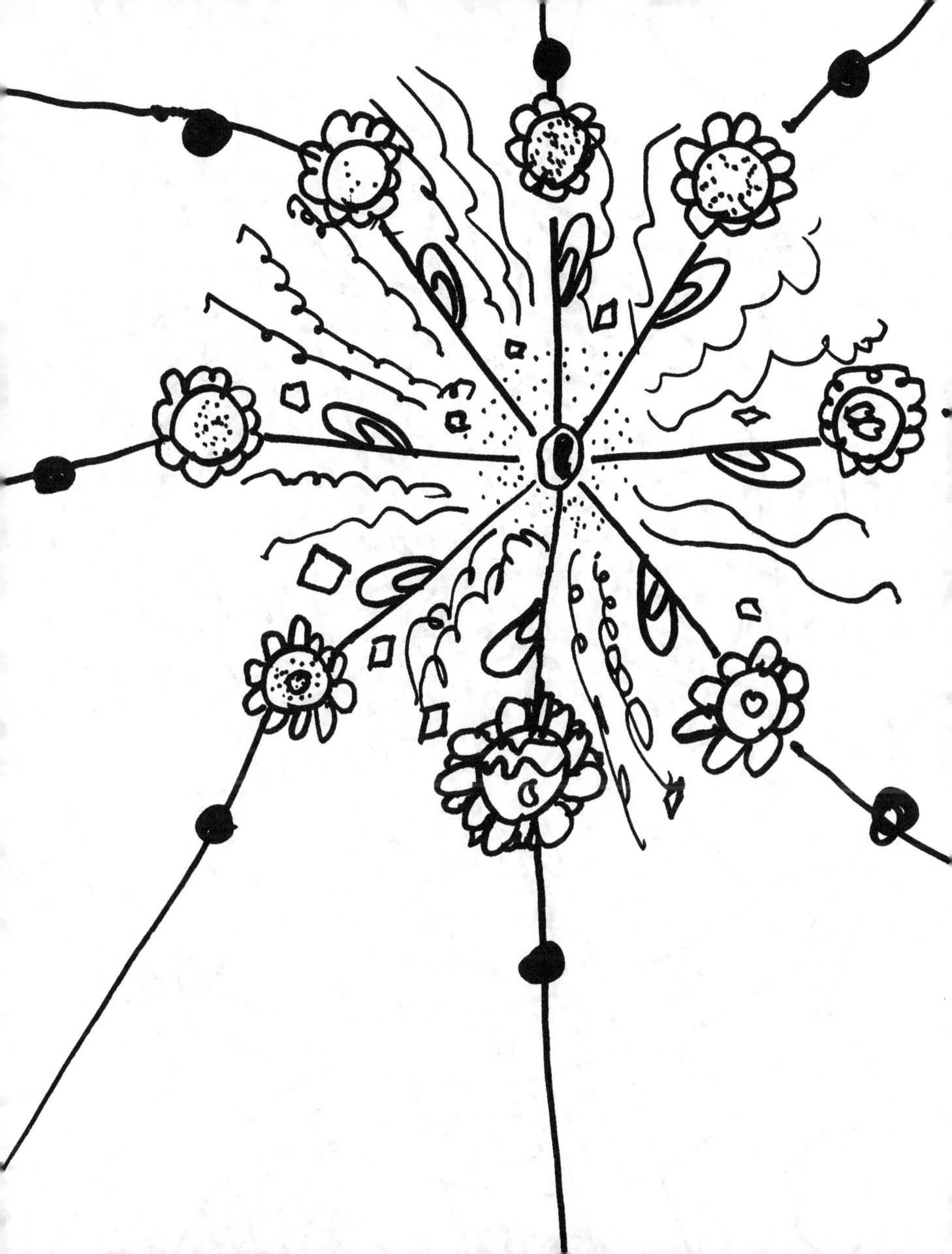

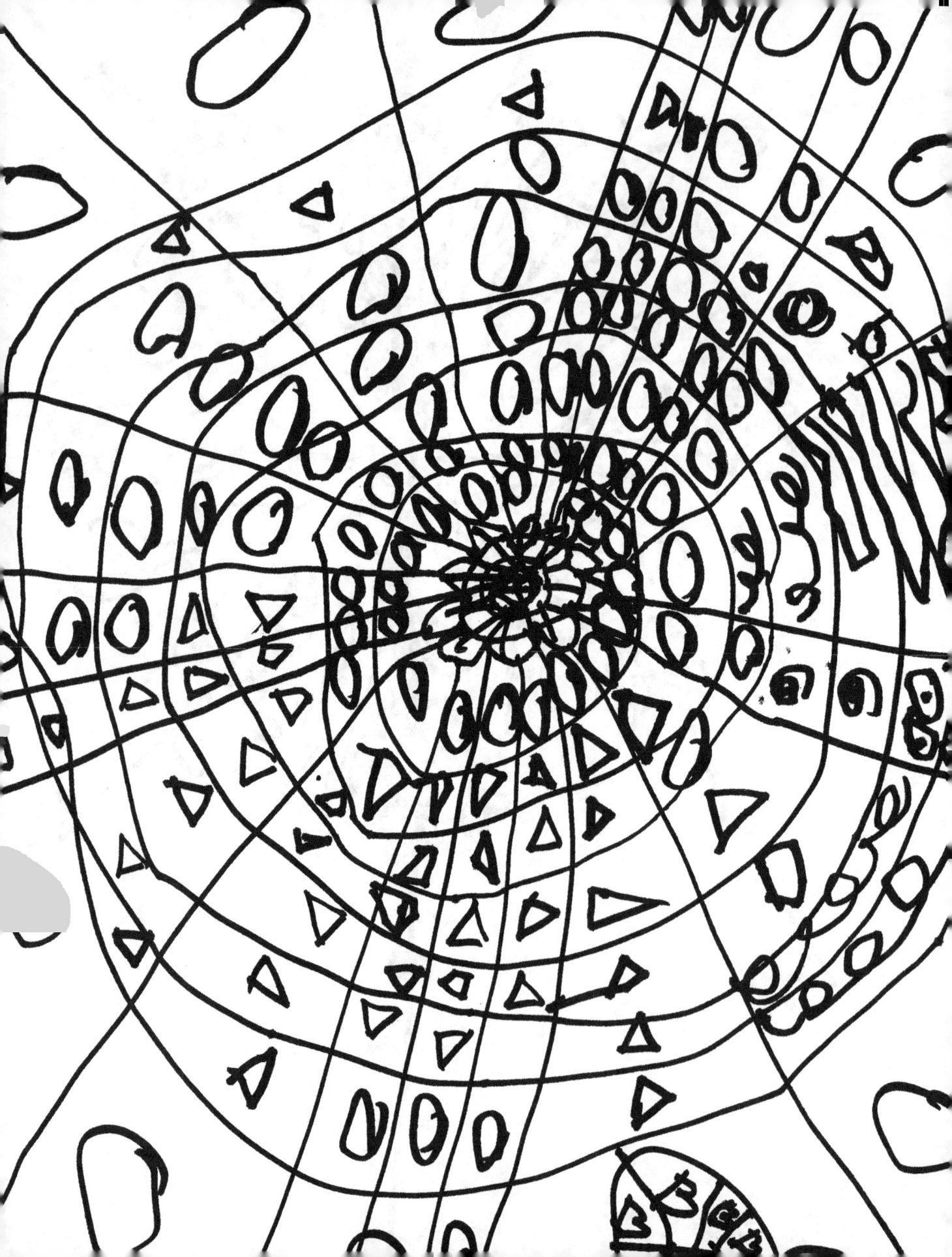

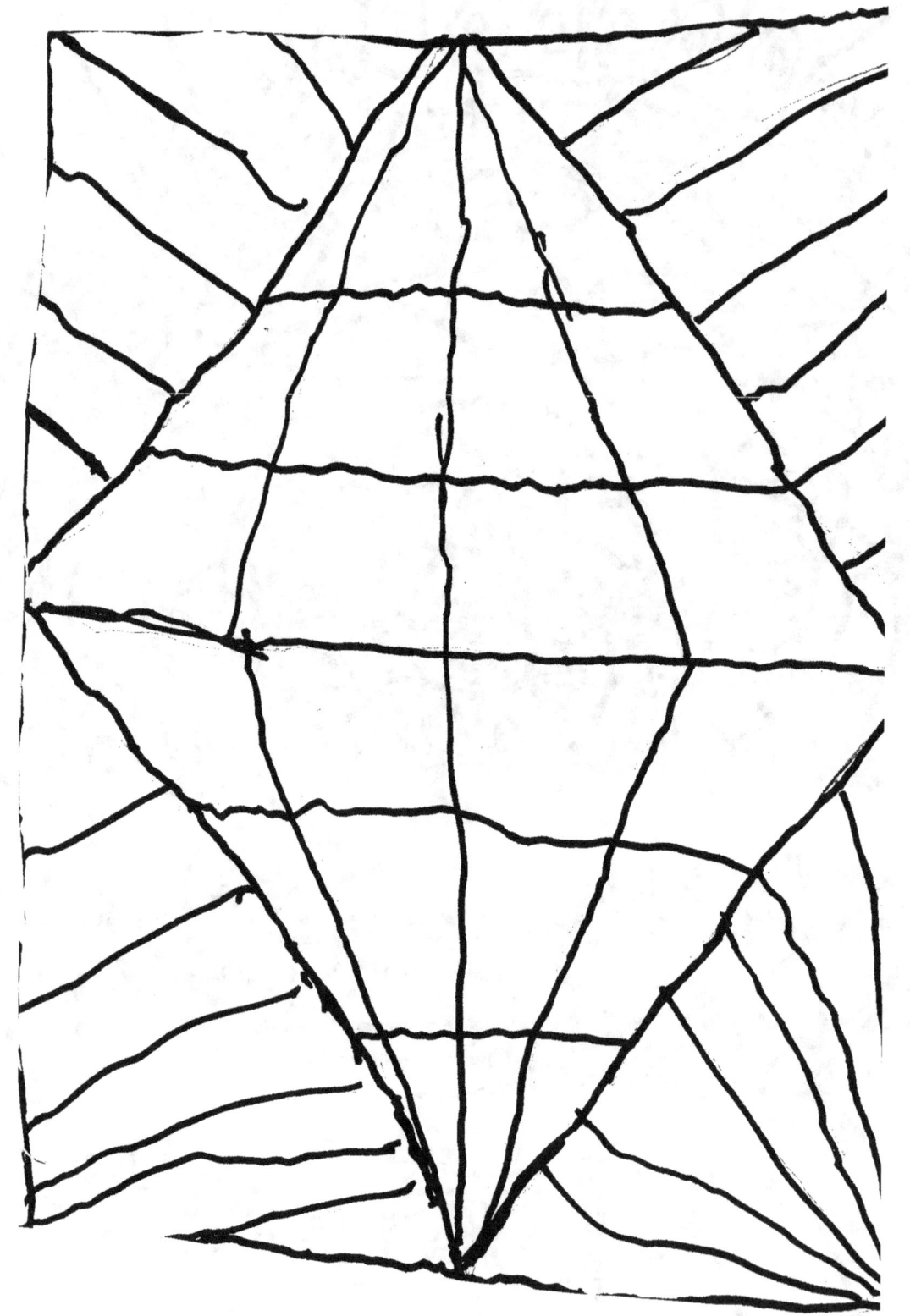

The End